WITHDRAWN

MODERN AMERICAN LITERATURE

EDITED WITH AN INTRODUCTION

AND NOTES BY

Bernard I. Duffey

———

New York RINEHART & CO. INC. *Toronto*

Second Printing, August, 1953

Introduction and Notes Copyright, 1951, by BERNARD I. DUFFEY
Typography and Cover Design by Stefan Salter
Printed in the United States of America

Introduction

The reader, it is hoped, will find in this book a selection of short fiction, poetry, and prose representative of American writing from 1900 to the present. Such a selection, of course, must be suggestive of the whole rather than comprehensive of it, and no doubt each critic will discover his own major omissions. He will see here, for example, no hint of the twentieth-century burgeoning of American drama—of its escape from the narrow conventions of the nineteenth-century stage to the productive freedom of the modern. Equally, he will miss any token of the astonishing fertility of American literary criticism in this century. Such major omissions as these may be forgiven on the grounds of necessity. What is to be found here, on the contrary, will stand or fall in the degree to which it reflects the most salient phenomena of American prose and poetry in the twentieth century.

What has happened in twentieth-century literature must be inferred from the writing itself rather than from more convenient but more arbitrary notions of what should have been. And from such a basis certain deductions seem inescapable. The writing of our half-century began in an act of rebellion against its own literary, intellectual, and social inheritance; it moved on, in various directions, to assert and establish an independence of that inheritance, and of less disaffected members of its society; and it has tentatively come to consider ways in which it might, without compromising its necessary independence, again put its talents to work on the home ground. Its progress, in fiction, may be plotted from Dreiser to Hemingway to Faulkner; or, in poetry, from Robinson to Pound to Hart Crane. The curves, of course, are not mathematical. They must be flexible enough to allow for exceptions, and most of all for countercurrents set in force by too overwhelming an assertion of one point of view only. But if we take as our center the proposition that modern American literature has been a literature of cultural disaffection and search, we shall be on tenable ground.

To an unusual degree, therefore, twentieth-century American writing has been shaped and characterized by conditions which are extraliterary and extraimaginative; not these wholly, of course, but these predominantly. Even in our poetry, where we have seen an epochal and intricate growth of strictly poetic and imaginative means, or in the writing of such a novelist as William Faulkner, concerned deeply as it is with enriching and enlarging the accepted methods of prose fiction, there has been a constant ground swell of social and cultural dissent. This dissent has developed to a point where the founder of our modern poetry stands accused of treason, its chief practitioner lives as an expatriate seeking for traditions which his native air could not nourish, and a most highly honored novelist devotes his writing to a re-turning and cultivation of a milieu thought previously to have expired in the Civil War and reconstruction. Modern American writing is not to be wholly explained, least of all explained away, by its refusal of its own cultural legacy, but an understanding of it does well to begin with a recognition of that refusal, for much follows therefrom.

Within our culture three large sectors have especially incurred the condemnation of our writers: its economics, its mores, and its taste. Out of opposition to the first has grown the considerable bulk of literature written in the vein of social protest. This has been predominantly left wing, sometimes explicitly revolutionary, in its emphasis. It was given an enormous impetus, of course, by the suffering and unrest of the great depression of the thirties, but it was far from finding its origins in that decade. Among only those writers represented in this selection, we find that Theodore Dreiser's *Sister Carrie*, first published in 1900, rests upon a foundation of economic protest as did his *Jennie Gerhardt* of 1911. Much of the poetry of Carl Sandburg, equally, dating from about 1912, was written out of the highly developed social and economic awareness of a Socialist party worker. Scott Fitzgerald, in the booming twenties, was cognizant of the importance, and convinced of the harm of, a conformity of the individual life to the hard rack of a culture of wealth. And to a degree not yet sufficiently explored, Ezra Pound's hostility to America involved from an early date the kind of distrust of the American economy displayed in *The Cantos*. The later development of socially conscious fiction in Dos Passos, Farrell, and Steinbeck was thus extensively anticipated in an America whose economic pains were seen first as those of a wildcat wealth rather than a wildcat poverty. The depression made apparent the dramatic urgency of economic theory and practice, but it was the modern business culture in its self-proclaimed glory which first caught our writers' attention and drew their attack.

Along with American business went the whole complex of prudential manners, values, and cultural habits received by our society at the turn of the century. Here, equally, the writers took exception, perhaps out of an intuition of their own need for freedom of expression. The efflorescence of Midwestern writing, represented for us by Sherwood Anderson, put a strident and revolutionary emphasis upon the importance of the individual above all else. A required conformity was established as the root of all evil; and the fulfillment of individual destinies, short only of individual tyranny, was elevated as the greatest good. Something of this same romanticism was reflected in Van Wyck Brooks' early writing and in the characteristic diatribes of Mencken against any and all restrictions laid upon its more gifted citizens by the republic. A main stream of American philosophy, received from Emerson and the early romantics through William James by John Dewey, systematized this individualism in the name of "pragmatism," or "instrumentalism." Just as James had once exulted in the possession of a new house because it had eleven doors, "all opening outward," so did Dewey bring to an America in romantic protest the assurance that in the freely chosen satisfaction of individual possibilities and needs lay the essence of the national salvation.

But the protest in mores took other directions too. Irving Babbitt and the New Humanists made urgent exception to nineteenth-century individualism, and to twentieth-century romanticism as well, in their doctrine of "the inner check," the supreme necessity for self-control, a reliance upon a common sense rather than an individual sense of what was right and necessary. T. S. Eliot adopted as his own the religious traditionalism of the Catholic movement in the Anglican communion and from its vantage point saw secularized life as a waste land of chaos and pain. Ernest Hemingway, carrying the rhetoric of disillusion and dissent to one kind of ultimate, seized in a grim hug the brute facts of personal endurance, suffering, and death which he found the sole realities of the century's wars and increasingly of its whole texture of life. William Faulkner diagnosed the decay at the heart of American society precisely in the esteemed characteristics of its materialistic and bourgeois elements.

A third line of protest, often combined with one or both of the first two, lay in the increasingly strong demand of the writer for his freedom from a submission to "what the public wants," to a vulgar and standardized taste. When Margaret Anderson began her *Little Review* in 1914 she took as a motto for the magazine the flamboyant, "No Compromise with the Public Taste," and though by no means all modern writers would have approved her magazine, few could have denied their own attachment, in varying ways, to her slogan. Our decades have been those of the "little" magazine and the avant-garde publisher. Much of the writing contained in these pages first saw light by their means or as a result of their influence upon old-line institutions. Freed from a need to conform, the writer thus had thrust upon him the opportunity for experiment with the materials of his craft, and of our poets and storytellers few have refused. Their directions have ranged from the deliberate neoprimitivism of a Sherwood Anderson to the supersubtle exploitation of the creative faculty displayed by Wallace Stevens, even to a point where the means of a particular poem become the subject of the poem as in "Esthétique du Mal." The result of such freedom of taste, coupled with a constant concern for taste, has been to give twentieth-century writing, despite its vast disparities, a most marked stylistic quality. It is engrainedly and perennially "experimental."

By such analytic means as this one of the threefold alienation of modern American writers from the prevailing economy, mores, and taste are we able most clearly to pick out the chief characteristics of their work. A detailed history, to the contrary, put down in strict chronological order would lead more to confusion than to clarity. Within a period of fifty years there is more than sufficient opportunity for overlapping, backtracking, and procedure by fits and starts. In its separate facts, a chronology of our decades confounds us overwhelmingly with the characteristic refusal of historical reality to conform neatly to historical theory. If, however, one is prepared for approximations and exceptions, a generalized narrative may be of a certain use.

Our modern period can thus be said to have begun with the impact on its more sensitive souls of the despairing naturalistic visions growing out of post-Darwinian thinking and with the concrete facts of the modern life which seemed to give them so overwhelming a reality. Here we would see Henry Adams, standing awe-struck before the giant dynamo of the Paris Exposition, seeing in the machine nothing less than a totally inhuman and anarchic force of the cosmos itself, which required of him an impossible new set of responses and which set at naught all he had been able to learn of modern man. His conclusions that force, force only, was the reality of modern human existence echoed through the work of such otherwise unrelated contemporaries as Frank Norris and Jack London, whether they brought their sensibilities to bear on the new behemoths of American business or the eternal problem of mankind's place in nature. Theodore Dreiser accepted such a naturalism implicitly and set out in his early novels to give it concrete form. As he worried the question throughout his life, he turned new elements of it to the light and made important changes in his conclusions. But the Dreiser of the first four novels was a confounded and saddened expositor of the naturalistic idea—that mankind was wholly a creature of a heartless universe and stood wholly a victim of its merciless mercy. Much of the same attitude was shared by as different a figure as Edwin Arlington Robinson. Though, unlike Dreiser, he wrote about discrete and individual human beings rather than representative cases, he could see little in the human situation except what must be dealt with ironically, bitterly, and with a full sense of futility as the common lot. Robinson's second volume of poems, *Children of the Night,* published in 1897, Dreiser's *Sister Carrie* of 1900, and *The Education of Henry Adams* of 1907 give us warrant for centering this first aspect of modern American writing in the turn of the century and its first decade.

Between 1910 and 1925, however, a second and then a third phase had largely replaced the first one. These revealed themselves, originally, as a renewed and romantic insistence upon individual expression, and, second, as the positive rejection, manifested in the exile movement of the second and third decades, of all American society and its ways. The naturalistic pessimism of the first decade, however, lay behind both these later movements as a kind of make-ready activity. Both the literary radicals and the exiles took up the original protest where the naturalistic writers and thinkers had left off. The second generation of our century did not repudiate the first. They accepted especially the proposition of the first generation—that the dominant and threefold American rationale of the benevolent inevitability of a free-enterprise economy, a prudentially related system of mores best phrased in Poor Richard's maxims, and a confinement of the faculties of imagination and taste to a sort of docile and well-mannered after-hours status was hopelessly irrelevant to the realities of the twentieth-century situation. The romantic and radical individualists set out to replace these dried pods of a trembling vine with the living fruit of individual expression and fulfillment.

It was John Dewey who began much of the process when, in 1891, in his *Outlines of a Critical Theory of Ethics,* he gave the radical heart of his new philosophy, instrumentalism, its first statement. No institution, he claimed, and no human faculty could be given status or honor without a demonstration of its value to the true goals of human living. Unlike the earlier English utilitarians, who had proposed "the greatest good of the greatest number" as the grand idea of a similar ethical plan, Dewey always remained vague as to what his ideas of the best ends of human life might be. His ethical philosophy, both in its theory and in its application (which latter he stressed especially), remained a curiously truncated affair. Perhaps, however, because it so well represented the intellectuals' general inability to agree upon ends, while suiting the equally general desire to be on the march to somewhere (it was the bravery of the march rather than its direction that was important), Dewey's instrumentalism, particularly through its hold upon American public education, became almost as firmly set an official philosophy of our day as was the scholastic realism of the late Middle Ages. It was an agreement, in a generally muddled situation, to disagree: in effect, to let nature take its own inevitable course while man devoted himself to the melioristic occupation of making the best of things as it carried him along.

How far this program itself, through mensurable channels of influence, shaped the attitudes of the literary radicals, of how far these latter developed independently of Dewey but within the same cultural demands which formed his thought, cannot now be estimated. Certainly, however, there were great similarities. The work of Midwestern writers like Sherwood Anderson and Carl Sandburg in the Chicago Renaissance of 1912 to 1925 reiterated the vitalistic and romantic elements implicit in Dewey's thought, while the eastern branch of the movement, inaugurated by the essays of Randolph Bourne and Van Wyck Brooks, was active throughout the second decade, though with a distinctive tinge of intellectualization. In the second decade also a non-Deweyan force was at work, that of the archindividualism of the German philosopher, Friederich Nietzsche, which made itself felt in both East and Midwest. It was this, indeed, which most notably quickened the lavish vituperation of American society spewed forth by that noisiest of literary radicals,

H. L. Mencken, and which colored the attitudes, directly or indirectly, of the whole radical movement. Then, through the breach in American conservatism cut by naturalism, Dewey, and the Nietzschean influence tumbled a whole spate of heterodox and individualizing influences: intellectual anarchism, womens' freedom, Freudianism, and romantic socialism being only a few.

The exiles, unlike the literary radicals, showed no similarity to Dewey and only a slight one to Nietzsche. Their concerns were mixed, but most apparent among them lay the need felt by artist and writer to withdraw to a society of their own peers. Europe offered this to them not so much by opposing a different kind of culture to the American, as by allowing within its own bourgeois structure a more commodious place for the spiritual rebel. Europe was more used to and more tolerant of the intellectual or artistic bohemian than America. The number of exiles who, like Eliot and Gertrude Stein, settled and took root in a foreign culture was small. For the most part, the exiles were drifters over the face of Europe, following the favorable exchange rates from country to country, disliking the bourgeoisie in each of them, and resting only in the hospitable areas like the Left Bank and the summer Riviera. Theirs was not so much an exile from America as from the twentieth-century world. Ezra Pound's vituperation of this country can be matched almost word for word by his vituperation of England and France. They shared with the literary radicals, with whom they were otherwise frequently at odds, a common alienation from the business culture. Their method of response, however, was that of forming a world within a world rather than one of criticism, reform, and individual adaptation. Their literary work, not surprisingly, was international in character. Eliot and Pound wrote in various languages as did the contributors to the exile's chief magazine (one among many), *transition*.

There came a reaction, however, and again of a twofold kind, against both literary radicals and exiles. The New Humanism, an academic critical movement, had prepared much of its ground during the second decade and the twenties. And by the late twenties and early thirties the Marxist influence in American thought had prepared for the novels of social consciousness precipitated by the paradox of boom and depression. Again, these two newer loyalties were impatient and critical of each other, but they shared a common distrust of what now seemed the irresponsibility and vacuousness of much of the earlier activity.

The response of the New Humanists, summed up in Irving Babbitt's *Rousseau and Romanticism* of 1919, was to reject the whole current of modern individualism set in force by Dewey and Nietzsche in favor of a renewed emphasis upon the rational governance of self. This faculty, the Humanists declared, was the one which especially set off humanity from the lower animals, and, without its exercise, man plunged himself hopelessly back into the moral chaos described by the naturalists. The followers of Dewey, the romantics, the Nietzschean radicals, and the exiles—all these failed in Humanistic eyes by trying to substitute self-expression and self-satisfaction for an adherence to the common moral and rational ground of humanity itself.

The New Humanists, however, somewhat like the Deweyites whom they criticized, were indefinite about what exactly constituted man's moral and rational community. They lacked definition. This want, in particular, was supplied by the Marxists. Their philosophy, a naturalistic one, was definite. It was, further, complemented by a course of action leading to the creation of a tangible and earthly state of affairs which seemed to promise in clear-cut ways to alleviate some of mankind's most apparent plagues. When we are driven at this late date to consider why Communism has had such a widespread appeal in the twentieth century despite its harshness and illiberality, we may well remember its seeming positiveness, clarity, and actionability in the midst of so many random and equivocal voices. It has spoken in a modern vocabulary to the modern condition.

Such sureness is best exemplified in John Steinbeck's *In Dubious Battle,* published in 1936, but it is reflected, though less fully, in the earliest characteristic work of John Dos Passos, *Manhattan Transfer* of 1925, and James Farrell's *Young Lonigan* of 1932, as well as in their later novels. In Marxism, a whole generation of writers found place, purpose, and vocabulary. Though they largely outgrew this early attachment, they did, by its means, succeed in grounding themselves for a time in what seemed the pressing realities of American Life.

The new writing of the late thirties and the last decade has largely failed to assume any very definite shape. But, partly in deference to a new intellectual force which has made its way over the Western world in the forties, and more so because of a larger area of meaning in the term, we may characterize it as "existential" in character. It has, that is, tried to bend back the curve established in the early century to a point where the writer could again phrase his material and his point of view in the terms of his particular existence and his individual will without recourse to romantic vision-making. We have had William Faulkner, in this way, deeply absorbed in the complex and particular qualities of life in his native South. His admirer, Robert Penn Warren, after turning to fiction from poetry in 1939 with his first novel, *Night Rider*, has followed Faulkner's methods closely while attempting to broaden the import of his work. The Second World War has brought forth much writing, fiction and verse as well as prose, engaged not with ideas about the war or lessons drawn from it, but with the texture of war itself. Karl Shapiro is a case in point here. There has been a renewed intellectual interest in religion, but one manifest not so much in preaching or in detached theological speculation as in a way of apprehending the nature of man's existence itself through religion, as being concerned with experiential truths rather than rationalistic or hortatory ones per se.

Thus has the general course of our century turned back and forth, hither and yon, in its effort to find within itself a place for imaginative and intellectual expression. There have been many, of course, who would not fit our categories. Robert Frost, with his sensitive and redoubtable imagination, has been content with his own region and his own experience as an excuse for his poetic being. Robinson Jeffers, a naturalist born out of due time, writes bleak verse in a lonely tower and exclaims upon the hideousness of the human spectacle. These, and many more, will not be bound in classification. There are few, however, who have not in their writing left abundant traces of the century's literary preoccupation—that of the estranged writer in search of character and stability. This, through all, has been the saddening and the enlivening literary business of our decades.

Only a brief word remains, that of absolute significance. Have we been living through a major, perhaps an unparalleled period of literary productivity as one extreme wing of our criticism has declared? Or, given the uneasiness of our days and the closeness of our writers' preoccupation with them, have we only succeeded in producing a literature which, however directly it speaks to us now, will eventually lose its force—one which lacks the ultimate qualities of literary authenticity and literary objectivity. One must make the usual caveats: certainly our literature will finally be evaluated only in terms of its particular productions, and the conclusive judgments will be made after our time. But one may hazard the opinion that there has been much to cause the best of it to stand. We have succeeded in finding unique voices for all our major genres despite our highly developed awareness of the past. And some genres, poetry especially, have worked consistently toward the desirable end of literary integrity—the establishment of literature on its own grounds of imaginative power rather than the leaseholds of historical, social, ideational, or ethical significance. The relatively greater absorption of our novelists with the conflicts of their own milieu may ultimately cost them status just as we today are inclined to distinguish between the documentary parts, or the temporal parts, and the absolute parts of a Dickens or a Dryden. The steadfast honesty of Dreiser at his best may finally suffice. The skilled rhetoric of a Dos Passos or a Steinbeck may at some future date sufficiently excuse their contemporaneity. It seems more certain, however, that the purer literary achievement of an Eliot or a Faulkner, like that of a Milton, may finally outweigh more completely their concern with a troublesome world, though the justification may not be an epic one.

Meanwhile we have had an indubitably original and ambitious half-century. It has been one especially devoted to exploration and discovery. Whatever its fulfillments may be, they will stand exclusively as its own.

Bernard I. Duffey

East Lansing, Michigan
September, 1951

Contents

INTELLECTUAL CURRENTS

Sanctuary

THEODORE DREISER

I

Primarily, there were the conditions under which she was brought to fifteen years of age: the crowded, scummy tenements; the narrow green-painted halls with their dim gas-jets, making the entrance look more like that of a morgue than a dwelling-place; the dirty halls and rooms with their green or blue or brown walls painted to save the cost of paper; the bare wooden floors, long since saturated with every type of grease and filth from oleomargarine and suet leaked from cheap fats or meats, to beer and whiskey and tobacco-juice. A little occasional scrubbing by some would-be hygienic tenant was presumed to keep or make clean some of the chambers and halls.

And then the streets outside—any of the streets by which she had ever been surrounded—block upon block of other red, bare, commonplace tenements crowded to the doors with human life, the space before them sped over by noisy, gassy trucks and vehicles of all kinds. And stifling in summer, dusty and icy in winter; decorated on occasion by stray cats and dogs, pawing in ashcans, watched over by lordly policemen, and always running with people, people, people—who made their living heaven only knows how, existing in such a manner as their surroundings suggested.

In this atmosphere were always longshoremen, wagon-drivers, sweepers of floors, washers of dishes, waiters, janitors, workers in laundries, factories—mostly in indifferent or decadent or despairing conditions. And all of these people existed, in so far as she ever knew, upon that mysterious, evanescent and fluctuating something known as the weekly wage.

Always about her there had been drunkenness, fighting, complaining, sickness or death; the police coming in, and arresting one and another; the gas man, the rent man, the furniture man, hammering at doors for their due—and not getting it—in due time the undertaker also arriving amid a great clamor, as though lives were the most precious things imaginable.

It is entirely conceivable that in viewing or in meditating upon an atmosphere such as this, one might conclude that no good could come out of it. What! a dung-heap grow a flower? Exactly, and often, a flower—but not to grow to any glorious maturity probably. Nevertheless a flower of the spirit at least might have its beginnings there. And if it shrank or withered in the miasmatic atmosphere—well, conceivably, that might be normal, although in reality all flowers thus embedded in infancy do not so wither. There are flowers and flowers.

Viewing Madeleine Kinsella at the ages of five, seven, eleven and thirteen even, it might have been conceded that she was a flower of sorts—admittedly not a brave, lustrous one of the orchid or gardenia persuasion, but a flower nevertheless. Her charm was simpler, more retiring, less vivid than is usually accorded the compliment of beauty. She was never rosy, never colorful in the high sense, never daring or aggressive. Always, from her infancy on, she seemed to herself and others to be slipping about the corners and out-of-the-way places of life, avoiding it, staring at it with wide, lamblike eyes, wondering at things, often fearfully.

Her face, always delicately oval and pale, was not of the force which attracted. Her eyes, a milkish blue-gray with a suggestion of black in the iris, her hair black, her hands long-fingered and slim, were not of a type which would appeal to the raw youth of her world. Unconsciously, and ever, her slender, longish body sank into graceful poses. Beside the hard, garish, colorful, strident types of her neighborhoods—the girls whom the boys liked —she was not fascinating, and yet, contemplated at odd moments as she grew, she was appealing enough—at times beautiful.

What most affected her youth and her life was the internal condition of her family, the poverty and general worthlessness of her parents. They were as poor as their poorest neighbors, and quarrelsome, unhappy and mean-spirited into the bargain. Her father came dimly into her understanding at somewhere near her seventh or eighth year as an undersized, contentious and drunken and wordy man, always more or less out of a job, irritated with her mother and her sister and brother, and always, as her mother seemed to think, a little the worse for drink.

"You're a liar! You're a liar! You're a liar! You're a liar!"—how well she remembered this sing-song echoing reiteration of his, in whatever basement or hole they were living at the time. "You're a liar! I never did it! You're a liar! I wasn't there!"

Her mother, often partially intoxicated or morose because of her own ills, was only too willing to rejoin in kind. Her elder sister and brother, much more agreeable in their way and as much put upon as herself, were always coming in or running out somewhere and staying while the storm lasted; while she, shy and always a little frightened, seemed to look upon it all as unavoidable, possibly even essential. The world was always so stern, so mysterious, so non-understandable to Madeleine.

Again it might be, and often was, "Here, you, you brat, go an' get me a can o' beer! Gwan, now!" which she did quickly and fearfully enough, running to the nearest wretched corner saloon with the "can" or "growler," her slim little fingers closed tightly over the five-cent piece or dime entrusted to her, her eyes taking in the wonders and joys of the street even as she ran. She was so small at the time that her little arms were unable to reach quite the level of the bar, and she had to accept the aid of the bartender or some drinker. Then she would patiently wait while one of them teased her as to her size or until the beer was handed down.

Once, and once only, three "bad boys," knowing what she was going for and how wretched and shabby was her father, not able to revenge himself on any one outside his family, had seized her en route, forced open her hand and run away with the dime, leaving her to return fearsomely to her father, rubbing her eyes, and to be struck and abused soundly and told to fight—"Blank-blank you, what the hell are you good for if you can't do that?"

Only the vile language and the defensive soberness of her mother at the time saved her from a worse fate. As for the boys who had stolen the money, they only received curses and awful imprecations, which harmed no one.

Wretched variations of this same existence were endured by the other two members of the family, her brother Frank and her sister Tina.

The former was a slim and nervous youth, given to fits of savage temper like his father and not to be ordered and controlled exactly as his father would have him. At times, as Madeleine recalled, he appeared terribly resentful of the conditions that surrounded him and cursed and swore and even threatened to leave; at other times he was placid enough, at least not inclined to share the dreadful scenes which no one could avoid where her father was.

At the age of twelve or thirteen he secured work in a box-factory somewhere and for a while brought his wages home. But often there was no breakfast or dinner for him, and when his father and mother were deep in their cups or quarreling things were so generally neglected that even where home ties were strong no one of any worldly experience could have endured them, and he ran away.

His mother was always complaining of "the lumbago" and of not being able to get up, even when he and Tina were working and bringing home a portion of their weekly wage or all of it. If she did, it was only to hover over the wretched cookstove and brew herself a little tea and complain as before.

Madeleine had early, in her ignorant and fearsome way, tried to help, but she did not always know how and her mother was either too ill or too disgruntled with life to permit her to assist, had she been able.

As it had been with Frank so it was with Tina, only it came sooner.

When Madeleine was only five Tina was a grown girl of ten, with yellow hair and a pretty, often smiling face, and was already working somewhere—in a candy store—for a dollar and a half a week. Later, when Madeleine was eight and Tina thirteen, the latter had graduated to a button-works and was earning three.

There was something rather admirable and yet disturbing connected dimly with Tina in Madeleine's mind, an atmosphere of rebelliousness and courage which she could not have described, lacking as she did a mind that registered the facts of life clearly. She only saw Tina, pretty and strong, coming and going from her ninth to her thirteenth year, refusing to go for beer at her father's order and being cursed for it, even struck at or thrown at by him, sometimes by her mother, and often standing at the foot of the stairs after work hours or on a Sunday afternoon or evening, looking at the crowded street or walking up and down with other girls and boys, when her mother wanted her to be doing things in the house—sweeping, washing dishes, making beds —dreary, gray tasks all.

"Fixin' your hair again! Fixin' your hair again! Fixin' your hair again!" she could hear her father screaming whenever she paused before the one cracked mirror to arrange her hair. "Always in front of that blank-blank mirror fixin' her hair! If you don't get away from in front of it I'll throw you an' the mirror in the street! What the hell are you always fixin' your hair for? Say? What're you always fixin' your hair for? Say! What? What're you always fixin' your hair for?"

But Tina was never cast down apparently, only silent. At times she sang and walked with an air. She dressed herself as attractively as possible, as if with the few things she had she was attempting to cast off the burden of the life by which she was surrounded. Always she was hiding things away from the others, never wanting them to touch anything of hers. And how she had hated her father as she grew, in bitter moments calling him a "sot" and a "fool."

Tina had never been very obedient, refusing to go to church or to do much of anything about the house. Whenever her father and mother were drinking or fighting she would slip away and stay with some girl in the neighborhood that she knew. And in spite of all this squalor and misery and the fact that they moved often and the food was bad, Tina, once she was twelve or thirteen, always seemed able to achieve an agreeable appearance.

Madeleine often remembered her in a plaid skirt she had got somewhere, which looked beautiful on her, and a little gilt pin which she wore at her neck. And she had a way of doing her yellow hair high on her head, which had stuck in Madeleine's mind perhaps because of her father's rude comments on it.

II

It is not surprising that Madeleine came to her twelfth and thirteenth years without any real understanding of the great world about her and without any definite knowledge or skill. Her drunken mother was now more or less dependent upon her, her father having died of pneumonia and her brother and sister having disappeared to do for themselves.

Aside from petty beginners' tasks in shops or stores, or assisting her mother at washing or cleaning, there was little that she could do at first. Mrs. Kinsella, actually compelled by the need for rent or food or fuel after a time, would get occasional work in a laundry or kitchen or at scrubbing or window-cleaning, but not for long. The pleasure of drink would soon rob her of that.

At these tasks Madeleine helped until she secured work in a candy factory in her thirteenth year at the wage of three-thirty a week. But even with this little money paid in regularly there was no assurance that her mother would add sufficient to it to provide either food or warmth. Betimes, and when Madeleine was working, her mother cheered her all too obvious sorrows with the bottle, and at nights or week-ends rewarded Madeleine with a gabble which was all the more painful because no material comfort came with it.

The child actually went hungry at times. Usually, after a few drinks, her mother would begin to weep and recite her past ills: a process which reduced her timorous and very sympathetic daughter to complete misery. In sheer desperation the child sought for some new way in her own mind. A reduction in the working-force of the candy factory, putting her back in the ranks of the work-seekers once more, and a neighbor perceiving her wretched state and suggesting that some extra helpers were wanted in a department store at Christmas time, she applied there, but so wretched were her clothes by now that she was not even considered.

Then a man who had a restaurant in a nearby street gave her mother and Madeleine positions as dishwashers, but he was compelled to discharge her mother, although he wished to retain Madeleine. From this last, however, because of the frightening attentions of the cook, she had to flee, and without obtaining a part of the small pittance which was due her. Again, and because in times past she had aided her mother to clean in one place and another, she was able to get a place as servant in a family.

Those who know anything of the life of a domestic know how thoroughly unsatisfactory it is—the leanness, the lack of hope. As a domestic, wherever she was—and she obtained no superior places for the time being—she had only the kitchen for her chief chamber or a cubbyhole under the roof. Here, unless she was working elsewhere in the house or chose to visit her mother occasionally she was expected to remain. Pots and pans and scrubbing and cleaning and bed-making were her world. If any one aside from her mother ever wanted to see her (which was rare) he or she could only come into the kitchen, an ugly and by day inconvenient realm.

She had, as she soon came to see, no privileges whatsoever. In the morning she was expected to be up before any one else, possibly after working late the night before. Breakfast had to be served for others before she herself could eat—what was left. Then came the sweeping and cleaning. In one place which she obtained in her fifteenth year the husband annoyed her so, when his wife was not looking, that she had to leave; in another it was the son. By now she was becoming more attractive, although by no means beautiful or daring.

But wherever she was and whatever she was doing, she could not help thinking of her mother and Tina and Frank and her father, and of the grim necessities and errors and vices which had seemed to dominate them. Neither her brother nor her sister did she ever see again. Her mother, she felt (and this was due to a sensitiveness and a sympathy which she could not possibly overcome), she would have with her for the rest of her days unless, like the others, she chose to run away.

Daily her mother was growing more inadequate and less given to restraint or consideration. As "bad" as she was, Madeleine could not help thinking what a "hard" time she had had. From whatever places she obtained work in these days (and it was not often any more) she was soon discharged, and then she would come inquiring after Madeleine, asking to be permitted to see her. Naturally, her shabby dress and shawl and rag of a hat, as well as her wastrel appearance, were an affront to any well-ordered household. Once in her presence, whenever Madeleine was permitted to see her, she would begin either a cozening or a lachrymose account of her great needs.

"It's out o' oil I am, me dear," or "Wurra, I have no wood" or "bread" or "meat"—never drink. "Ye won't let yer pore old mother go cold or hungry, now, will ye? That's the good girl now. Fifty cents now, if ye have it, me darlin', or a quarter, an' I'll not be troublin' ye soon again. Even a dime, if ye can spare me no more. God'll reward ye. I'll have work o' me own tomorra. That's the good girl now—ye won't let me go away without anything."

Oscillating between shame and sympathy, her daughter would

take from the little she had and give it to her, trembling for fear the disturbing figure would prove her undoing. Then the old woman would go out, lurching sometimes in her cups, and disappear, while an observant fellow servant was probably seeing and reporting to the mistress, who, of course, did not want her to come there and so told the girl, or more practical still, discharged her.

Thus from her fourteenth to her sixteenth year she was shunted from house to house and from shop to shop, always in the vain hope that this time her mother might let her alone.

And at the very same time, life, sweetened by the harmonies of youth in the blood, was calling—that exterior life which promised everything because so far it had given nothing. The little simple things of existence, the very ordinary necessities of clothing and ornament, with which the heart of youth and the inherent pride of appearance are gratified, had a value entirely disproportionate to their worth. Yes, already she had turned the age wherein the chemic harmonies in youth begin to sing, thought to thought, color to color, dream to dream. She was being touched by the promise of life itself.

And then, as was natural, love in the guise of youth, a rather sophisticated gallant somewhat above the world in which she was moving, appeared and paid his all but worthless court to her. He was physically charming, the son of a grocer of some means in the vicinity in which she was working, a handsome youth with pink cheeks and light hair and blue eyes, and vanity enough for ten. Because she was shy and pretty he became passingly interested in her.

"Oh, I saw you cleaning the windows yesterday," this with a radiant, winning smile; or "You must live down toward Blake Street. I see you going down that way once in a while."

Madeleine acknowledged rather shamefacedly that it was true: That so dashing a boy should be interested in her was too marvelous.

In the evenings, or at any time, it was easy for a youth of his

skill and *savoir-faire* to pick her out of the bobbing stream of
humanity in which she occasionally did errands or visited her
mother in her shabby room, and to suggest that he be permitted
to call upon her. Or, failing that, because of her mother's shabby
quarters and her mother herself, that the following Sunday
would be ideal for an outing to one of those tawdry, noisy
beaches to which he liked to go with other boys and girls in a
car.

A single trip to Wonderland, a single visit to one of its halls
where music sounded to the splash of the waves and where he
did his best to teach her to dance, a single meal in one of its
gaudy, noisy restaurants, a taste of its whirly pleasures, and a
new color and fillip were given to hope, a new and seemingly
realizable dream of happiness implanted in her young mind. The
world was happier than she had thought, or could be made so;
not all people fought and screamed at each other. There were
such things as tenderness, soft words, sweet words.

But the way of so sophisticated a youth with a maid was brief
and direct. His mind was of that order which finds in the fresh-
ness of womankind a mere passing delight, something to be
deflowered and then put aside. He was a part of a group that
secured its happiness in rifling youth, the youth of those whose
lives were so dull and bleak that a few words of kindness, a little
change of scene, the mere proximity of experience and force
such as they had never known, were pay ample for anything
which they might give or do.

And of these Madeleine was one.

Never having had anything in her own life, the mere thought
of a man so vigorous and handsome, one with knowledge enough
to show her more of life than she had ever dreamed of, to take
her to places of color and light, to assure her that she was fitted
for better things even though they were not immediately forth-
coming, was sufficient to cause her to place faith where it was
least worthy of being placed. To win his way there was even
talk of marriage later on, that love should be generous and have
faith—and then—

III

Plain-clothesman Amundsen, patrolling hawk-like the region of Fourteenth and K streets, not so far from Blake, where Madeleine had lived for a time, was becoming interested in and slightly suspicious of a new face.

For several days at odd hours, he had seen a girl half-slinking, half-brazening her way through a region the very atmosphere of which was blemishing to virtue. To be sure, he had not yet seen her speak to any one; nor was there that in her glance or manner which caused him to feel that she might.

Still—with the assurance of his authority and his past skill in trapping many he followed discreetly, seeing where she went, how she lingered for awhile nervously, then returned as she had come. She was very young, not more than seventeen.

He adjusted his tie and collar and decided to attempt his skill. "Excuse me, Miss. Out for a little stroll? So am I. Mind my walking along with you a little way? Wouldn't like to come and have a drink, would you? I work in an automobile place over here in Grey Street, and I'm just off for the afternoon. Live here in the neighborhood?"

Madeleine surveyed this stranger with troubled eyes. Since the day her youthful lover had deserted her, and after facing every conceivable type of ill, but never being willing to confess or fall back upon her drunken, dreaming mother for aid, she had tested every device. The necessities and expenses incident to a prospective, and to her degrading state, as well as the continued care of her mother, had compelled her, as she had finally seen it, to come to this—for a time anyhow. A street girl, finding her wandering and crying, had taken her in hand and shown her, after aiding her for weeks, how to make her way.

Her burden that she feared so much was artificially if ruthlessly and criminally disposed of. Then she was shown the way of the streets until she could gain a new foothold in life; only, as she had since learned, it was difficult for her to accommodate herself to this fell traffic. She was not of it spiritually. She really did not intend to continue in it; it was just a temporary make-shift, born of fear and a dumb despair.

But neither Detective Amundsen nor the law was ready to believe that. To the former she seemed as worthless as any—one of those curious, uncared-for flowers never understood by the dull.

In a nearby café she had listened to his inquiries, the fact that he had a room in a nearby hotel, or could secure one. Contemning a fate which drove her to such favors, and fully resolved to leave it soon, to make something better of her life in the future, she went with him.

Then came the scarring realization that he was an officer of the law, a cynical, contemptuous hawk smirking over her tears and her explanations. It was absolutely nothing to him that she was so young and could scarcely have been as hardened as he pretended. She was compelled to walk through the streets with him to the nearest police station, while he nodded to or stopped to explain to passing brothers of the cloth the nature of his latest conquest.

There was the registering of her under the false name that she chose, rather than be exposed under her true one, before a brusque and staring sergeant in shirtslceves; a cell with a wooden bench, the first she had ever known; a matron who searched her; then a ride somewhere in a closed vehicle, and the usual swift and confusing arraignment before a judge whose glance was seemingly so cold that it was frightening.

"Nellie Fitzpatrick; Officer Amundsen. Eighth Precinct."

The friend who had taught her the ways of the streets had warned her that if caught and arrested it might mean months of incarceration in some institution, the processes or corrective meaning of which she did not quite comprehend. All that she had grasped fully was that it meant a severance from her freedom, the few little things, pitiful as they were, that she could call her own. And now here she was, in the clutches of the law, and with no one to defend her.

The testimony of the officer was as it had been in hundreds of cases before this; he had been walking his beat and she had accosted him, as usual.

There being no legal alternative, the magistrate had held her for sentence, pending investigation, and the investigation proving, as it only could, that her life would be better were some corrective measures applied to it, she was sent away. She had never had any training worthy the name. Her mother was an irresponsible inebriate. A few months in some institution where she could be taught some trade or craft would be best.

And so it was that for a period of a year she was turned over to the care of the Sisterhood of the Good Shepherd.

IV

The gray and bony walls of that institution starkly dominated one of the barest and most unprepossessing regions of the city. Its northern façade fronted a stoneyard, beyond which were the rocks of the racing Sound and a lighthouse. To the east, rocks and the river, a gray expanse in winter picked over by gulls, mourned over by the horns of endless craft. To the south, bare coal-yards, wagon-yards, tenements.

Twice weekly, sentenced delinquents of various ages—the "children," of whom Madeleine was one; the "girls," ranging from eighteen to thirty; the "women," ranging from thirty to fifty; and the old people, ranging from fifty until the last years of life— were brought here in an all but air-tight cage, boxed like a great circus van, and with only small barred air-holes at the top. Inside the van were bare, hard benches, one against either wall. A representative of the probation and control system of the city, a gaunt female of many years, sat within; also an officer of such prodigious proportions that the mere sight of him might well raise the inquiry of why so much unnecessary luggage. For amusement in dull hours he smoothed his broad mouth with the back of his red, hairy hand, and dreamed of bygone days.

The institution itself was operated by a Mother Superior and thirty nuns, all of the order mentioned, all expert in their separate ways in cooking, housekeeping, laundering, buying, lace-making, teaching, and a half dozen other practical or applied arts.

Within the institution were separate wings or sections for each of the four groups before mentioned, sections in which each had its separate working, eating, sleeping and playing rooms. Only one thing was shared in common: the daily, and often twice or thrice daily, religious ceremonies in the great chapel, a lofty, magi-decorated and be-altered and be-candled chamber, whose tall, thin spire surmounted with a cross might easily be seen from many of the chambers in which the different groups worked. There were masses in the mornings, vespers and late prayers in the afternoons, often late prayers at night or on holidays, when additional services of one kind and another were held. To the religious-minded these were of course consoling. To the contrary-minded they became at times a strain.

Always, and over all the work and all the routine relaxations or pleasures of the institution, there hung the grim insistence of the law, its executive arm, upon order, seemliness, and, if not penance, at least a servility of mind which was the equivalent thereof. Let the voices of the nuns be never so soft, their footfalls light, their manners courteous, their ways gentle, persuasive, sympathetic, their mood tender; back of it all lay the shadow of the force which could forthwith return any or all to the rough hands of the police, the stern and not-to-be-evaded dictum of the courts.

This, much more than any look of disappointment or displeasure, if such were ever necessary, spoke to these delinquents or victims, whatever their mood, and quieted them in their most rebellious hours. Try as they would, they could not but remember that it was the law that had placed them here and now detained them. That there reigned here peace, order, sweetness and harmony, was well enough, comforting in cases, yet and always the life here had obviously a two-fold base: one the power of the law itself, the other the gentle, appealing, beautiful suasion of the nuns.

But to so inexperienced and as yet unreasoning a child as

Madeleine all of this savored at this time of but one thing: the sharp, crude, inconsiderate and uninquiring forces of law or life, which seemed never to stop and inquire how or why, but only to order how, and that without mercy. Like some frightened animal faced by a terrifying enemy, she had thus far been able to think only of some darksome corner into which she might slip and hide, a secret place so inconspicuous and minute that the great savage world without would not trouble or care to follow.

And well enough the majority of the Sisterhood, especially those in immediate authority over her, understood the probable direction and ramifications of her present thoughts.

They knew her mood, for had they not during years past dealt with many such? And stern as was the law, they were not unmindful of her welfare. So long as she was willing and obedient there was but one thing more: that somehow her troubled or resentful or congealed and probably cruelly injured mind should be wooed from its blind belief in the essential injustice of life, to be made to feel, as they themselves were ready to believe, that all paths were not closed, all forces not essentially dark or evil.

For them there was hope of sorts for all, a way out, and many —even she—might find ways and means of facing life, better possibly than any she had ever known.

v

Sister St. Agnes, for instance, who controlled the spotlessly clean but barnlike and bleak room in which were a hundred machines for the sewing of shirtwaists, was a creature of none too fortunate a history herself.

Returning at the age of eighteen and at the death of her father from a convent in which she had been placed by him in order to escape the atmosphere of a home which he himself had found unsatisfactory, she had found a fashionable mother leading a life of which she could scarcely conceive, let alone accept. The taint, the subterfuge, the self-indulgent waste, had as soon sickened her as had the streets Madeleine.

Disappointed, she felt herself after a time incapable of enduring it and had fled, seeking first to make her way in a world which offered only meagre wages and a barren life to those incapable of enduring its rugged and often shameless devices; later, again wearied of her own trials, she had returned to the convent in which she had been trained and asked to be schooled for service there. Finding the life too simple for a nature grown more rugged, she had asked to be, and had been, transferred to the House of the Good Shepherd, finding there for the first time, in this institution, duties and opportunities which somehow matched her ideals.

And by the same token the Mother Superior of this same institution, Mother St. Bertha, who often came through and inquired into the story of each one, was of a history and of an order of mind which was not unlike that of Sister St. Agnes, only it had even more of genuine pathos and suffering in it. The daughter of a shoe manufacturer, she had seen her father fail, her mother die of consumption, a favorite brother drink and carouse until he finally fell under the blight of disease and died. The subsequent death of her father, to whom she had devoted her years, and the failing of her own dreams of a personal love, had saddened her, and she sought out and was admitted to this order in the hope that she, too, might still make especial use of a life that promised all too little in the world outside.

Her great comfort was in having some one or something to love, the satisfaction of feeling that lives which otherwise might have come to nothing had by some service of hers been lifted to a better state. And in that thought she worked here daily, going about among those incarcerated in different quarters, seeing to it that their tasks were not too severe, their comforts and hopes, where hope still remained, in nowise betrayed.

But to Madeleine at first the solemn habits of the nuns, as well as the gray gingham apron she had to don, the grayer woolen dress, the severe manner in which she had to dress her hair, her very plain shoes, the fact that she had to rise at six-thirty, attend mass and then breakfast at eight, work from eight-thirty to twelve-thirty, and again from one-thirty to four; lunch regularly at twelve-thirty and sup at six, attend a form of prayer service at four-thirty, play at simple games with her new companions between five and six and again between seven and nine, and then promptly retire to a huge sleeping-ward set with small white iron beds in long rows, and lit, after the retiring bell had sounded, by small oil cups or candles burning faintly before various images, all smacked of penance, the more disturbing because it was strange, a form of personal control which she had not sought and could not at once accept.

Nor could she help thinking that some severer form of punishment was yet to be meted out to her, or might ensue by reason of one unavoidable error or another. Life had always been so with her. But, once here a time, things proved not so bad.

The large workroom with its hundred machines and its tall windows, which afforded a stark view of the coal-pockets to the south, and the river with its boats and gulls, proved not unpleasing. The clean, bright windows, polished floors and walls—washed and cleaned by the inmates themselves, the nuns not disdaining to do their share—and the habits of the Sisters, their white-fringed hoods, black robes and clinking beads and their silent tread and low speech, impressed her greatly.

The fact that there was no severe reproof of any failure to comprehend at first, but only slow and patient explanations of simple things, not difficult in themselves to do; that aside from the routine duties, the marching in line with hands crossed over breast and head up, as well as genuflections at mass, prayers before and after meals, at rising and on retiring, and at the peal of the Angelus, morning, noon and night, there was no real oppression, finally caused her to like it.

The girls who were here with her, shy or silent or cold or indifferent at first, and each with her world of past experiences, contacts, and relationships locked in her heart, were still, placed as they were elbow to elbow at work, at meals, at prayer, at retiring, incapable of not achieving some kind of remote fellowship which eventually led to speech and confidences.

Thus the young girl who sat next at her right in the sewing-room—Viola Patters by name, a brave, blonde, cheerful little thing—although she had endured much that might be called ill-fortune, was still intensely interested in life.

By degrees and as they worked the two reached an under-standing. Viola confessed that her father, who was a non-union painter by trade, had always worked well enough when he could get work, but that he managed badly and could not al-ways get it. Her mother was sickly and they were very poor and there were many children.

Viola had first worked in a box-factory, where she had been able to earn only three dollars or less at piece work—"pasting corners," as she described it—and once she had been sworn at and even thrown away from a table at which she had been working because she didn't do it right, and then she quit. Then her father in turn swearing at her for her "uppishness," she had got work in a five-and-ten-cent store, where she had received three dollars a week and a commission of one per cent on her sales, which were not sufficient to yield more than a dollar more. Then she had secured a better place in a department store at five dollars a week, and there it was that she had come by the handsome boy who had caused her so much trouble.

He was a taxi-driver, who always had a car at his disposal when he worked, only it was very seldom that he cared to work. Although he married her swiftly enough and took her away from her family, still he had not supported her very well, and shortly after they were married he was arrested and accused with two others of stealing a machine and selling it, and after months and months of jail life he had been sentenced to three years in the penitentiary.

In the meantime he had called upon her to aid him, pressed her to raise sums of which she had never previously dreamed—and by ways of which she had never previously dreamed—was pleaded with, all but ordered—and still she loved him. And then in executing the "how" of it she had been picked up by the po-lice and sent here, as had Madeleine, only she never told, not even to Madeleine, what the police had never discovered—that at the suggestion of her first love she had included robbery among her arts.

"But I don't care," she had whispered finally as they worked. "He was good to me, anyhow, when he had work. He was crazy about me, and he liked to go places and dance and eat and see shows when he had money, and he always took me. Gee, the times we've had! And if he wants me to stick to him when he gets out, I will. He ain't half as bad as some. Gee, you oughta hear some of the girls talk!"

And so it was finally that Madeleine was induced to tell her story.

There were other girls here who, once this bond of sympathy was struck, were keen enough to tell their tales—sad, unfortunate, harried lives all—and somehow the mere telling of them restored to Madeleine some of her earlier faint confidence or interest in life. It was "bad," but it was vivid. For in spite of their unfortunate beginnings, the slime in which primarily and without any willing of their own they had been embedded and from which nearly all were seeking to crawl upwards, and bravely enough, they had heart for and faith in life.

In all cases, apparently, love was their star as well as their bane. They thought chiefly of the joy that might be had in joining their lives with some man or being out in the free world, working again possibly, at least in touch in some feeble way with the beauty and gayety of life, as beauty and gayety manifested themselves to them.

And so by degrees, the crash of her own original hopes echoing less and less loudly in the distance, the pain of her great shame and rude awakening passed farther and farther from her. The smoothness and regularity of this austere life, indifferent as it seemed at times, consoled her by its very security and remoteness from the world. It was lean and spare, to be sure, but it offered safety and rest to the mind and heart. Now, rising in her dim, silent ward of a morning, repeating her instructed prayers, marching in silence to chapel, to breakfast, to work, hearing only the soft hum of the machines, marching again to chapel, playing each day, but not too noisily, and finally retiring in the same ordered and silent way to her tiny bed, she was soothed and healed.

And yet, or perhaps because of this, she could not help thinking of the clangor and crash of the world without. It had been grim and painful to her, but in its rude, brutal way it had been alive. The lighted streets at night! The cars! That dancing pavilion in which once she had been taught to dance by the great blue sea! The vanished touches of her faithless lover's hands—his kisses—brief, so soon over! Where was he now in the great strange world outside? With whom? What was she like? And would he tire of her as quickly? Treat her as badly? Where was Tina? Frank? Her mother? What had happened to her mother? Not a word had she heard.

To Sister St. Agnes, after a time, sensing her to be generous, faithful, patient, she had confided all concerning herself and her mother, crying on her shoulder, and the Sister had promised to learn what she could. But the investigation proving that her mother had been sent to the workhouse, she deemed it best to say nothing for the present. Madeleine would find her quickly enough on returning to the world. Why cloud the new budding life with so shameful a memory?

VI

And then once more, in due time, and with the memory of these things clinging fast to her, she was sent forth into the world, not quite as poorly-armed as before, perhaps, but still with the limited equipment which her own innate disposition compelled.

After many serious and presumably wise injunctions as to the snares and pitfalls of this world, and accompanied by a black-habited nun, who took her direct to one of those moral and religious families whose strict adherence to the tenets of this particular faith was held to provide an ideal example, she was left to her own devices and the type of work she had previously followed, the nuns themselves being hard put to it to discover any thing above the most menial forms of employment for their various charges. Theirs was a type of schooling and training which did not rise above a theory of morality requiring not so much skill as faith and blind obedience.

And again, here, as in the institution itself, the idea of a faith, a religion, a benign power above that of man and seeking his welfare, surrounded her as the very air itself or as an aura, although she personally was by no means ready to accept it, never having given it serious thought.

Everywhere here, as in the institution itself, were little images or colored pictures of saints, their brows circled by stars or crowns, their hands holding scepters or lilies, their bodies arrayed in graceful and soothing robes of white, blue, pink and gold. Their faces were serene, their eyes benignly contemplative, yet to Madeleine they were still images only, pretty and graceful, even comforting, but at so great variance to life as she knew it as to be little more than pretty pictures.

In the great church which they attended, and to which they persuaded her to accompany them, were more of these same candle-lit pictures of saints, images and altars starred with candles, many or few, at which she was wont to start in wonder and awe. The vestments of the priest and the acolytes, the white-and-gold and red-and-gold of the chasuble and the stole and the cope, the gold and silver crosses, chalices and winecups, overrawed her inexperienced and somewhat impressionable mind without convincing it of the immanence of superior forces whose significance or import she could in nowise guess. God, God, God —she heard of Him and the passion and death of the self-sacrificing Lord Jesus.

And here, as there, the silence, the order, the cleanliness and regularity, as well as simplicity, were the things which most invested her reason and offered the greatest contrasts to her old life.

She had not known or sensed the significance of these things before. Now, day by day, like the dripping of water, the ticking of time, they made an impression, however slight. Routine, rou-

tine, routine, and the habit and order and color of a vast and
autocratic religion, made their lasting impression upon her.

And yet, in spite of an occasional supervisory visit on the part
of one or other of the nuns of the probation department, she
was not only permitted but compelled to work out her life as
best she might, and upon such wages as she could command or
devise. For all the prayers and the good-will of the nuns, life was
as insistent and driving as ever. It did not appear to be so involved with religion. In spite of the admonitions of the church,
the family for whom she was working saw little more in its religious obligation than that she should be housed and fed according to her material merits. If she wished to better herself, as she
soon very clearly saw she must, she would have to develop a
skill which she did not now have and which, once developed,
would make her of small use here. At the same time, if the
months spent in the institution had conveyed to her the reason-
ableness of making something better of her life than hitherto
she had been able to do, the world, pleasure, hope, clanged as
insistently and as wooingly as ever before.

But how? How? was the great problem. Hers was no resource-
ful, valiant soul, capable of making its own interesting way
alone. Think as she would, and try, love, and love only, the admiration and ministering care of some capable and affectionate
man was the only thing that seemed likely to solve for her the
various earthly difficulties which beset her.

But even as to this, how, in what saving or perfect way, was
love to come to her? She had made one mistake which in the
development of any honest relationship with another would have
to be confessed. And how would it be then? Would love, admiration, forgive? Love, love, love, and the peace and comfort
of that happy routine home life which she imagined she saw
operative in the lives of others—how it glimmered afar, like a
star!

And again there was her mother.

It was not long after she had come from the institution that
sheer loneliness, as well as a sense of daughterly responsibility

and pity, had urged her to look up her mother, in order that she might restore to herself some little trace of a home, however wretched it might be. She had no one, as she proceeded to argue. At least in her own lonely life her mother provided, or would, an ear and a voice, sympathetic if begging, a place to go.

She had learned on returning to their last living-place on one of her afternoons off, that her mother had been sent away to the "Island," but had come back and since had been sent to the city poor-farm. This last inquiry led eventually to her mother's discovery of her and of her fixing herself upon her once more as a dependent, until her death somewhat over a year later.

But in the meantime, and after all, life continued to call and call and to drive her on, for she was still full of the hope and fever of youth.

Once, before leaving the institution in which they had worked together, Viola Patters had said to her in one of those bursts of confidence based on attraction:

"Once you're outa here an' I am, too, I'd like to see you again, only there ain't no use your writin' me here, for I don't believe they'd give it to me. I don't believe they'd want us to run together. I don't believe they like me as well as they do you. But you write me, wherever you are, care of—," and here she gave a definite address—"an' I'll get it when I get out."

She assured Madeleine that she would probably be able to get a good place, once she was free of the control of the sisters, and then she might be able to do something for her.

Often during these dark new days she thought of this, and being hard-pressed for diverting interests in her life she finally wrote her, receiving in due time a request to come and see her.

But, as it proved, Viola was no avenue of improvement for her in her new mood. She was, as Madeleine soon discovered, part of a small group which was making its way along a path which she had promised herself henceforth to avoid. Viola was more comfortably placed in quarters of her own than Madeleine had ever been, but the method by which she was forwarding her life she could not as readily accept.

Yet her own life, move about as she might and did after a time from one small position to another, in store or factory, in the hope of bettering herself, held nothing either. Day by day as she worked she sensed all the more clearly that the meagre tasks at which she toiled could bring her nothing of permanent value. Her mother was dead now, and she more alone than ever. During a period of several years, in which she worked and dreamed, leading a thin, underpaid life, her mind was ever on love and what it might do for her—the pressure of a seeking hand, the sanctuary of an enveloping heart.

And then, for the second time in her brief life, love came, or seemed to—at least in her own heart if nowhere else.

She had by now, and through her own efforts, attained to a clerkship in one of the great stores at the salary of seven dollars a week, on which she was trying to live. And then, behold, one day among her customers one of those suave and artful masters of the art of living by one's wits, with a fortune of looks, to whom womanhood is a thing to be taken by an upward curl of a pair of mustachios, the vain placement of ringed locks, spotless and conspicuous linen, and clothes and shoes of a newness and lustre all but disturbing to a very work-a-day world. His manners and glances were of a winsomeness which only the feminine heart—and that unschooled in the valuelessness of veneer—fully appreciates.

Yes, the sheer grace of the seeking male, his shallow and heartless courtesy, the lustre of his eye and skin, a certain something of shabby-grand manner, such as she had never known in the particularly narrow world in which she moved, was sufficient to arrest and fix her interest.

He leaned over and examined the stationery and pencils which she sold, commenting on prices, the routine of her work, smiled archly and suggested by his manner entire that she was one in whom he could be deeply interested. At the same time a certain animal magnetism, of the workings of which she was no more conscious than might be any stick or stone, took her in its tow. Here was one out of many, a handsome beau, who was inter-

ested in her and her little life. The oiled and curled hair became
the crown of a god; the mustachios and the sharp, cruel nose
harmonies of exquisite beauty. Even the muscular, prehensile
hands were rhythmic, musical in their movements. She had
time only to sense the wonder of his perfect self before he went
away. But it was to return another day, with an even more familiar and insinuating grace.

He was interested in her, as he frankly said the next time, and
she must be his friend. At lunch-time one day he was waiting to
take her to a better restaurant than she would ever have dreamed
of entering; on another day it was to dinner that she accompanied him.

According to him, she was beautiful, wonderful. Her flower-
like life was being wasted on so rude a task. She should marry
him, and then her difficulties would be solved. He was one who,
when fortune was with him, so he said, made much, much
money. He might even take her from the city at times to see
strange places and interesting scenes.

As for her own stunted life, from most of the details of which
she forbore, he seemed in nowise interested. It was not due to
any lack on her part in the past that her life had been so ill. . . .

Love, love, love. . . . The old story. In a final burst of admiration and love for his generosity she told him of her one great
error, which caused him a few moments of solemn cogitation
and was then dismissed as nothing of importance, a pathetic,
childish mistake. Then there followed one of those swift and
seemingly unguarded unions, a commonplace of the tangled self-
preserving underworld of poverty. A clergyman was found
whose moral assurances seemed to make the union ideal. Then
a room in a commonplace boarding-house, and the newer and
better life which eventually was to realize all was begun.

VII

To those familiar with the brazen and relentless methods of a
certain type of hawk of the underworld, which picks fledglings
from the nest and springlings from the fields and finds life itself

only a hunting-ground in which those mentally or physically weaker than itself may be enslaved, this description will seem neither strained nor inadequate. Fagins of sex, creatures who change their women as they would their coats, they make an easy if reprehensible bed of their lives, and such of their victims as have known them well testify that for a while at least in their care or custody they were not unhappy.

So it was with Madeleine and her lover. With amused and laughing tolerance toward her natural if witless efforts to build up a home atmosphere about their presumably joint lives, to build for a future in which they should jointly share, he saw in them only something trivial or ridiculous, whereas to her it was as though the heavens had opened and she was surveying a new world. For in his love and care there was to be peace. Latterly, if not now—for already he complained of conditions which made it impossible for him to work—the results of their several labors were to be pooled in order to prepare for that something better which would soon be achieved—a home, an ideally happy state somewhere. Even children were in her mind.

The mere fact that he shortly complained of other temporary reverses which made it necessary for him and her to keep close watch over their resources, and that for the time being, until he "could arrange his affairs," she must find some employment which would pay much better than her old one, gave her no shock.

Indeed, it was an indescribable joy for her to do for her love, for love had come, that great solvent of all other earthly difficulties, that leveler of all but insurmountable barriers. Even now love was to make her life flower at last. There was an end to loneliness and the oppressive indifference of the great sea of life.

But, as in the first instance, so now the awakening was swift and disconcerting. Realizing the abject adoration in which she held his surface charms and that his thin, tricky soul was the beginning and the end of things for her, it was all the easier to assure her, and soon insist, that the easiest and swiftest way of making money, of which she was unfortunately aware, must be resorted to, for a great necessity had come upon him. The usual tale of a threatening disaster, a sudden loss at cards which might end in imprisonment for him and their enforced separation, was enough.

Swiftly he filled her ears with tales of rescues by women of many of his men friends similarly circumstanced, of the "fools" and "marks" that filled the thoroughfares to be captured and preyed upon by women. Why hesitate? Consider the meagre, beggarly wages she had previously earned, the nothingness of her life before. Why jeopardize their future now? Why be foolish, dull? Plainly it was nothing to love, as he saw it. Should it be so much to her? In this wise she was persuaded.

But now it was not the shame and the fear of arrest that troubled her, but the injury which love had done and was doing to her, that cut and burned and seared and scarred.

Love, as she now began dimly to realize once more, should not be so. More than anything else, if love was what she had always dreamed, should it not protect and save and keep her for itself? And now see. Love was sending her out again to loiter in doorways and before windows and to "make eyes."

It was this that turned like a wheel in her brain and heart. For in spite of the roughness of her emotional experiences thus far, she had faith to believe that love should not be so, should not do so.

Those features which to this hour, and long after, like those features of her first love, seemed so worship-worth, those eyes that had seemed to beam on her with love, the lips that had smiled so graciously and kissed hers, the hands and arms that had petted and held her, should not be part of the compulsion that sent her here.

No, love should be better than that. He himself had told her so at first—that she was worth more than all else to him—and now see!

And then one night, fully a year and a half later, the climax. Being particularly irritated by some money losses and the need of enduring her at all, even though she might still prove of some value as a slave, he turned on her with a savage fury.

"What, only . . . ! Get to hell outa here! What do you think I am—a sucker? And let go my arm. Don't come that stuff on me. I'm sick of it. Don't hang on my arm, I tell yah! I'm tired, damned tired! Get out! Go on—beat it, an' don't come back, see? I'm through—through—yuh hear me? I mean what I say. I'm through, once an' fer all. Beat it, an' fer good. Don't come back. I've said that before, but this time it *goes!* Go on, now quick— Scat!—an' don't ever let me see yah around here any more, yah hear?—yah damned piece o' mush, yah!"

He pushed her away, throwing open the door as he did so, and, finding her still pleading and clinging, threw her out with such force that she cut her left eye and the back of her left hand against the jamb of the door.

There was a cry of "Fred! Fred! Please! Please!"—and then the door was slammed and she was left leaning disconsolately and brokenly against the stair-rail outside.

And now, as before, the cruelty and inscrutability of life weighed on her, only now, less than before, had she hope wherewith to buoy herself. It was all so dark, so hopeless. Often in this hour she thought of the swift, icy waters of the river, glistening under a winter moon, and then again of the peace and quiet of the House of the Good Shepherd, its shielding remoteness from life, the only true home or sanctuary she had ever known. And so, brooding and repressing occasional sobs, she made her way toward it, down the long streets, thinking of the pathetically debasing love-life that was now over—the dream of love that never, never could be again, for her.

VIII

The stark red walls of the institution stood as before, only dim and gray and cold under a frosty winter moon. It was three of a chill, cold morning. She had come a long way, drooping, brooding, half-freezing and crying. More than once on the way the hopelessness of her life and her dreams had given her pause, causing her to turn again with renewed determination toward the river—only the vivid and reassuring picture she had retained of this same grim and homely place, its restricted peace and quiet, the sympathy of Sister St. Agnes and Mother St. Bertha, had carried her on.

En route she speculated as to whether they would receive her now, so objectionable and grim was her tale. And yet she could not resist continuing toward it, so reassuring was its memory, only to find it silent, not a single light burning. But, after all, there was one, at a side door—not the great cold gate by which she had first been admitted but another to one side, to her an all but unknown entrance; and to it after some brooding hesitation she made her way, ringing a bell and being admitted by a drowsy nun, who ushered her into the warmth and quiet of the inner hallway. Once in she mechanically followed to the bronze grille which, as prison bars, obstructed the way, and here on one of the two plain chairs placed before a small aperture she now sank wearily and looked through.

Her cut eye was hurting her and her bruised hands. On the somewhat faded jacket and crumpled hat, pulled on indifferently because she was too hurt to think or care, there was some blown snow. And when the Sister Secretary in charge of the room after midnight, hearing footsteps, came to the grille, she looked up wanly, her little red, rough hands crossed on her lap.

"Mother," she said beseechingly, "may I come in?"

Then remembering that only Mother St. Bertha could admit her, added wearily:

"Is Mother St. Bertha here? I was here before. She will know me."

The Sister Secretary surveyed her curiously, sensing more of the endless misery that was ever here, but seeing that she was sick or in despair hastened to call her superior, whose rule it was that all such requests for admission should be referred to her. There was no stir in the room in her absence. Presently pattened feet were heard, and the face of Mother St. Bertha, wrinkled and a-weary, appeared at the square opening.

"What is it, my child?" she asked curiously if softly, wondering at the crumpled presence at this hour.

"Mother," began Madeleine tremulously, looking up and recognizing her, "don't you remember me? It is Madeleine. I was here four years ago. I was in the girls' ward. I worked in the sewing-room."

She was so beaten by life, the perpetual endings to her never more than tremulous hopes, that even now and here she expected little more than an indifference which would send her away again.

"Why, yes, of course I remember you, my child. But what is it that brings you now, dear? Your eye is cut, and your hand."

"Yes, Mother, but please don't ask—just now. Oh, please let me come in! I am so tired! I've had such a hard time!"

"Of course, my child," said the Mother, moving to the door and opening it. "You may come in. But what has happened, child? How is it that your cheek is cut, and your hands?"

"Mother," pleaded Madeleine wearily, "must I answer now? I am so unhappy! Can't I just have my old dress and my bed for tonight—that little bed under the lamp?"

"Why, yes, dear, you may have them, of course," said the nun, tactfully sensing a great grief. "And you need not talk now. I think I know how it is. Come with me."

She led the way along bare, dimly lit corridors and up cold solid iron stairs, echoing to the feet, until once more, as in the old days, the severe but spotless room in which were the baths and the hampers for soiled clothes was reached.

"Now, my child," she said, "you may undress and bathe. I will get something for your eye."

And so here at last, once more, Madeleine put aside the pathetic if showy finery that for a time had adorned and shamed her: a twilled skirt she had only recently bought in the pale hope of interesting *him*, the commonplace little hat for which she had paid ten dollars, the striped shirtwaist, once a pleasure to her in the hope that it would please *him*.

In a kind of dumbness of despair she took off her shoes and

stockings and, as the Mother left, entered the warm, clean bath which had been provided. She stifled a sob as she did so, and others as she bathed. Then she stepped out and dried her body and covered it with the clean, simple slip of white which had been laid on a chair, brushing her hair and touching her eye, until the Mother Sister returned with an unguent wherewith to dress it.

Then she was led along other silent passages, once dreary enough but now healing in their sense of peace and rest, and so into the great room set with row upon row of simple white iron beds, covered with their snowy linen and illuminated only by the minute red lamps or the small candles burning before their idealistic images here and there, beneath which so many like herself were sleeping. Over the bed which she had once occupied, and which by chance was then vacant, burned the one little lamp which she recognized as of old—her lamp, as she had always thought of it—a thin and flickering flame, before an image of the Virgin. At sight of it she repressed a sob.

"You see, my child," said the Mother Superior poetically, "it must have been waiting for you. Anyhow it is empty. Perhaps it may have known you were coming."

She spoke softly so that the long rows of sleepers might not be disturbed, then proceeded to turn down the coverlets.

"Oh, Mother," Madeleine suddenly whispered softly as she stood by the bed, "won't you let me stay always? I never want to go out any more. I have had such a hard time. I will work so hard for you if you will let me stay!"

The experienced Sister looked at her curiously. Never before had she heard such a plea.

"Why, yes, my child," she said. "If you wish to stay I'm sure it can be arranged. It is not as we usually do, but you are not the only one who has gone out in the past and come back to us. I am sure God and the Blessed Virgin will hear your prayer for whatever is right. But now go to bed and sleep. You need rest. I can see that. And tomorrow, or any time, or never, as you choose you may tell me what has happened."

She urged her very gently to enter and then tucked the covers about her, laying finally a cool, wrinkled hand on her forehead. For answer Madeleine seized and put it to her lips, holding it so.

"Oh, Mother," she sobbed as the Sister bent over her, "don't ever make me go out in the world again, will you? You won't, will you? I'm so tired! I'm so tired!"

"No dear, no," soothed the Sister, "not unless you wish it. And now rest. You need never go out into the world again unless you wish."

And withdrawing the hand from the kissing lips, she tiptoed silently from the room.

Death in the Woods

SHERWOOD ANDERSON

I

She was an old woman and lived on a farm near the town in which I lived. All country and small-town people have seen such old women, but no one knows much about them. Such an old woman comes into town driving an old worn-out horse or she comes afoot carrying a basket. She may own a few hens and have eggs to sell. She brings them in a basket and takes them to a grocer. There she trades them in. She gets some salt pork and some beans. Then she gets a pound or two of sugar and some flour.

Afterwards she goes to the butcher's and asks for some dog-meat. She may spend ten or fifteen cents, but when she does she asks for something. Formerly the butchers gave liver to anyone who wanted to carry it away. In our family we were always hav-

From *Death in the Woods and Other Stories*, by Sherwood Anderson. Published by Liveright Publishing Corp. Copyright, 1933, by Sherwood Anderson.

ing it. Once one of my brothers got a whole cow's liver at the slaughterhouse near the fair grounds in our town. We had it until we were sick of it. It never cost a cent. I have hated the thought of it ever since.

The old farm woman got some liver and a soup-bone. She never visited with anyone, and as soon as she got what she wanted she lit out for home. It made quite a load for such an old body. No one gave her a lift. People drive right down a road and never notice an old woman like that.

There was such an old woman who used to come into town past our house one summer and fall when I was a young boy and was sick with what was called inflammatory rheumatism. She went home later carrying a heavy pack on her back. Two or three large gaunt-looking dogs followed at her heels.

The old woman was nothing special. She was one of the nameless ones that hardly anyone knows, but she got into my thoughts. I have just suddenly now, after all these years, remembered her and what happened. It is a story. Her name was Grimes, and she lived with her husband and son in a small unpainted house on the bank of a small creek four miles from town.

The husband and son were a tough lot. Although the son was but twenty-one, he had already served a term in jail. It was whispered about that the woman's husband stole horses and ran them off to some other county. Now and then, when a horse turned up missing, the man had also disappeared. No one ever caught him. Once, when I was loafing at Tom Whitehead's livery-barn, the man came there and sat on the bench in front. Two or three other men were there, but no one spoke to him. He sat for a few minutes and then got up and went away. When he was leaving he turned around and stared at the men. There was a look of defiance in his eyes. "Well, I have tried to be friendly. You don't want to talk to me. It has been so wherever I have gone in this town. If, some day, one of your fine horses turns up missing, well, then what?" He did not say anything actually. "I'd like to bust one of you on the jaw," was about what his eyes said. I remember how the look in his eyes made me shiver.

The old man belonged to a family that had had money once. His name was Jake Grimes. It all comes back clearly now. His father, John Grimes, had owned a sawmill when the country was new, and had made money. Then he got to drinking and running after women. When he died there wasn't much left.

Jake blew in the rest. Pretty soon there wasn't any more lumber to cut and his land was nearly all gone.

He got his wife off a German farmer, for whom he went to work one June day in the wheat harvest. She was a young thing then and scared to death. You see, the farmer was up to something with the girl—she was, I think, a bound girl and his wife had her suspicions. She took it out on the girl when the man wasn't around. Then, when the wife had to go off to town for supplies, the farmer got after her. She told young Jake that nothing really ever happened, but he didn't know whether to believe it or not.

He got her pretty easy himself, the first time he was out with her. He wouldn't have married her if the German farmer hadn't tried to tell him where to get off. He got her to go riding with him in his buggy one night when he was threshing on the place, and then he came for her the next Sunday night.

She managed to get out of the house without her employer's seeing, but when she was getting into the buggy he showed up. It was almost dark, and he just popped up suddenly at the horse's head. He grabbed the horse by the bridle and Jake got out his buggy-whip.

They had it out all right! The German was a tough one. Maybe he didn't care whether his wife knew or not. Jake hit him over the face and shoulders with the buggy-whip, but the horse got to acting up and he had to get out.

Then the two men went for it. The girl didn't see it. The horse started to run away and went nearly a mile down the road before the girl got him stopped. Then she managed to tie him to a tree beside the road. (I wonder how I know all this. It must have stuck in my mind from small-town tales when I was a boy.) Jake found her there after he got through with the German. She was huddled up in the buggy seat, crying, scared to death. She told Jake a lot of stuff, how the German had tried to get her, how he chased her once into the barn, how another time, when they happened to be alone in the house together, he tore her dress open clear down the front. The German, she said, might have got her that time if he hadn't heard his old woman drive in at the gate. She had been off to town for supplies. Well, she would be putting the horse in the barn. The German managed to sneak off to the fields without his wife seeing. He told the girl he would kill her if she told. What could she do? She told a lie about ripping her dress in the barn when she was feeding the stock. I remember now that she was a bound girl and did not know where her father and mother were. Maybe she did not have any father. You know what I mean.

Such bound children were often enough cruelly treated. They were children who had no parents, slaves really. There were very few orphan homes then. They were legally bound into some home. It was a matter of pure luck how it came out.

II

She married Jake and had a son and daughter, but the daughter died.

Then she settled down to feed stock. That was her job. At the German's place she had cooked the food for the German and his wife. The wife was a strong woman with big hips and worked most of the time in the fields with her husband. She fed them and fed the cows in the barn, fed the pigs, the horses and the chickens. Every moment of every day, as a young girl, was spent feeding something.

Then she married Jake Grimes and he had to be fed. She was a slight thing, and when she had been married for three or four years, and after the two children were born, her slender shoulders became stooped.

Jake always had a lot of big dogs around the house, that stood near the unused sawmill near the creek. He was always trading horses when he wasn't stealing something and had a lot of poor bony ones about. Also he kept three or four pigs and a cow. They were all pastured in the few acres left of the Grimes place and Jake did little enough work.

He went into debt for a threshing outfit and ran it for several years, but it did not pay. People did not trust him. They were afraid he would steal the grain at night. He had to go a long way off to get work and it cost too much to get there. In the winter he hunted and cut a little firewood, to be sold in some nearby town. When the son grew up he was just like the father. They got drunk together. If there wasn't anything to eat in the house when they came home the old man gave his old woman a cut over the head. She had a few chickens of her own and had to kill one of them in a hurry. When they were all killed she wouldn't have any eggs to sell when she went to town, and then what would she do?

She had to scheme all her life about getting things fed, getting the pigs fed so they would grow fat and could be butchered in the fall. When they were butchered her husband took most of the meat off to town and sold it. If he did not do it first the boy did. They fought sometimes and when they fought the old woman stood aside trembling.

She had got the habit of silence anyway—that was fixed. Sometimes, when she began to look old—she wasn't forty yet— and when the husband and son were both off, trading horses or drinking or hunting or stealing, she went around the house and the barnyard muttering to herself.

How was she going to get everything fed?—that was her problem. The dogs had to be fed. There wasn't enough hay in the barn for the horses and the cow. If she didn't feed the chickens how could they lay eggs? Without eggs to sell how could she get things in town, things she had to have to keep the life of the farm going? Thank heaven, she did not have to feed her husband—in a certain way. That hadn't lasted long after their marriage and after the babies came. Where he went on his long trips she did not know. Sometimes he was gone from home for weeks, and after the boy grew up they went off together.

They left everything at home for her to manage and she had no money. She knew no one. No one ever talked to her in town. When it was winter she had to gather sticks of wood for her fire, had to try to keep the stock fed with very little grain.

The stock in the barn cried to her hungrily, the dogs followed her about. In the winter the hens laid few enough eggs. They huddled in the corners of the barn and she kept watching them. If a hen lays an egg in the barn in the winter and you do not find it, it freezes and breaks.

One day in winter the old woman went off to town with a few eggs and the dogs followed her. She did not get started until nearly three o'clock and the snow was heavy. She hadn't been feeling very well for several days and so she went muttering along, scantily clad, her shoulders stooped. She had an old grain bag in which she carried her eggs, tucked away down in the bottom. There weren't many of them, but in winter the price of eggs is up. She would get a little meat in exchange for the eggs, some salt pork, a little sugar, and some coffee perhaps. It might be the butcher would give her a piece of liver.

When she had got to town and was trading in her eggs the dogs lay by the door outside. She did pretty well, got the things she needed, more than she had hoped. Then she went to the butcher and he gave her some liver and some dog-meat.

It was the first time anyone had spoken to her in a friendly way for a long time. The butcher was alone in his shop when she came in and was annoyed by the thought of such a sick-looking old woman out on such a day. It was bitter cold and the snow, that had let up during the afternoon, was falling again. The butcher said something about her husband and her son, swore at them, and the old woman stared at him, a look of mild surprise in her eyes as he talked. He said that if either the husband or the son were going to get any of the liver or the heavy bones with scraps of meat hanging to them that he had put into the grain bag, he'd see him starve first.

Starve, eh? Well, things had to be fed. Men had to be fed, and the horses that weren't any good but maybe could be traded off, and the poor thin cow that hadn't given any milk for three months.

Horses, cows, pigs, dogs, men.

III

The old woman had to get back before darkness came if she could. The dogs followed at her heels, sniffing at the heavy grain bag she had fastened on her back. When she got to the edge of town she stopped by a fence and tied the bag on her back with a piece of rope she had carried in her dress-pocket for just that purpose. That was an easier way to carry it. Her arms ached. It was hard when she had to crawl over fences and once she fell over and landed in the snow. The dogs went frisking about. She had to struggle to get to her feet again, but she made it. The point of climbing over the fences was that there was a short cut over a hill and through a woods. She might have gone around by the road, but it was a mile farther that way. She was afraid she couldn't make it. And then, besides, the stock had to be fed. There was a little hay left and a little corn. Perhaps her husband and son would bring some home when they came. They had driven off in the only buggy the Grimes family had, a rickety thing, a rickety horse hitched to the buggy, two other rickety horses led by halters. They were going to trade horses, get a little money if they could. They might come home drunk. It would be well to have something in the house when they came back.

The son had an affair on with a woman at the county seat, fifteen miles away. She was a rough enough woman, a tough one. Once, in the summer, the son had brought her to the house. Both she and the son had been drinking. Jake Grimes was away and the son and his woman ordered the old woman about like a servant. She didn't mind much; she was used to it. Whatever happened she never said anything. That was her way of getting along. She had managed that way when she was a young girl at the German's and ever since she had married Jake. That time her son brought his woman to the house they stayed all night, sleeping together just as though they were married. It hadn't shocked the old woman, not much. She had got past being shocked early in life.

With the pack on her back she went painfully along across an open field, wading in the deep snow, and got into the woods.

There was a path, but it was hard to follow. Just beyond the top of the hill, where the woods was thickest, there was a small clearing. Had someone once thought of building a house there? The clearing was as large as a building lot in town, large enough for a house and a garden. The path ran along the side of the clearing, and when she got there the old woman sat down to rest at the foot of a tree.

It was a foolish thing to do. When she got herself placed, the pack against the tree's trunk, it was nice, but what about getting up again? She worried about that for a moment and then quietly closed her eyes.

She must have slept for a time. When you are about so cold you can't get any colder. The afternoon grew a little warmer and the snow came thicker than ever. Then after a time the weather cleared. The moon even came out.

There were four Grimes dogs that had followed Mrs. Grimes into town, all tall gaunt fellows. Such men as Jake Grimes and his son always keep just such dogs. They kick and abuse them, but they stay. The Grimes dogs, in order to keep from starving, had to do a lot of foraging for themselves, and they had been at it while the old woman slept with her back to the tree at the side of the clearing. They had been chasing rabbits in the woods and in adjoining fields and in their ranging had picked up three other farm dogs.

After a time all the dogs came back to the clearing. They were excited about something. Such nights, cold and clear and with a moon, do things to dogs. It may be that some old instinct, come down from the time when they were wolves and ranged the woods in packs on winter nights, comes back into them.

The dogs in the clearing, before the old woman, had caught two or three rabbits and their immediate hunger had been satisfied. They began to play, running in circles in the clearing.

Round and round they ran, each dog's nose at the tail of the next dog. In the clearing, under the snow-laden trees and under the wintry moon they made a strange picture, running thus silently, in a circle their running had beaten in the soft snow. The dogs made no sound. They ran around and around in the circle.

It may have been that the old woman saw them doing that before she died. She may have awakened once or twice and looked at the strange sight with dim old eyes.

She wouldn't be very cold now, just drowsy. Life hangs on a long time. Perhaps the old woman was out of her head. She may have dreamed of her girlhood, at the German's, and before that, when she was a child and before her mother lit out and left her.

Her dreams couldn't have been very pleasant. Not many pleasant things had happened to her. Now and then one of the Grimes dogs left the running circle and came to stand before her. The dog thrust his face close to her face. His red tongue was hanging out.

The running of the dogs may have been a kind of death ceremony. It may have been that the primitive instinct of the wolf, having been aroused in the dogs by the night and the running, made them somehow afraid.

"Now we are no longer wolves. We are dogs, the servants of men. Keep alive, man! When man dies we become wolves again."

When one of the dogs came to where the old woman sat with her back against the tree and thrust his nose close to her face he seemed satisfied and went back to run with the pack. All the Grimes dogs did it at some time during the evening, before she died. I knew all about it afterward, when I grew to be a man, because once in a woods in Illinois, on another winter night, I saw a pack of dogs act just like that. The dogs were waiting for me to die as they had waited for the old woman that night when I was a child, but when it happened to me I was a young man and had no intention whatever of dying.

The old woman died softly and quietly. When she was dead and when one of the Grimes dogs had come to her and had found her dead all the dogs stopped running.

They gathered about her.

Well, she was dead now. She had fed the Grimes dogs when she was alive, what about now?

There was the pack on her back, the grain bag containing the piece of salt pork, the liver the butcher had given her, the dog-meat, the soup bones. The butcher in town, having been suddenly overcome with a feeling of pity, had loaded her grain bag heavily. It had been a big haul for the old woman.

It was a big haul for the dogs now.

IV

One of the Grimes dogs sprang suddenly out from among the others and began worrying the pack on the old woman's back. Had the dogs really been wolves that one would have been the leader of the pack. What he did, all the others did.

All of them sank their teeth into the grain bag the old woman had fastened with ropes to her back.

They dragged the old woman's body out into the open clearing. The worn-out dress was quickly torn from her shoulders. When she was found, a day or two later, the dress had been torn from her body clear to the hips, but the dogs had not touched her body. They had got the meat out of the grain bag, that was all. Her body was frozen stiff when it was found, and the shoulders were so narrow and the body so slight that in death it looked like the body of some charming young girl.

Such things happened in towns of the Middle West, on farms near town, when I was a boy. A hunter out after rabbits found the old woman's body and did not touch it. Something, the beaten round path in the little snow-covered clearing, the silence of the place, the place where the dogs had worried the body trying to pull the grain bag away or tear it open—something startled the man and he hurried off to town.

I was in Main Street with one of my brothers who was town newsboy and who was taking the afternoon papers to the stores. It was almost night.

The hunter came into a grocery and told his story. Then he went to a hardware shop and into a drugstore. Men began to gather on the sidewalks. Then they started out along the road to the place in the woods.

My brother should have gone on about his business of distributing papers but he didn't. Everyone was going to the woods. The undertaker went and the town marshal. Several men got on a dray and rode out to where the path left the road and went into the woods, but the horses weren't very sharply shod and slid about on the slippery roads. They made no better time than those of us who walked.

The town marshal was a large man whose leg had been injured in the Civil War. He carried a heavy cane and limped rapidly along the road. My brother and I followed at his heels, and as we went other men and boys joined the crowd.

It had grown dark by the time we got to where the old woman had left the road but the moon had come out. The marshal was thinking there might have been a murder. He kept asking the hunter questions. The hunter went along with his gun across his shoulders, a dog following at his heels. It isn't often a rabbit hunter has a chance to be so conspicuous. He was taking full advantage of it, leading the procession with the town marshal. "I didn't see any wounds. She was a beautiful young girl. Her face was buried in the snow. No, I didn't know her." As a matter of fact, the hunter had not looked closely at the body. He had been frightened. She might have been murdered and someone might spring out from behind a tree and murder him. In a woods, in the late afternoon, when the trees are all bare and there is white snow on the ground, when all is silent, something creepy steals over the mind and body. If something strange or uncanny has happened in the neighborhood all you think about is getting away from there as fast as you can.

The crowd of men and boys had got to where the old woman had crossed the field and went, following the marshal and the hunter, up the slight incline and into the woods.

My brother and I were silent. He had his bundle of papers in a bag slung across his shoulder. When he got back to town he would have to go on distributing his papers before he went home to supper. If I went along, as he had no doubt already determined I should, we would both be late. Either mother or our older sister would have to warm our supper.

Well, we would have something to tell. A boy did not get such a chance very often. It was lucky we just happened to go into the grocery when the hunter came in. The hunter was a country fellow. Neither of us had ever seen him before.

Now the crowd of men and boys had got to the clearing. Darkness comes quickly on such winter nights, but the full moon made everything clear. My brother and I stood near the tree, beneath which the old woman had died.

She did not look old, lying there in that light, frozen and still. One of the men turned her over in the snow and I saw everything. My body trembled with some strange mystical feeling and so did my brother's. It might have been the cold.

Neither of us had ever seen a woman's body before. It may have been the snow, clinging to the frozen flesh, that made it look so white and lovely, so like marble. No woman had come with the party from town; but one of the men, he was the town blacksmith, took off his overcoat and spread it over her. Then he gathered her into his arms and started off to town, all the others following silently. At that time no one knew who she was.

v

I had seen everything, had seen the oval in the snow, like a miniature race track, where the dogs had run, had seen how the men were mystified, had seen the white bare young-looking shoulders, had heard the whispered comments of the men.

The men were simply mystified. They took the body to the undertaker's, and when the blacksmith, the hunter, the marshal and several others had got inside they closed the door. If father had been there perhaps he could have got in, but we boys couldn't.

I went with my brother to distribute the rest of his papers and when we got home it was my brother who told the story.

I kept silent and went to bed early. It may have been I was not satisfied with the way he told it.

Later, in the town, I must have heard other fragments of the old woman's story. She was recognized the next day and there was an investigation.

The husband and son were found somewhere and brought to town and there was an attempt to connect them with the woman's death, but it did not work. They had perfect enough alibis.

However, the town was against them. They had to get out. Where they went I never heard.

I remember only the picture there in the forest, the men standing about, the naked girlish-looking figure, face down in the snow, the tracks made by the running dogs and the clear cold winter sky above. White fragments of clouds were drifting across the sky. They went racing across the little open space among the trees.

The scene in the forest had become for me, without my knowing it, the foundation for the real story I am now trying to tell. The fragments, you see, had to be picked up slowly, long afterwards.

Things happened. When I was a young man I worked on the farm of a German. The hired-girl was afraid of her employer. The farmer's wife hated her.

I saw things at that place. Once later, I had a half-uncanny, mystical adventure with dogs in an Illinois forest on a clear, moonlit winter night. When I was a schoolboy, and on a summer day, I went with a boy friend out along a creek some miles from town and came to the house where the old woman had lived. No one had lived in the house since her death. The doors were broken from the hinges; the window lights were all broken. As the boy and I stood in the road outside, two dogs, just roving farm dogs no doubt, came running around the corner of the house. The dogs were tall, gaunt fellows and came down to the fence and glared through at us, standing in the road.

The whole thing, the story of the old woman's death, was to me as I grew older like music heard from far off. The notes had to be picked up slowly one at a time. Something had to be understood.

The woman who died was one destined to feed animal life. Anyway, that is all she ever did. She was feeding animal life before she was born, as a child, as a young woman working on the farm of the German, after she married, when she grew old and when she died. She fed animal life in cows, in chickens, in pigs, in horses, in dogs, in men. Her daughter had died in childhood and with her one son she had no articulate relations. On the night when she died she was hurrying homeward, bearing on her body food for animal life.

She died in the clearing in the woods and even after her death continued feeding animal life.

You see it is likely that, when my brother told the story, that night when we got home and my mother and sister sat listening, I did not think he got the point. He was too young and so was I. A thing so complete has its own beauty.

I shall not try to emphasize the point. I am only explaining why I was dissatisfied then and have been ever since. I speak of that only that you may understand why I have been impelled to try to tell the simple story over again.

The Rich Boy

F. SCOTT FITZGERALD

———

I

Begin with an individual, and before you know it you find that you have created a type; begin with a type, and you find that you have created—nothing. That is because we are all queer fish, queerer behind our faces and voices than we want any one to know or than we know ourselves. When I hear a man proclaiming himself an "average, honest, open fellow," I feel pretty sure that he has some definite and perhaps terrible abnormality which he has agreed to conceal—and his protestation of being average and honest and open is his way of reminding himself of his misprision.

There are no types, no plurals. There is a rich boy, and this is his and not his brothers' story. All my life I have lived among his brothers but this one has been my friend. Besides, if I wrote about his brothers I should have to begin by attacking all the lies that the poor have told about the rich and the rich have told about themselves—such a wild structure they have erected that when we pick up a book about the rich, some instinct prepares us for unreality. Even the intelligent and impassioned reporters of life have made the country of the rich as unreal as fairy-land.

Let me tell you about the very rich. They are different from you and me. They possess and enjoy early, and it does something to them, makes them soft where we are hard, and cynical where we are trustful, in a way that, unless you were born rich, it is very difficult to understand. They think, deep in their hearts, that they are better than we are because we had to discover the compensations and refuges of life for ourselves. Even when they enter deep into our world or sink below us, they still think that they are better than we are. They are different. The only way I can describe young Anson Hunter is to approach him as if he were a foreigner and cling stubbornly to my point of view. If I accept his for a moment I am lost—I have nothing to show but a preposterous movie.

II

Anson was the eldest of six children who would some day divide a fortune of fifteen million dollars, and he reached the age of reason—is it seven?—at the beginning of the century when daring young women were already gliding along Fifth Avenue in electric "mobiles." In those days he and his brother had an English governess who spoke the language very clearly and crisply and well, so that the two boys grew to speak as she did —their words and sentences were all crisp and clear and not run together as ours are. They didn't talk exactly like English children but acquired an accent that is peculiar to fashionable people in the city of New York.

In the summer the six children were moved from the house on 71st Street to a big estate in northern Connecticut. It was not a fashionable locality—Anson's father wanted to delay as long as possible his children's knowledge of that side of life. He was a man somewhat superior to his class, which composed New York society, and to his period, which was the snobbish and formalized vulgarity of the Gilded Age, and he wanted his sons to learn habits of concentration and have sound constitutions and grow up into right-living and successful men. He and his wife kept an eye on them as well as they were able until the two older boys went away to school, but in huge establishments this is difficult—it was much simpler in the series of small and medium-sized houses in which my own youth was spent—I was never far out of the reach of my mother's voice, of the sense of her presence, her approval or disapproval.

Anson's first sense of his superiority came to him when he realized the half-grudging American deference that was paid to him in the Connecticut village. The parents of the boys he played with always inquired after his father and mother, and were vaguely excited when their own children were asked to the Hunters' house. He accepted this as the natural state of things, and a sort of impatience with all groups of which he was not the centre—in money, in position, in authority—remained with him for the rest of his life. He disdained to struggle with other boys for precedence—he expected it to be given him freely, and when it wasn't he withdrew into his family. His family was sufficient, for in the East money is still a somewhat feudal thing, a clan-forming thing. In the snobbish West, money separates families to form "sets."

At eighteen, when he went to New Haven, Anson was tall and thick-set, with a clear complexion and a healthy color from the ordered life he had led in school. His hair was yellow and grew in a funny way on his head, his nose was beaked—these two things kept him from being handsome—but he had a confident charm and a certain brusque style, and the upper-class men who passed him on the street knew without being told that he was a rich boy and had gone to one of the best schools. Nevertheless, his very superiority kept him from being a success in college— the independence was mistaken for egotism, and the refusal to accept Yale standards with the proper awe seemed to belittle all those who had. So, long before he graduated, he began to shift the centre of his life to New York.

He was at home in New York—there was his own house with "the kind of servants you can't get any more"—and his own family, of which, because of his good humor and a certain ability to make things go, he was rapidly becoming the centre, and the débutante parties, and the correct manly world of the men's clubs, and the occasional wild spree with the gallant girls whom New Haven only knew from the fifth row. His aspirations were conventional enough—they included even the irreproachable shadow he would some day marry, but they differed from the aspirations of the majority of young men in that there was no mist over them, none of that quality which is variously known as "idealism" or "illusion." Anson accepted without reservation the world of high finance and high extravagance, of divorce and dissipation, of snobbery and of privilege. Most of our lives end as a compromise—it was as a compromise that his life began.

He and I first met in the late summer of 1917 when he was just out of Yale, and, like the rest of us, was swept up into the systematized hysteria of the war. In the blue-green uniform of the naval aviation he came down to Pensacola, where the hotel orchestras played "I'm sorry, dear," and we young officers danced with the girls. Every one liked him, and though he ran with the drinkers and wasn't an especially good pilot, even the instructors treated him with a certain respect. He was always having long talks with them in his confident, logical voice— talks which ended by his getting himself, or, more frequently,

another officer, out of some impending trouble. He was convivial, bawdy, robustly avid for pleasure, and we were all surprised when he fell in love with a conservative and rather proper
girl.

Her name was Paula Legendre, a dark, serious beauty from
somewhere in California. Her family kept a winter residence
just outside of town, and in spite of her primness she was enormously popular; there is a large class of men whose egotism
can't endure humor in a woman. But Anson wasn't that sort, and
I couldn't understand the attraction of her "sincerity"—that was
the thing to say about her—for his keen and somewhat sardonic
mind.

Nevertheless, they fell in love—and on her terms. He no longer
joined the twilight gathering at the De Soto bar, and whenever
they were seen together they were engaged in a long, serious
dialogue, which must have gone on several weeks. Long afterward he told me that it was not about anything in particular but
was composed on both sides of immature and even meaningless
statements—the emotional content that gradually came to fill it
grew up not out of the words but out of its enormous seriousness. It was a sort of hypnosis. Often it was interrupted, giving
way to that emasculated humor we call fun; when they were
alone it was resumed again, solemn, low-keyed, and pitched so
as to give each other a sense of unity in feeling and thought.
They came to resent any interruptions of it, to be unresponsive
to facetiousness about life, even to the mild cynicism of their
contemporaries. They were only happy when the dialogue was
going on, and its seriousness bathed them like the amber glow
of an open fire. Toward the end there came an interruption they
did not resent—it began to be interrupted by passion.

Oddly enough, Anson was as engrossed in the dialogue as she
was and as profoundly affected by it, yet at the same time aware
that on his side much was insincere, and on hers much was
merely simple. At first, too, he despised her emotional simplicity
as well, but with his love her nature deepened and blossomed,
and he could despise it no longer. He felt that if he could enter

into Paula's warm safe life he would be happy. The long preparation of the dialogue removed any constraint—he taught her some of what he had learned from more adventurous women, and she responded with a rapt holy intensity. One evening after a dance they agreed to marry, and he wrote a long letter about her to his mother. The next day Paula told him that she was rich, that she had a personal fortune of nearly a million dollars.

III

It was exactly as if they could say "Neither of us has anything: we shall be poor together"—just as delightful that they should be rich instead. It gave them the same communion of adventure. Yet when Anson got leave in April, and Paula and her mother accompanied him North, she was impressed with the standing of his family in New York and with the scale on which they lived. Alone with Anson for the first time in the rooms where he had played as a boy, she was filled with a comfortable emotion, as though she were pre-eminently safe and taken care of. The pictures of Anson in a skull cap at his first school, of Anson on horseback with the sweetheart of a mysterious forgotten summer, of Anson in a gay group of ushers and bridesmaids at a wedding, made her jealous of his life apart from her in the past, and so completely did his authoritative person seem to sum up and typify these possessions of his that she was inspired with the idea of being married immediately and returning to Pensacola as his wife.

But an immediate marriage wasn't discussed—even the engagement was to be secret until after the war. When she realized that only two days of his leave remained, her dissatisfaction crystallized in the intention of making him as unwilling to wait as she was. They were driving to the country for dinner and she determined to force the issue that night.

Now a cousin of Paula's was staying with them at the Ritz, a severe, bitter girl who loved Paula but was somewhat jealous of her impressive engagement, and as Paula was late in dressing, the cousin, who wasn't going to the party, received Anson in the parlor of the suite.

Anson had met friends at five o'clock and drunk freely and indiscreetly with them for an hour. He left the Yale Club at a proper time, and his mother's chauffeur drove him to the Ritz, but his usual capacity was not in evidence, and the impact of the steam-heated sitting-room made him suddenly dizzy. He knew it, and he was both amused and sorry.

Paula's cousin was twenty-five, but she was exceptionally naïve, and at first failed to realize what was up. She had never met Anson before, and she was surprised when he mumbled strange information and nearly fell off his chair, but until Paula appeared it didn't occur to her that what she had taken for the odor of a dry-cleaned uniform was really whiskey. But Paula understood as soon as she appeared; her only thought was to get Anson away before her mother saw him, and at the look in her eyes the cousin understood too.

When Paula and Anson descended to the limousine they found two men inside, both asleep; they were the men with whom he had been drinking at the Yale Club, and they were also going to the party. He had entirely forgotten their presence in the car. On the way to Hempstead they awoke and sang. Some of the songs were rough, and though Paula tried to reconcile herself to the fact that Anson had few verbal inhibitions, her lips tightened with shame and distaste.

Back at the hotel the cousin, confused and agitated, considered the incident, and then walked into Mrs. Legendre's bedroom, saying: "Isn't he funny?"

"Who is funny?"

"Why—Mr. Hunter. He seemed so funny."

Mrs. Legendre looked at her sharply.

"How is he funny?"

"Why, he said he was French. I didn't know he was French."

"That's absurd. You must have misunderstood." She smiled: "It was a joke."

The cousin shook her head stubbornly.

"No. He said he was brought up in France. He said he couldn't speak any English, and that's why he couldn't talk to me. And he couldn't!"

Mrs. Legendre looked away with impatience just as the cousin added thoughtfully, "Perhaps it was because he was so drunk," and walked out of the room.

This curious report was true. Anson, finding his voice thick and uncontrollable, had taken the unusual refuge of announce-ing that he spoke no English. Years afterwards he used to tell that part of the story, and he invariably communicated the up-roarious laughter which the memory aroused in him.

Five times in the next hour Mrs. Legendre tried to get Hemp-stead on the phone. When she succeeded, there was a ten-min-ute delay before she heard Paula's voice on the wire.

"Cousin Jo told me Anson was intoxicated."

"Oh, no. . . ."

"Oh, yes. Cousin Jo says he was intoxicated. He told her he was French, and fell off his chair and behaved as if he was very intoxicated. I don't want you to come home with him."

"Mother, he's all right! Please don't worry about——"

"But I do worry. I think it's dreadful. I want you to promise me not to come home with him."

"I'll take care of it, Mother. . . ."

"I don't want you to come home with him."

"All right, Mother. Good-by."

"Be sure now, Paula. Ask some one to bring you."

Deliberately Paula took the receiver from her ear and hung it up. Her face was flushed with helpless annoyance. Anson was stretched asleep out in a bedroom up-stairs, while the dinner-party below was proceeding lamely toward conclusion.

The hour's drive had sobered him somewhat—his arrival was merely hilarious—and Paula hoped that the evening was not spoiled, after all, but two imprudent cocktails before dinner completed the disaster. He talked boisterously and somewhat offensively to the party at large for fifteen minutes, and then slid silently under the table; like a man in an old print—but, unlike an old print, it was rather horrible without being at all quaint. None of the young girls present remarked upon the incident—it seemed to merit only silence. His uncle and two other men carried him up-stairs, and it was just after this that Paula was called to the phone.

An hour later Anson awoke in a fog of nervous agony, through which he perceived after a moment the figure of his Uncle Robert standing by the door.

". . . I said are you better?"

"What?"

"Do you feel better, old man?"

"Terrible," said Anson.

"I'm going to try you on another bromo-seltzer. If you can hold it down, it'll do you good to sleep."

With an effort Anson slid his legs from the bed and stood up.

"I'm all right," he said dully.

"Take it easy."

"I thin' if you gave me a glassbrandy I could go down-stairs."

"Oh, no——"

"Yes, that's the only thin'. I'm all right now. . . . I suppose I'm in Dutch dow' there."

"They know you're a little under the weather," said his uncle deprecatingly. "But don't worry about it. Schuyler didn't even get here. He passed away in the locker-room over at the Links."

Indifferent to any opinion, except Paula's, Anson was nevertheless determined to save the débris of the evening, but when after a cold bath he made his appearance most of the party had already left. Paula got up immediately to go home.

In the limousine the old serious dialogue began. She had known that he drank, she admitted, but she had never expected anything like this—it seemed to her that perhaps they were not suited to each other, after all. Their ideas about life were too different, and so forth. When she finished speaking, Anson spoke in turn, very soberly. Then Paula said she'd have to think it over; she wouldn't decide to-night; she was not angry but she was terribly sorry. Nor would she let him come into the hotel with her, but just before she got out of the car she leaned and kissed him unhappily on the cheek.

The next afternoon Anson had a long talk with Mrs. Legendre while Paula sat listening in silence. It was agreed that Paula was to brood over the incident for a proper period and then, if mother and daughter thought it best, they would follow Anson to Pensacola. On his part he apologized with sincerity and dignity—that was all; with every card in her hand Mrs. Legendre was unable to establish any advantage over him. He made no promises, showed no humility, only delivered a few serious comments on life which brought him off with rather a moral superiority at the end. When they came South three weeks later, neither Anson in his satisfaction nor Paula in her relief at the reunion realized that the psychological moment had passed forever.

IV

He dominated and attracted her, and at the same time filled her with anxiety. Confused by his mixture of solidity and self-indulgence, of sentiment and cynicism—incongruities which her gentle mind was unable to resolve—Paula grew to think of him as two alternating personalities. When she saw him alone, or at a formal party, or with his casual inferiors, she felt a tremendous pride in his strong, attractive presence, the paternal, understanding stature of his mind. In other company she became uneasy when what had been a fine imperviousness to mere gentility showed its other face. The other face was gross, humorous, reckless of everything but pleasure. It startled her mind temporarily away from him, even led her into a short covert experiment with an old beau, but it was no use—after four months of Anson's enveloping vitality there was an anaemic pallor in all other men.

In July he was ordered abroad, and their tenderness and desire reached a crescendo. Paula considered a last-minute marriage—decided against it only because there were always cocktails on his breath now, but the parting itself made her physically ill with grief. After his departure she wrote him long letters of regret for the days of love they had missed by waiting. In August Anson's plane slipped down into the North Sea. He was pulled onto a destroyer after a night in the water and sent to hospital with pneumonia; the armistice was signed before he was finally sent home.

Then, with every opportunity given back to them, with no material obstacle to overcome, the secret weavings of their temperaments came between them, drying up their kisses and their tears, making their voices less loud to one another, muffling the intimate chatter of their hearts until the old communication was only possible by letters, from far away. One afternoon a society reporter waited for two hours in the Hunters' house for a confirmation of their engagement. Anson denied it; nevertheless an early issue carried the report as a leading paragraph—they were "constantly seen together at Southampton, Hot Springs, and Tuxedo Park." But the serious dialogue had turned a corner into a long-sustained quarrel, and the affair was almost played out. Anson got drunk flagrantly and missed an engagement with her, whereupon Paula made certain behavioristic demands. His despair was helpless before his pride and his knowledge of himself: the engagement was definitely broken.

"Dearest," said their letters now, "Dearest, Dearest, when I wake up in the middle of the night and realize that after all it was not to be, I feel that I want to die. I can't go on living any more. Perhaps when we meet this summer we may talk things over and decide differently—we were so excited and sad that day, and I don't feel that I can live all my life without you. You speak of other people. Don't you know there are no other people for me, but only you. . . ."

But as Paula drifted here and there around the East she would sometimes mention her gaieties to make him wonder. Anson was too acute to wonder. When he saw a man's name in her letters he felt more sure of her and a little disdainful—he was always superior to such things. But he still hoped that they would some day marry.

Meanwhile he plunged vigorously into all the movement and glitter of post-bellum New York, entering a brokerage house, joining half a dozen clubs, dancing late, and moving in three worlds—his own world, the world of young Yale graduates, and that section of the half-world which rests one end on Broadway. But there was always a thorough and infractible eight hours devoted to his work in Wall Street, where the combination of his influential family connection, his sharp intelligence, and his abundance of sheer physical energy brought him almost immediately forward. He had one of those invaluable minds with partitions in it; sometimes he appeared at his office refreshed by less than an hour's sleep, but such occurrences were rare. So early as 1920 his income in salary and commissions exceeded twelve thousand dollars.

As the Yale tradition slipped into the past he became more and more of a popular figure among his classmates in New York, more popular than he had ever been in college. He lived in a great house, and had the means of introducing young men into other great houses. Moreover, his life already seemed secure, while theirs, for the most part, had arrived again at precarious beginnings. They commenced to turn to him for amusement and escape, and Anson responded readily, taking pleasure in helping people and arranging their affairs.

There were no men in Paula's letters now, but a note of tenderness ran through them that had not been there before. From several sources he heard that she had "a heavy beau," Lowell Thayer, a Bostonian of wealth and position, and though he was sure she still loved him, it made him uneasy to think that he might lose her, after all. Save for one unsatisfactory day she had not been in New York for almost five months, and as the rumors multiplied he became increasingly anxious to see her. In February he took his vacation and went down to Florida.

Palm Beach sprawled plump and opulent between the sparkling sapphire of Lake Worth, flawed here and there by house-boats at anchor, and the great turquoise bar of the Atlantic Ocean. The huge bulks of the Breakers and the Royal Poinciana rose as twin paunches from the bright level of the sand, and around them clustered the Dancing Glade, Bradley's House of Chance, and a dozen modistes and milliners with goods at triple prices from New York. Upon the trellised veranda of the Break-ers two hundred women stepped right, stepped left, wheeled, and slid in that then celebrated calisthenic known as the double-shuffle, while in half-time to the music two thousand bracelets clicked up and down on two hundred arms.

At the Everglades Club after dark Paula and Lowell Thayer and Anson and a casual fourth played bridge with hot cards. It seemed to Anson that her kind, serious face was wan and tired —she had been around now for four, five, years. He had known her for three.

"Two spades."

"Cigarette? . . . Oh, I beg your pardon. By me."

"By."

"I'll double three spades."

There were a dozen tables of bridge in the room, which was filling up with smoke. Anson's eyes met Paula's, held them per-sistently even when Thayer's glance fell between them. . . .

"What was bid?" he asked abstractedly.

"Rose of Washington Square"

sang the young people in the corners:

> *"I'm withering there*
> *In basement air——"*

The smoke banked like fog, and the opening of a door filled the room with blown swirls of ectoplasm. Little Bright Eyes streaked past the tables seeking Mr. Conan Doyle among the Englishmen who were posing as Englishmen about the lobby.

"You could cut it with a knife."

". . . cut it with a knife."

". . . a knife."

At the end of the rubber Paula suddenly got up and spoke to Anson in a tense, low voice. With scarcely a glance at Lowell Thayer, they walked out the door and descended a long flight of stone steps—in a moment they were walking hand in hand along the moonlit beach.

"Darling, darling. . . ." They embraced recklessly, passionately, in a shadow. . . . Then Paula drew back her face to let his lips say what she wanted to hear—she could feel the words forming as they kissed again. . . . Again she broke away, listening, but as he pulled her close once more she realized that he had said nothing—only *"Darling! Darling!"* in that deep, sad whisper that always made her cry. Humbly, obediently, her emotions yielded to him and the tears streamed down her face, but her heart kept on crying: "Ask me—oh, Anson, dearest, ask me!"

"Paula. . . . *Paula!*"

The words wrung her heart like hands, and Anson, feeling her tremble, knew that emotion was enough. He need say no more, commit their destinies to no practical enigma. Why should he, when he might hold her so, biding his own time, for another year—forever? He was considering them both, her more than himself. For a moment, when she said suddenly that she must go back to her hotel, he hesitated, thinking, first, "This is the moment, after all," and then: "No, let it wait—she is mine. . . ."

He had forgotten that Paula too was worn away inside with the strain of three years. Her mood passed forever in the night.

He went back to New York next morning filled with a certain restless dissatisfaction. Late in April, without warning, he received a telegram from Bar Harbor in which Paula told him that she was engaged to Lowell Thayer, and that they would be married immediately in Boston. What he never really believed could happen had happened at last.

Anson filled himself with whiskey that morning, and going to the office, carried on his work without a break—rather with a fear of what would happen if he stopped. In the evening he went out as usual, saying nothing of what had occurred; he was cordial, humorous, unabstracted. But one thing he could not help—for three days, in any place, in any company, he would suddenly bend his head into his hands and cry like a child.

V

In 1922 when Anson went abroad with the junior partner to investigate some London loans, the journey intimated that he was to be taken into the firm. He was twenty-seven now, a little heavy without being definitely stout, and with a manner older than his years. Old people and young people liked him and trusted him, and mothers felt safe when their daughters were in his charge, for he had a way, when he came into a room, of putting himself on a footing with the oldest and most conservative people there. "You and I," he seemed to say, "we're solid. We understand."

He had an instinctive and rather charitable knowledge of the weaknesses of men and women, and, like a priest, it made him the more concerned for the maintenance of outward forms. It was typical of him that every Sunday morning he taught in a fashionable Episcopal Sunday-school—even though a cold shower and a quick change into a cutaway coat were all that separated him from the wild night before.

After his father's death he was the practical head of his family, and, in effect, guided the destinies of the younger children. Through a complication his authority did not extend to his father's estate, which was administrated by his Uncle Robert, who was the horsey member of the family, a good-natured, hard-drinking member of that set which centres about Wheatley Hills.

Uncle Robert and his wife, Edna, had been great friends of Anson's youth, and the former was disappointed when his nephew's superiority failed to take a horsey form. He backed him for a city club which was the most difficult in America to enter—one could only join if one's family had "helped to build up New York" (or, in other words, were rich before 1880)—and when Anson, after his election, neglected it for the Yale Club, Uncle

Robert gave him a little talk on the subject. But when on top of that Anson declined to enter Robert Hunter's own conservative and somewhat neglected brokerage house, his manner grew cooler. Like a primary teacher who has taught all he knew, he slipped out of Anson's life.

There were so many friends in Anson's life—scarcely one for whom he had not done some unusual kindness and scarcely one whom he did not occasionally embarrass by his bursts of rough conversation or his habit of getting drunk whenever and however he liked. It annoyed him when any one else blundered in that regard—about his own lapses he was always humorous. Odd things happened to him and he told them with infectious laughter.

I was working in New York that spring, and I used to lunch with him at the Yale Club, which my university was sharing until the completion of our own. I had read of Paula's marriage, and one afternoon, when I asked him about her, something moved him to tell me the story. After that he frequently invited me to family dinners at his house and behaved as though there was a special relation between us, as though with his confidence a little of that consuming memory had passed into me.

I found that despite the trusting mothers, his attitude toward girls was not indiscriminately protective. It was up to the girl —if she showed an inclination toward looseness, she must take care of herself, even with him.

"Life," he would explain sometimes, "has made a cynic of me."

By life he meant Paula. Sometimes, especially when he was drinking, it became a little twisted in his mind, and he thought that she had callously thrown him over.

This "cynicism," or rather his realization that naturally fast girls were not worth sparing, led to his affair with Dolly Karger. It wasn't his only affair in those years, but it came nearest to touching him deeply, and it had a profound effect upon his attitude toward life.

Dolly was the daughter of a notorious "publicist" who had

married into society. She herself grew up into the Junior League, came out at the Plaza, and went to the Assembly; and only a few old families like the Hunters could question whether or not she "belonged," for her picture was often in the papers, and she had more enviable attention than many girls who undoubtedly did. She was dark-haired, with carmine lips and a high, lovely color, which she concealed under pinkish-gray powder all through the first year out, because high color was unfashionable—Victorian-pale was the thing to be. She wore black, severe suits and stood with her hands in her pockets leaning a little forward, with a humorous restraint on her face. She danced exquisitely—better than anything she liked to dance—better than anything except making love. Since she was ten she had always been in love, and, usually, with some boy who didn't respond to her. Those who did—and there were many—bored her after a brief encounter, but for her failures she reserved the warmest spot in her heart. When she met them she would always try once more—sometimes she succeeded, more often she failed.

It never occurred to this gypsy of the unattainable that there was a certain resemblance in those who refused to love her—they shared a hard intuition that saw through to her weakness, not a weakness of emotion but a weakness of rudder. Anson perceived this when he first met her, less than a month after Paula's marriage. He was drinking rather heavily, and he pretended for a week that he was falling in love with her. Then he dropped her abruptly and forgot—immediately he took up the commanding position in her heart.

Like so many girls of that day Dolly was slackly and indiscreetly wild. The unconventionality of a slightly older generation had been simply one facet of a post-war movement to discredit obsolete manners—Dolly's was both older and shabbier, and she saw in Anson the two extremes which the emotionally shiftless woman seeks, an abandon to indulgence alternating with a protective strength. In his character she felt both the sybarite and the solid rock, and these two satisfied every need of her nature.

She felt that it was going to be difficult, but she mistook the reason—she thought that Anson and his family expected a more spectacular marriage, but she guessed immediately that her advantage lay in his tendency to drink.

They met at the large débutante dances, but as her infatuation increased they managed to be more and more together. Like most mothers, Mrs. Karger believed that Anson was exceptionally reliable, so she allowed Dolly to go with him to distant country clubs and suburban houses without inquiring closely into their activities or questioning her explanations when they came in late. At first these explanations might have been accurate, but Dolly's worldly ideas of capturing Anson were soon engulfed in the rising sweep of her emotion. Kisses in the back of taxis and motor-cars were no longer enough; they did a curious thing:

They dropped out of their world for a while and made another world just beneath it where Anson's tippling and Dolly's irregular hours would be less noticed and commented on. It was composed, this world, of varying elements—several of Anson's Yale friends and their wives, two or three young brokers and bond salesmen and a handful of unattached men, fresh from college, with money and a propensity to dissipation. What this world lacked in spaciousness and scale it made up for by allowing them a liberty that it scarcely permitted itself. Moreover, it centred around them and permitted Dolly the pleasure of a faint condescension—a pleasure which Anson, whose whole life was a condescension from the certitudes of his childhood, was unable to share.

He was not in love with her, and in the long feverish winter of their affair he frequently told her so. In the spring he was weary—he wanted to renew his life at some other source—moreover, he saw that either he must break with her now or accept the responsibility of a definite seduction. Her family's encouraging attitude precipitated his decision—one evening when Mr. Karger knocked discreetly at the library door to announce that he had left a bottle of old brandy in the dining-room,

Anson felt that life was hemming him in. That night he wrote her a short letter in which he told her that he was going on his vacation, and that in view of all the circumstances they had better meet no more.

It was June. His family had closed up the house and gone to the country, so he was living temporarily at the Yale Club. I had heard about his affair with Dolly as it developed—accounts salted with humor, for he despised unstable women, and granted them no place in the social edifice in which he believed —and when he told me that night that he was definitely breaking with her I was glad. I had seen Dolly here and there, and each time with a feeling of pity at the hopelessness of her struggle, and of shame at knowing so much about her that I had no right to know. She was what is known as "a pretty little thing," but there was a certain recklessness which rather fascinated me. Her dedication to the goddess of waste would have been less obvious had she been less spirited—she would most certainly throw herself away, but I was glad when I heard that the sacrifice would not be consummated in my sight.

Anson was going to leave the letter of farewell at her house next morning. It was one of the few houses left open in the Fifth Avenue district, and he knew that the Kargers, acting upon erroneous information from Dolly, had foregone a trip abroad to give their daughter her chance. As he stepped out the door of the Yale Club into Madison Avenue the postman passed him, and he followed back inside. The first letter that caught his eye was in Dolly's hand.

He knew what it would be—a lonely and tragic monologue, full of the reproaches he knew, the invoked memories, the "I wonder if's"—all the immemorial intimacies that he had communicated to Paula Legendre in what seemed another age. Thumbing over some bills, he brought it on top again and opened it. To his surprise it was a short, somewhat formal note, which said that Dolly would be unable to go to the country with him for the week-end, because Perry Hull from Chicago had unexpectedly come to town. It added that Anson had brought this on himself: "—if I felt that you loved me as I love you I would go with you at any time, any place, but Perry is *so* nice, and he so much wants me to marry him——"

Anson smiled contemptuously—he had had experience with such decoy epistles. Moreover, he knew how Dolly had labored over this plan, probably sent for the faithful Perry and calculated the time of his arrival—even labored over the note so that it would make him jealous without driving him away. Like most compromises, it had neither force nor vitality but only a timorous despair.

Suddenly he was angry. He sat down in the lobby and read it again. Then he went to the phone, called Dolly and told her in his clear, compelling voice that he had received her note and would call for her at five o'clock as they had previously planned. Scarcely waiting for the pretended uncertainty of her "Perhaps I can see you for an hour," he hung up the receiver and went down to his office. On the way he tore his own letter into bits and dropped it in the street.

He was not jealous—she meant nothing to him—but at her pathetic ruse everything stubborn and self-indulgent in him came to the surface. It was a presumption from a mental inferior and it could not be overlooked. If she wanted to know to whom she belonged she would see.

He was on the door-step at quarter past five. Dolly was dressed for the street, and he listened in silence to the paragraph of "I can only see you for an hour," which she had begun on the phone.

"Put on your hat, Dolly," he said, "we'll take a walk."

They strolled up Madison Avenue and over to Fifth while Anson's shirt dampened upon his portly body in the deep heat. He talked little, scolding her, making no love to her, but before they had walked six blocks she was his again, apologizing for the note, offering not to see Perry at all as an atonement, offering anything. She thought that he had come because he was beginning to love her.

"I'm hot," he said when they reached 71st Street. "This is a winter suit. If I stop by the house and change, would you mind waiting for me down-stairs? I'll only be a minute."

She was happy; the intimacy of his being hot, of any physical fact about him, thrilled her. When they came to the iron-grated door and Anson took out his key she experienced a sort of delight.

Down-stairs it was dark, and after he ascended in the lift Dolly raised a curtain and looked out through opaque lace at the houses over the way. She heard the lift machinery stop, and with the notion of teasing him pressed the button that brought it down. Then on what was more than an impulse she got into it and sent it up to what she guessed was his floor.

"Anson," she called, laughing a little.

"Just a minute," he answered from his bedroom . . . then after a brief delay: "Now you can come in."

He had changed and was buttoning his vest.

"This is my room," he said lightly. "How do you like it?"

She caught sight of Paula's picture on the wall and stared at it in fascination, just as Paula had stared at the pictures of Anson's childish sweethearts five years before. She knew something about Paula—sometimes she tortured herself with fragments of the story.

Suddenly she came close to Anson, raising her arms. They embraced. Outside the area window a soft artificial twilight already hovered, though the sun was still bright on a back roof across the way. In half an hour the room would be quite dark. The uncalculated opportunity overwhelmed them, made them both breathless, and they clung more closely. It was imminent, inevitable. Still holding one another, they raised their heads—their eyes fell together upon Paula's picture, staring down at them from the wall.

Suddenly Anson dropped his arms, and sitting down at his desk tried the drawer with a bunch of keys.

"Like a drink?" he asked in a gruff voice.

"No, Anson."

He poured himself half a tumbler of whiskey, swallowed it, and then opened the door into the hall.

"Come on," he said.

Dolly hesitated.

"Anson—I'm going to the country with you tonight, after all. You understand that, don't you?"

"Of course," he answered brusquely.

In Dolly's car they rode on to Long Island, closer in their emotions than they had ever been before. They knew what would happen—not with Paula's face to remind them that something was lacking, but when they were alone in the still, hot Long Island night they did not care.

The estate in Port Washington where they were to spend the week-end belonged to a cousin of Anson's who had married a Montana copper operator. An interminable drive began at the lodge and twisted under imported poplar saplings toward a huge, pink Spanish house. Anson had often visited there before.

After dinner they danced at the Linx Club. About midnight Anson assured himself that his cousins would not leave before two—then he explained that Dolly was tired; he would take her home and return to the dance later. Trembling a little with excitement, they got into a borrowed car together and drove to Port Washington. As they reached the lodge he stopped and spoke to the night-watchman.

"When are you making a round, Carl?"

"Right away."

"Then you'll be here till everybody's in?"

"Yes, sir."

"All right. Listen: if any automobile, no matter whose it is, turns in at this gate, I want you to phone the house immediately." He put a five-dollar bill into Carl's hand. "Is that clear?"

"Yes, Mr. Anson." Being of the Old World, he neither winked nor smiled. Yet Dolly sat with her face turned slightly away.

Anson had a key. Once inside he poured a drink for both of

them—Dolly left hers untouched—then he ascertained definitely the location of the phone, and found that it was within easy hearing distance of their rooms, both of which were on the first floor.

Five minutes later he knocked at the door of Dolly's room.

"Anson?" He went in, closing the door behind him. She was in bed, leaning up anxiously with elbows on the pillow; sitting beside her he took her in his arms.

"Anson, darling."

He didn't answer.

"Anson. . . . Anson! I love you. . . . Say you love me. Say it now—can't you say it now? Even if you don't mean it?"

He did not listen. Over her head he perceived that the picture of Paula was hanging here upon this wall.

He got up and went close to it. The frame gleamed faintly with thrice-reflected moonlight—within was a blurred shadow of a face that he saw he did not know. Almost sobbing, he turned around and stared with abomination at the little figure on the bed.

"This is all foolishness," he said thickly. "I don't know what I was thinking about. I don't love you and you'd better wait for somebody that loves you. I don't love you a bit, can't you understand?"

His voice broke, and he went hurriedly out. Back in the salon he was pouring himself a drink with uneasy fingers, when the front door opened suddenly, and his cousin came in.

"Why, Anson, I hear Dolly's sick," she began solicitously. "I hear she's sick. . . ."

"It was nothing," he interrupted, raising his voice so that it would carry into Dolly's room. "She was a little tired. She went to bed."

For a long time afterward Anson believed that a protective God sometimes interfered in human affairs. But Dolly Karger, lying awake and staring at the ceiling, never again believed in anything at all.

VI

When Dolly married during the following autumn, Anson was in London on business. Like Paula's marriage, it was sudden, but it affected him in a different way. At first he felt that it was funny, and had an inclination to laugh when he thought of it. Later it depressed him—it made him feel old.

There was something repetitive about it—why, Paula and Dolly had belonged to different generations. He had a foretaste of the sensation of a man of forty who hears that the daughter of an old flame has married. He wired congratulations and, as was not the case with Paula, they were sincere—he had never really hoped that Paula would be happy.

When he returned to New York, he was made a partner in the firm, and, as his responsibilities increased, he had less time on his hands. The refusal of a life-insurance company to issue him a policy made such an impression on him that he stopped drinking for a year, and claimed that he felt better physically, though I think he missed the convivial recounting of those Celliniesque adventures which, in his early twenties, had played such a part in his life. But he never abandoned the Yale Club. He was a figure there, a personality, and the tendency of his class, who were now seven years out of college, to drift away to more sober haunts was checked by his presence.

His day was never too full nor his mind too weary to give any sort of aid to any one who asked it. What had been done at first through pride and superiority had become a habit and a passion. And there was always something—a younger brother in trouble at New Haven, a quarrel to be patched up between a friend and his wife, a position to be found for this man, an investment for that. But his specialty was the solving of problems for young married people. Young married people fascinated him and their apartments were almost sacred to him—he knew the story of their love-affair, advised them where to live and how, and remembered their babies' names. Toward young wives his attitude was circumspect: he never abused the trust which their

husbands—strangely enough in view of his unconcealed irregu-
larities—invariably reposed in him.

He came to take a vicarious pleasure in happy marriages, and
to be inspired to an almost equally pleasant melancholy by those
that went astray. Not a season passed that he did not witness the
collapse of an affair that perhaps he himself had fathered. When
Paula was divorced and almost immediately remarried to another Bostonian, he talked about her to me all one afternoon.
He would never love any one as he had loved Paula, but he insisted that he no longer cared.

"I'll never marry," he came to say; "I've seen too much of it,
and I know a happy marriage is a very rare thing. Besides, I'm
too old."

But he did believe in marriage. Like all men who spring from
a happy and successful marriage, he believed in it passionately
—nothing he had seen would change his belief, his cynicism dissolved upon it like air. But he did really believe he was too old.
At twenty-eight he began to accept with equanimity the pros-
pect of marrying without romantic love; he resolutely chose a
New York girl of his own class, pretty, intelligent, congenial,
above reproach—and set about falling in love with her. The
things he had said to Paula with sincerity, to other girls with
grace, he could no longer say at all without smiling, or with the
force necessary to convince.

"When I'm forty," he told his friends, "I'll be ripe. I'll fall for
some chorus girl like the rest."

Nevertheless, he persisted in his attempt. His mother wanted
to see him married, and he could now well afford it—he had a
seat on the Stock Exchange, and his earned income came to
twenty-five thousand a year. The idea was agreeable: when his
friends—he spent most of his time with the set he and Dolly
had evolved—closed themselves in behind domestic doors at
night, he no longer rejoiced in his freedom. He even wondered if
he should have married Dolly. Not even Paula had loved him
more, and he was learning the rarity, in a single life, of encoun-
tering true emotion.

Just as this mood began to creep over him a disquieting story reached his ear. His Aunt Edna, a woman just this side of forty, was carrying on an open intrigue with a dissolute, hard-drinking young man named Cary Sloane. Every one knew of it except Anson's Uncle Robert, who for fifteen years had talked long in clubs and taken his wife for granted.

Anson heard the story again and again with increasing annoyance. Something of his old feeling for his uncle came back to him, a feeling that was more than personal, a reversion toward that family solidarity on which he had based his pride. His intuition singled out the essential point of the affair, which was that his uncle shouldn't be hurt. It was his first experiment in unsolicited meddling, but with his knowledge of Edna's character he felt that he could handle the matter better than a district judge or his uncle.

His uncle was in Hot Springs. Anson traced down the sources of the scandal so that there should be no possibility of mistake and then he called Edna and asked her to lunch with him at the Plaza next day. Something in his tone must have frightened her, for she was reluctant, but he insisted, putting off the date until she had no excuse for refusing.

She met him at the appointed time in the Plaza lobby, a lovely, faded, gray-eyed blonde in a coat of Russian sable. Five great rings, cold with diamonds and emeralds, sparkled on her slender hands. It occurred to Anson that it was his father's intelligence and not his uncle's that had earned the fur and the stones, the rich brilliance that buoyed up her passing beauty.

Though Edna scented his hostility, she was unprepared for the directness of his approach.

"Edna, I'm astonished at the way you've been acting," he said in a strong, frank voice. "At first I couldn't believe it."

"Believe what?" she demanded sharply.

"You needn't pretend with me, Edna. I'm talking about Cary Sloane. Aside from any other consideration, I didn't think you could treat Uncle Robert——"

"Now look here, Anson—" she began angrily, but his peremptory voice broke through hers:

"—and your children in such a way. You've been married eighteen years, and you're old enough to know better."

"You can't talk to me like that! You——"

"Yes, I can. Uncle Robert has always been my best friend." He was tremendously moved. He felt a real distress about his uncle, about his three young cousins.

Edna stood up, leaving her crab-flake cocktail untasted.

"This is the silliest thing——"

"Very well, if you won't listen to me I'll go to Uncle Robert and tell him the whole story—he's bound to hear it sooner or later. And afterward I'll go to old Moses Sloane."

Edna faltered back into her chair.

"Don't talk so loud," she begged him. Her eyes blurred with tears. "You have no idea how your voice carries. You might have chosen a less public place to make all these crazy accusations."

He didn't answer.

"Oh, you never liked me, I know," she went on. "You're just taking advantage of some silly gossip to try and break up the only interesting friendship I've ever had. What did I ever do to make you hate me so?"

Still Anson waited. There would be the appeal to his chivalry, then to his pity, finally to his superior sophistication—when he had shouldered his way through all these there would be admissions, and he could come to grips with her. By being silent, by being impervious, by returning constantly to his main weapon, which was his own true emotion, he bullied her into frantic despair as the luncheon hour slipped away. At two o'clock she took out a mirror and a handkerchief, shined away the marks of her tears and powdered the slight hollows where they had lain. She had agreed to meet him at her own house at five.

When he arrived she was stretched on a *chaise-longue* which was covered with cretonne for the summer, and the tears he had called up at luncheon seemed still to be standing in her eyes.

Then he was aware of Cary Sloane's dark anxious presence upon the cold hearth.

"What's this idea of yours?" broke out Sloane immediately. "I understand you invited Edna to lunch and then threatened her on the basis of some cheap scandal."

Anson sat down.

"I have no reason to think it's only scandal."

"I hear you're going to take it to Robert Hunter, and to my father."

Anson nodded.

"Either you break it off—or I will," he said.

"What God damned business is it of yours, Hunter?"

"Don't lose your temper, Cary," said Edna nervously. "It's only a question of showing him how absurd——"

"For one thing, it's my name that's being handed around," interrupted Anson. "That's all that concerns you, Cary."

"Edna isn't a member of your family."

"She most certainly is!" His anger mounted. "Why—she owes this house and the rings on her fingers to my father's brains. When Uncle Robert married her she didn't have a penny."

They all looked at the rings as if they had a significant bearing on the situation. Edna made a gesture to take them from her hand.

"I guess they're not the only rings in the world," said Sloane.

"Oh, this is absurd," cried Edna. "Anson, will you listen to me? I've found out how the silly story started. It was a maid I discharged who went right to the Chilicheffs—all these Russians pump things out of their servants and then put a false meaning on them." She brought down her fist angrily on the table: "And after Robert lent them the limousine for a whole month when we were South last winter——"

"Do you see?" demanded Sloane eagerly. "This maid got hold of the wrong end of the thing. She knew that Edna and I were friends, and she carried it to the Chilicheffs. In Russia they assume that if a man and a woman——"

He enlarged the theme to a disquisition upon social relations in the Caucasus.

"If that's the case it better be explained to Uncle Robert," said Anson dryly, "so that when the rumors do reach him he'll know they're not true."

Adopting the method he had followed with Edna at luncheon he let them explain it all away. He knew that they were guilty and that presently they would cross the line from explanation into justification and convict themselves more definitely than he could ever do. By seven they had taken the desperate step of telling him the truth—Robert Hunter's neglect, Edna's empty life, the casual dalliance that had flamed up into passion—but like so many true stories it had the misfortune of being old, and its enfeebled body beat helplessly against the armor of Anson's will. The threat to go to Sloane's father sealed their helplessness, for the latter, a retired cotton broker out of Alabama, was a notorious fundamentalist who controlled his son by a rigid allowance and the promise that at his next vagary the allowance would stop forever.

They dined at a small French restaurant, and the discussion continued—at one time Sloane resorted to physical threats, a little later they were both imploring him to give them time. But Anson was obdurate. He saw that Edna was breaking up, and that her spirit must not be refreshed by any renewal of their passion.

At two o'clock in a small night-club on 53d Street, Edna's nerves suddenly collapsed, and she cried to go home. Sloane had been drinking heavily all evening, and he was faintly maudlin, leaning on the table and weeping a little with his face in his hands. Quickly Anson gave them his terms. Sloane was to leave town for six months, and he must be gone within forty-eight hours. When he returned there was to be no resumption of the affair, but at the end of a year Edna might, if she wished, tell Robert Hunter that she wanted a divorce and go about it in the usual way.

He paused, gaining confidence from their faces for his final word.

"Or there's another thing you can do," he said slowly, "if Edna wants to leave her children, there's nothing I can do to prevent your running off together."

"I want to go home!" cried Edna again. "Oh, haven't you done enough to us for one day?"

Outside it was dark, save for a blurred glow from Sixth Avenue down the street. In that light those two who had been lovers looked for the last time into each other's tragic faces, realizing that between them there was not enough youth and strength to avert their eternal parting. Sloane walked suddenly off down the street and Anson tapped a dozing taxi-driver on the arm.

It was almost four; there was a patient flow of cleaning water along the ghostly pavement of Fifth Avenue, and the shadows of two night woman flitted over the dark façade of St. Thomas's church. Then the desolate shrubbery of Central Park where Anson had often played as a child, and the mounting numbers, significant as names, of the marching streets. This was his city, he thought, where his name had flourished through five generations. No change could alter the permanence of its place here, for change itself was the essential substratum by which he and those of his name identified themselves with the spirit of New York. Resourcefulness and a powerful will—for his threats in weaker hands would have been less than nothing—had beaten the gathering dust from his uncle's name, from the name of his family, from even this shivering figure that sat beside him in the car.

Cary Sloane's body was found next morning on the lower shelf of a pillar of Queensboro Bridge. In the darkness and in his excitement he had thought that it was the water flowing black beneath him, but in less than a second it made no possible difference—unless he had planned to think one last thought of Edna, and call out her name as he struggled feebly in the water.

VII

Anson never blamed himself for his part in this affair—the situation which brought it about had not been of his making. But the just suffer with the unjust, and he found that his oldest and somehow his most precious friendship was over. He never knew what distorted story Edna told, but he was welcome in his uncle's house no longer.

Just before Christmas Mrs. Hunter retired to a select Episcopal heaven, and Anson became the responsible head of his family. An unmarried aunt who had lived with them for years ran the house, and attempted with helpless inefficiency to chaperone the younger girls. All the children were less self-reliant than Anson, more conventional both in their virtues and in their short-comings. Mrs. Hunter's death had postponed the début of one daughter and the wedding of another. Also it had taken some-thing deeply material from all of them, for with her passing the quiet, expensive superiority of the Hunters came to an end.

For one thing, the estate, considerably diminished by two inheritance taxes and soon to be divided among six children, was not a notable fortune any more. Anson saw a tendency in his youngest sisters to speak rather respectfully of families that hadn't "existed" twenty years ago. His own feeling of precedence was not echoed in them—sometimes they were conventionally snobbish, that was all. For another thing, this was the last summer they would spend on the Connecticut estate; the clamor against it was too loud: "Who wants to waste the best months of the year shut up in that dead old town?" Reluctantly he yielded —the house would go into the market in the fall, and next summer they would rent a smaller place in Westchester County. It was a step down from the expensive simplicity of his father's idea, and, while he sympathized with the revolt, it also annoyed him; during his mother's lifetime he had gone up there at least every other week-end—even in the gayest summers.

Yet he himself was part of this change, and his strong instinct for life had turned him in his twenties from the hollow obsequies of that abortive leisure class. He did not see this clearly—he still felt that there was a norm, a standard of society. But there was no norm, it was doubtful if there ever had been a true norm in New York. The few who still paid and fought to enter a particular set succeeded only to find that as a society it scarcely functioned—or, what was more alarming, that the Bohemia from which they fled sat above them at table.

At twenty-nine Anson's chief concern was his own growing loneliness. He was sure now that he would never marry. The number of weddings at which he had officiated as best man or usher was past all counting—there was a drawer at home that bulged with the official neckties of this or that wedding-party, neckties standing for romances that had not endured a year, for couples who had passed completely from his life. Scarf-pins, gold pencils, cuff-buttons, presents from a generation of grooms had passed through his jewel-box and been lost—and with every ceremony he was less and less able to imagine himself in the groom's place. Under his hearty good-will toward all those marriages there was despair about his own.

And as he neared thirty he became not a little depressed at the inroads that marriage, especially lately, had made upon his friendships. Groups of people had a disconcerting tendency to dissolve and disappear. The men from his own college—and it was upon them he had expended the most time and affection—were the most elusive of all. Most of them were drawn deep into domesticity, two were dead, one lived abroad, one was in Hollywood writing continuities for pictures that Anson went faithfully to see.

Most of them, however, were permanent commuters with an intricate family life centring around some suburban country club, and it was from these that he felt his estrangement most keenly.

In the early days of their married life they had all needed him; he gave them advice about their slim finances, he exorcised their doubts about the advisability of bringing a baby into two rooms and a bath, especially he stood for the great world outside. But now their financial troubles were in the past and the fearfully expected child had evolved into an absorbing family. They were always glad to see old Anson, but they dressed up for him and tried to impress him with their present importance, and kept their troubles to themselves. They needed him no longer.

A few weeks before his thirtieth birthday the last of his early and intimate friends was married. Anson acted in his usual rôle of best man, gave his usual silver tea-service, and went down to the usual *Homeric* to say good-by. It was a hot Friday afternoon in May, and as he walked from the pier he realized that Saturday closing had begun and he was free until Monday morning.

"Go where?" he asked himself.

The Yale Club, of course; bridge until dinner, then four or five raw cocktails in somebody's room and a pleasant confused evening. He regretted that this afternoon's groom wouldn't be along —they had always been able to cram so much into such nights: they knew how to attach women and how to get rid of them, how much consideration any girl deserved from their intelligent hedonism. A party was an adjusted thing—you took certain girls to certain places and spent just so much on their amusement; you drank a little, not much, more than you ought to drink, and at a certain time in the morning you stood up and said you were going home. You avoided college boys, sponges, future engagements, fights, sentiment, and indiscretions. That was the way it was done. All the rest was dissipation.

In the morning you were never violently sorry—you made no resolutions, but if you had overdone it and your heart was slightly out of order, you went on the wagon for a few days without saying anything about it, and waited until an accumulation of nervous boredom projected you into another party.

The lobby of the Yale Club was unpopulated. In the bar three very young alumni looked up at him, momentarily and without curiosity.

"Hello, there, Oscar," he said to the bartender. "Mr. Cahill been around this afternoon?"

"Mr. Cahill's gone to New Haven."

"Oh . . . that so?"

"Gone to the ball game. Lot of men gone up."

Anson looked once again into the lobby, considered for a moment, and then walked out and over to Fifth Avenue. From the broad window of one of his clubs—one that he had scarcely visited in five years—a gray man with watery eyes stared down at him. Anson looked quickly away—that figure sitting in vacant resignation, in supercilious solitude, depressed him. He stopped and, retracing his steps, started over 47th Street toward Teak Warden's apartment. Teak and his wife had once been his most familiar friends—it was a household where he and Dolly Karger had been used to go in the days of their affair. But Teak had taken to drink, and his wife had remarked publicly that Anson was a bad influence on him. The remark reached Anson in an exaggerated form—when it was finally cleared up, the delicate spell of intimacy was broken, never to be renewed.

"Is Mr. Warden at home?" he inquired.

"They've gone to the country."

The fact unexpectedly cut at him. They were gone to the country and he hadn't known. Two years before he would have known the date, the hour, come up at the last moment for a final drink, and planned his first visit to them. Now they had gone without a word.

Anson looked at his watch and considered a week-end with his family, but the only train was a local that would jolt through the aggressive heat for three hours. And to-morrow in the country, and Sunday—he was in no mood for porch-bridge with polite undergraduates, and dancing after dinner at a rural roadhouse, a diminutive of gaiety which his father had estimated too well.

"Oh, no," he said to himself. . . . "No."

He was a dignified, impressive young man, rather stout now, but otherwise unmarked by dissipation. He could have been cast for a pillar of something—at times you were sure it was not society, at others nothing else—for the law, for the church. He stood for a few minutes motionless on the sidewalk in front of a 47th Street apartment-house; for almost the first time in his life he had nothing whatever to do.

Then he began to walk briskly up Fifth Avenue, as if he had just been reminded of an important engagement there. The necessity of dissimulation is one of the few characteristics that we share with dogs, and I think of Anson on that day as some well-bred specimen who had been disappointed at a familiar back door. He was going to see Nick, once a fashionable bartender in demand at all private dances, and now employed in cooling non-alcoholic champagne among the labyrinthine cellars of the Plaza Hotel.

"Nick," he said, "what's happened to everything?"

"Dead," Nick said.

"Make me a whiskey sour." Anson handed a pint bottle over the counter. "Nick, the girls are different; I had a little girl in Brooklyn and she got married last week without letting me know."

"That a fact? Ha-ha-ha," responded Nick diplomatically. "Slipped it over on you."

"Absolutely," said Anson. "And I was out with her the night before."

"Ha-ha-ha," said Nick, "ha-ha-ha!"

"Do you remember the wedding, Nick, in Hot Springs where I had the waiters and the musicians singing 'God save the King'?"

"Now where was that, Mr. Hunter?" Nick concentrated doubtfully. "Seems to me that was——"

"Next time they were back for more, and I began to wonder how much I'd paid them," continued Anson.

"—seems to me that was at Mr. Trenholm's wedding."

"Don't know him," said Anson decisively. He was offended that a strange name should intrude upon his reminiscences; Nick perceived this.

"Na—aw—" he admitted, "I ought to know that. It was one of *your* crowd—Brakins . . . Baker——"

"Bicker Baker," said Anson responsively. "They put me in a hearse after it was over and covered me up with flowers and drove me away."

"Ha-ha-ha," said Nick. "Ha-ha-ha."

Nick's simulation of the old family servant paled presently and Anson went up-stairs to the lobby. He looked around—his eyes met the glance of an unfamiliar clerk at the desk, then fell upon a flower from the morning's marriage hesitating in the mouth of a brass cuspidor. He went out and walked slowly toward the blood-red sun over Columbus Circle. Suddenly he turned around and, retracing his steps to the Plaza, immured himself in a telephone-booth.

Later he said that he tried to get me three times that afternoon, that he tried every one who might be in New York—men and girls he had not seen for years, an artist's model of his college days whose faded number was still in his address book—Central told him that even the exchange existed no longer. At length his quest roved into the country, and he held brief disappointing conversations with emphatic butlers and maids. So-and-so was out, riding, swimming, playing golf, sailed to Europe last week. Who shall I say phoned?

It was intolerable that he should pass the evening alone—the private reckonings which one plans for a moment of leisure lose every charm when the solitude is enforced. There were always women of a sort, but the ones he knew had temporarily vanished, and to pass a New York evening in the hired company of a stranger never occurred to him—he would have considered that that was something shameful and secret, the diversion of a travelling salesman in a strange town.

Anson paid the telephone bill—the girl tried unsuccessfully to joke with him about its size—and for the second time that afternoon started to leave the Plaza and go he knew not where. Near the revolving door the figure of a woman, obviously with child, stood sideways to the light—a sheer beige cape fluttered at her shoulders when the door turned and, each time, she looked impatiently toward it as if she were weary of waiting. At the first sight of her a strong nervous thrill of familiarity went over him, but not until he was within five feet of her did he realize that it was Paula.

"Why, Anson Hunter!"

His heart turned over.

"Why, Paula——"

"Why, this is wonderful. I can't believe it, *Anson!*"

She took both his hands, and he saw in the freedom of the gesture that the memory of him had lost poignancy to her. But not to him—he felt that old mood that she evoked in him stealing over his brain, that gentleness with which he had always met her optimism as if afraid to mar its surface.

"We're at Rye for the summer. Pete had to come East on business—you know of course I'm Mrs. Peter Hagerty now—so we brought the children and took a house. You've got to come out and see us."

"Can I?" he asked directly. "When?"

"When you like. Here's Pete." The revolving door functioned, giving up a fine tall man of thirty with a tanned face and a trim mustache. His immaculate fitness made a sharp contrast with Anson's increasing bulk, which was obvious under the faintly tight cut-away coat.

"You oughtn't to be standing," said Hagerty to his wife. "Let's sit down here." He indicated lobby chairs, but Paula hesitated.

"I've got to go right home," she said. "Anson, why don't you—why don't you come out and have dinner with us to-night? We're just getting settled, but if you can stand that——"

Hagerty confirmed the invitation cordially.

"Come out for the night."

Their car waited in front of the hotel, and Paula with a tired gesture sank back against silk cushions in the corner.

"There's so much I want to talk to you about," she said, "it seems hopeless."

"I want to hear about you."

"Well"—she smiled at Hagerty—"that would take a long time too. I have three children—by my first marriage. The oldest is

five, then four, then three." She smiled again. "I didn't waste
much time having them, did I?"

"Boys?"

"A boy and two girls. Then—oh, a lot of things happened, and
I got a divorce in Paris a year ago and married Pete. That's all—
except that I'm awfully happy."

In Rye they drove up to a large house near the Beach Club,
from which there issued presently three dark, slim children who
broke from an English governess and approached them with an
esoteric cry. Abstractedly and with difficulty Paula took each one
into her arms, a caress which they accepted stiffly, as they had
evidently been told not to bump into Mummy. Even against their
fresh faces Paula's skin showed scarcely any weariness—for all
her physical languor she seemed younger than when he had
last seen her at Palm Beach seven years ago.

At dinner she was preoccupied, and afterward, during the
homage to the radio, she lay with closed eyes on the sofa, until
Anson wondered if his presence at this time were not an intrusion. But at nine o'clock, when Hagerty rose and said pleasantly
that he was going to leave them by themselves for a while, she
began to talk slowly about herself and the past.

"My first baby," she said—"the one we call darling, the biggest
little girl—I wanted to die when I knew I was going to have her,
because Lowell was like a stranger to me. It didn't seem as
though she could be my own. I wrote you a letter and tore it up.
Oh, you were *so* bad to me, Anson."

It was the dialogue again, rising and falling. Anson felt a sudden quickening of memory.

"Weren't you engaged once?" she asked—"a girl named Dolly
something?"

"I wasn't ever engaged. I tried to be engaged, but I never
loved anybody but you, Paula."

"Oh," she said. Then after a moment: "This baby is the first
one I ever really wanted. You see, I'm in love now—at last."

He didn't answer, shocked at the treachery of her remembrance. She must have seen that the "at last" bruised him, for she continued:

"I was infatuated with you, Anson—you could make me do anything you liked. But we wouldn't have been happy. I'm not smart enough for you. I don't like things to be complicated like you do." She paused. "You'll never settle down," she said.

The phrase struck at him from behind—it was an accusation that of all accusations he had never merited.

"I could settle down if women were different," he said. "If I didn't understand so much about them, if women didn't spoil you for other women, if they had only a little pride. If I could go to sleep for a while and wake up into a home that was really mine —why, that's what I'm made for, Paula, that's what women have seen in me and liked in me. It's only that I can't get through the preliminaries any more."

Hagerty came in a little before eleven; after a whiskey Paula stood up and announced that she was going to bed. She went over and stood by her husband.

"Where did you go, dearest?" she demanded.

"I had a drink with Ed Saunders."

"I was worried. I thought maybe you'd run away."

She rested her head against his coat.

"He's sweet, isn't he, Anson?" she demanded.

"Absolutely," said Anson, laughing.

She raised her face to her husband.

"Well, I'm ready," she said. She turned to Anson: "Do you want to see our family gymnastic stunt?"

"Yes," he said in an interested voice.

"All right. Here we go!"

Hagerty picked her up easily in his arms.

"This is called the family acrobatic stunt," said Paula. "He carries me up-stairs. Isn't it sweet of him?"

"Yes," said Anson.

Hagerty bent his head slightly until his face touched Paula's.

"And I love him," she said. "I've just been telling you, haven't I, Anson?"

"Yes," he said.

"He's the dearest thing that ever lived in this world; aren't you, darling? . . . Well, good night. Here we go. Isn't he strong?"

"Yes," Anson said.

"You'll find a pair of Pete's pajamas laid out for you. Sweet dreams—see you at breakfast."

"Yes," Anson said.

VIII

The older members of the firm insisted that Anson should go abroad for the summer. He had scarcely had a vacation in seven years, they said. He was stale and needed a change. Anson resisted.

"If I go," he declared, "I won't come back any more."

"That's absurd, old man. You'll be back in three months with all this depression gone. Fit as ever."

"No." He shook his head stubbornly. "If I stop, I won't go back to work. If I stop, that means I've given up—I'm through."

"We'll take a chance on that. Stay six months if you like—we're not afraid you'll leave us. Why, you'd be miserable if you didn't work."

They arranged his passage for him. They liked Anson—every one liked Anson—and the change that had been coming over him cast a sort of pall over the office. The enthusiasm that had invariably signalled up business, the consideration toward his equals and his inferiors, the lift of his vital presence—within the past four months his intense nervousness had melted down these qualities into the fussy pessimism of a man of forty. On every transaction in which he was involved he acted as a drag and a strain.

"If I go I'll never come back," he said.

Three days before he sailed Paula Legendre Hagerty died in childbirth. I was with him a great deal then, for we were crossing together, but for the first time in our friendship he told me not a word of how he felt, nor did I see the slightest sign of emotion. His chief preoccupation was with the fact that he was thirty years old—he would turn the conversation to the point where he could remind you of it and then fall silent, as if he assumed that the statement would start a chain of thought sufficient to itself. Like his partners, I was amazed at the change in him, and I was glad when the *Paris* moved off into the wet space between the worlds, leaving his principality behind.

"How about a drink?" he suggested.

We walked into the bar with that defiant feeling that characterizes the day of departure and ordered four Martinis. After one cocktail a change came over him—he suddenly reached across and slapped my knee with the first joviality I had seen him exhibit for months.

"Did you see that girl in the red tam?" he demanded, "the one with the high color who had the two police dogs down to bid her good-by."

"She's pretty," I agreed.

"I looked her up in the purser's office and found out that she's alone. I'm going down to see the steward in a few minutes. We'll have dinner with her to-night."

After a while he left me, and within an hour he was walking up and down the deck with her, talking to her in his strong, clear voice. Her red tam was a bright spot of color against the steel-green sea, and from time to time she looked up with a flashing bob of her head, and smiled with amusement and interest, and anticipation. At dinner we had champagne, and were very joyous—afterward Anson ran the pool with infectious gusto, and several people who had seen me with him asked me his name. He and the girl were talking and laughing together on a lounge in the bar when I went to bed.

I saw less of him on the trip than I had hoped. He wanted to arrange a foursome, but there was no one available, so I saw him only at meals. Sometimes, though, he would have a cocktail in the bar, and he told me about the girl in the red tam, and his adventures with her, making them all bizarre and amusing, as he had a way of doing, and I was glad that he was himself again, or at least the self that I knew, and with which I felt at home. I don't think he was ever happy unless some one was in love with him, responding to him like filings to a magnet, helping him to explain himself, promising him something. What it was I do not know. Perhaps they promised that there would always be women in the world who would spend their brightest, freshest, rarest hours to nurse and protect that superiority he cherished in his heart.

The Snows of Kilimanjaro

ERNEST HEMINGWAY

Kilimanjaro is a snow-covered mountain 19,710 feet high, and is said to be the highest mountain in Africa. Its western summit is called the Masai "Ngàje Ngài," the House of God. Close to the western summit there is the dried and frozen carcass of a leopard. No one has explained what the leopard was seeking at that altitude.

"The marvellous thing is that it's painless," he said. "That's how you know when it starts."

"Is it really?"

"Absolutely. I'm awfully sorry about the odor though. That must bother you."

"Don't! Please don't."

"Look at them," he said. "Now is it sight or is it scent that brings them like that?"

The cot the man lay on was in the wide shade of a mimosa

Reprinted from *The Fifth Column & The First Forty-nine Stories* by Ernest Hemingway; copyright, 1938, by Ernest Hemingway; used by permission of the publishers, Charles Scribner's Sons.

tree and as he looked out past the shade onto the glare of the plain there were three of the big birds squatted obscenely, while in the sky a dozen more sailed, making quick-moving shadows as they passed.

"They've been there since the day the truck broke down," he said. "Today's the first time any have lit on the ground. I watched the way they sailed very carefully at first in case I ever wanted to use them in a story. That's funny now."

"I wish you wouldn't," she said.

"I'm only talking," he said. "It's much easier if I talk. But I don't want to bother you."

"You know it doesn't bother me," she said. "It's that I've gotten so very nervous not being able to do anything. I think we might make it as easy as we can until the plane comes."

"Or until the plane doesn't come."

"Please tell me what I can do. There must be something I can do."

"You can take the leg off and that might stop it, though I doubt it. Or you can shoot me. You're a good shot now. I taught you to shoot, didn't I?"

"Please don't talk that way. Couldn't I read to you?"

"Read what?"

"Anything in the book bag that we haven't read."

"I can't listen to it," he said. "Talking is the easiest. We quarrel and that makes the time pass."

"I don't quarrel. I never want to quarrel. Let's not quarrel any more. No matter how nervous we get. Maybe they will be back with another truck today. Maybe the plane will come."

"I don't want to move," the man said. "There is no sense in moving now except to make it easier for you."

"That's cowardly."

"Can't you let a man die as comfortably as he can without calling him names? What's the use of slanging me?"

"You're not going to die."

"Don't be silly. I'm dying now. Ask those bastards." He looked

over to where the huge, filthy birds sat, their naked heads sunk
in the hunched feathers. A fourth planed down, to run quick-
legged and then waddle slowly toward the others.

"They are around every camp. You never notice them. You
can't die if you don't give up."

"Where did you read that? You're such a bloody fool."

"You might think about some one else."

"For Christ's sake," he said. "That's been my trade."

He lay then and was quiet for a while and looked across the
heat shimmer of the plain to the edge of the bush. There were
a few Tommies that showed minute and white against the yellow and, far off, he saw a herd of zebra, white against the green
of the bush. This was a pleasant camp under big trees against a
hill, with good water, and close by, a nearly dry water hole
where sand grouse flighted in the mornings.

"Wouldn't you like me to read?" she asked. She was sitting on
a canvas chair beside his cot. "There's a breeze coming up."

"No thanks."

"Maybe the truck will come."

"I don't give a damn about the truck."

"I do."

"You give a damn about so many things that I don't."

"Not so many, Harry."

"What about a drink?"

"It's supposed to be bad for you. It said in Black's to avoid all
alcohol. You shouldn't drink."

"Molo!" he shouted.

"Yes Bwana."

"Bring whiskey-soda."

"Yes Bwana."

"You shouldn't," she said. "That's what I mean by giving up.
It says it's bad for you. I know it's bad for you."

"No," he said. "It's good for me."

So now it was all over, he thought. So now he would never
have a chance to finish it. So this was the way it ended in a bick-
ering over a drink. Since the gangrene started in his right leg he

had no pain and with the pain the horror had gone and all he felt now was a great tiredness and anger that this was the end of it. For this, that now was coming, he had very little curiosity. For years it had obsessed him; but now it meant nothing in itself. It was strange how easy being tired enough made it.

Now he would never write the things that he had saved to write until he knew enough to write them well. Well, he would not have to fail at trying to write them either. Maybe you could never write them, and that was why you put them off and delayed the starting. Well he would never know, now.

"I wish we'd never come," the woman said. She was looking at him holding the glass and biting her lip. "You never would have gotten anything like this in Paris. You always said you loved Paris. We could have stayed in Paris or gone anywhere. I'd have gone anywhere. I said I'd go anywhere you wanted. If you wanted to shoot we could have gone shooting in Hungary and been comfortable."

"Your bloody money," he said.

"That's not fair," she said. "It was always yours as much as mine. I left everything and I went wherever you wanted to go and I've done what you wanted to do. But I wish we'd never come here."

"You said you loved it."

"I did when you were all right. But now I hate it. I don't see why that had to happen to your leg. What have we done to have that happen to us?"

"I suppose what I did was to forget to put iodine on it when I first scratched it. Then I didn't pay any attention to it because I never infect. Then, later, when it got bad, it was probably using that weak carbolic solution when the other antiseptics ran out that paralyzed the minute blood vessels and started the gangrene." He looked at her, "What else?"

"I don't mean that."

"If we would have hired a good mechanic instead of a half baked kikuyu driver, he would have checked the oil and never burned out that bearing in the truck."

"I don't mean that."

"If you hadn't left your own people, your goddamned Old Westbury, Saratoga, Palm Beach people to take me on—"

"Why, I loved you. That's not fair. I love you now. I'll always love you. Don't you love me?"

"No," said the man. "I don't think so. I never have."

"Harry, what are you saying? You're out of your head."

"No. I haven't any head to go out of."

"Don't drink that," she said. "Darling, please don't drink that. We have to do everything we can."

"You do it," he said. "I'm tired."

Now in his mind he saw a railway station at Karagatch and he was standing with his pack and that was the headlight of the Simplon-Orient cutting the dark now and he was leaving Thrace then after the retreat. That was one of the things he had saved to write, with, in the morning at breakfast, looking out the window and seeing snow on the mountains in Bulgaria and Nansen's Secretary asking the old man if it were snow and the old man looking at it and saying, No, that's not snow. It's too early for snow. And the Secretary repeating to the other girls, No, you see. It's not snow and them all saying, It's not snow we were mistaken. But it was the snow all right and he sent them on into it when he evolved exchange of populations. And it was snow they tramped along in until they died that winter.

It was snow too that fell all Christmas week that year up in the Gauertal, that year they lived in the woodcutter's house with the big square porcelain stove that filled half the room, and they slept on mattresses filled with beech leaves, the time the deserter came with his feet bloody in the snow. He said the police were right behind him and they gave him woolen socks and held the gendarmes talking until the tracks had drifted over.

In Schrunz, on Christmas day, the snow was so bright it hurt your eyes when you looked out from the weinstube and saw every one coming home from church. That was where they walked up the sleigh-smoothed urine-yellowed road along the *river with the steep pine hills, skis heavy on the shoulder, and where they ran that great run down the glacier above the Mad-lener-Haus, the snow as smooth to see as cake frosting and as light as powder and he remembered the noiseless rush the speed made as you dropped down like a bird.*

They were snow-bound a week in the Madlener-Haus that time in the blizzard playing cards in the smoke by the lantern light and stakes were higher all the time as Herr Lent lost more. Finally he lost it all. Everything, the ski-schule money and all the season's profit and then his capital. He could see him with his long nose, picking up the cards and then opening, "Sans Voir." There was always gambling then. When there was no snow you gambled and when there was too much you gambled. He thought of all the time in his life he had spent gambling.

But he had never written a line of that, nor of that cold, bright Christmas day with the mountains showing across the plain that Barker had flown across the lines to bomb the Austrian officers' leave train, machine-gunning them as they scattered and ran. He remembered Barker afterwards coming into the mess and start-ing to tell about it. And how quiet it got and then somebody saying, "You bloody murderous bastard."

Those were the same Austrians they killed then that he skied with later. No not the same. Hans, that he skied with all that year, had been in the Kaiser-Jagers and when they went hunting hares together up the little valley above the saw-mill they had talked of the fighting on Pasubio and of the attack on Pertica and Asalone and he had never written a word of that. Nor of Monte Corno, nor the Siete Commum, nor of Arsiedo.

How many winters had he lived in the Voralberg and the Arl-berg? It was four and then he remembered the man who had the fox to sell when they had walked into Bludenz, that time to buy presents, and the cherry-pit taste of good kirsch, the fastslipping rush of running powder-snow on crust, singing "Hi! Ho! said Rolly!" as you ran down the last stretch to the steep drop, taking it straight, then running the orchard in three turns and out across the ditch and onto the icy road behind the inn. Knocking your bindings loose kicking the skis free and leaning them up against the wooden wall of the inn, the lamplight coming from the window, where inside, in the smoky, new-wine smelling warmth, they were playing the accordion.

"Where did we stay in Paris?" he asked the woman who was sitting by him in a canvas chair, now, in Africa.

"At the Crillon. You know that."

"That's where we always stayed."

"No. Not always."

"There and at the Pavillion Henri-Quatre in St. Germain. You said you loved it there."

"Love is a dunghill," said Harry. "And I'm the sock that gets on it to crow."

"If you have to go away," she said, "is it absolutely necessary to kill off everything you leave behind? I mean do you have to take away everything? Do you have to kill your horse, and your wife and burn your saddle and your armour?"

"Yes," he said. "Your damned money was my armour. My Swift and my Armour."

"Don't."

"All right. I'll stop that. I don't want to hurt you."

"It's a little bit late now."

"All right then. I'll go on hurting you. It's more amusing. The only thing I ever really liked to do with you I can't do now."

"No, that's not true. You liked to do many things and everything you wanted to do I did."

"Oh, for Christ sake stop bragging, will you?"

He looked at her and saw her crying.

"Listen," he said. "Do you think that it is fun to do this? I don't know why I'm doing it. It's trying to kill to keep yourself alive, I imagine. I was all right when we started talking. I didn't mean to start this, and now I'm crazy as a coot and being as cruel to you as I can be. Don't pay any attention, darling, to what I say. I love you, really. You know I love you. I've never loved any one else the way I love you."

He slipped into the familiar lie he made his bread and butter by.

"You're sweet to me."

"You bitch," he said. "You rich bitch. That's poetry. I'm full of poetry now. Rot and poetry. Rotten poetry."

"Stop it. Harry, why do you have to turn into a devil now?"

"I don't like to leave anything," the man said. "I don't like to leave things behind."

It was evening now and he had been asleep. The sun was gone behind the hill and there was a shadow all across the plain and the small animals were feeding close to camp; quick dropping heads and switching tails, he watched them keeping well out away from the bush now. The birds no longer waited on the ground. They were all perched heavily in a tree. There were many more of them. His personal boy was sitting by the bed.

"Memsahib's gone to shoot," the boy said. "Does Bwana want?"

"Nothing."

She had gone to kill a piece of meat and, knowing how he liked to watch the game, she had gone well away so she would not disturb this little pocket of the plain that he could see. She was always thoughtful, he thought. On anything she knew about, or had read, or that she had ever heard.

It was not her fault that when he went to her he was already over. How could a woman know that you meant nothing that you said; that you spoke only from habit and to be comfortable? After he no longer meant what he said, his lies were more successful with women than when he had told them the truth.

It was not so much that he lied as that there was no truth to tell. He had had his life and it was over and then he went on living it again with different people and more money, with the best of the same places, and some new ones.

You kept from thinking and it was all marvellous. You were equipped with good insides so that you did not go to pieces that way, the way most of them had, and you made an attitude that you cared nothing for the work you used to do, now that you could no longer do it. But, in yourself, you said that you would write about these people; about the very rich; that you were really not of them but a spy in their country; that you would leave it and write of it and for once it would be written by some one who knew what he was writing of. But he would never do it, because each day of not writing, of comfort, of being that which he despised, dulled his ability and softened his will to work so that, finally, he did no work at all. The people he knew now were all much more comfortable when he did not work. Africa was where he had been happiest in the good time of his life, so he had come out here to start again. They had made this safari with the minimum of comfort. There was no hardship; but there was no luxury and he had thought that he could get back into training that way. That in some way he could work the fat off his soul the way a fighter went into the mountains to work and train in order to burn it out of his body.

She had liked it. She said she loved it. She loved anything that was exciting, that involved a change of scene, where there were new people and where things were pleasant. And he had felt the illusion of returning strength of will to work. Now if this was how it ended, and he knew it was, he must not turn like some snake biting itself because its back was broken. It wasn't this woman's fault. If it had not been she it would have been another. If he lived by a lie he should try to die by it. He heard a shot beyond the hill.

She shot very well this good, this rich bitch, this kindly caretaker and destroyer of his talent. Nonsense. He had destroyed his talent himself. Why should he blame this woman because she kept him well? He had destroyed his talent by not using it, by betrayals of himself and what he believed in, by drinking so much that he blunted the edge of his perceptions, by laziness, by sloth, and by snobbery, by pride and by prejudice, by hook and by crook. What was this? A catalogue of old books? What was his talent anyway? It was a talent all right but instead of using it, he had traded on it. It was never what he had done, but always what he could do. And he had chosen to make his living with something else instead of a pen or a pencil. It was strange, too, wasn't it, that when he fell in love with another woman, that woman should always have more money than the last one? But when he no longer was in love, when he was only lying, as to this woman, now, who had the most money of all, who had all the money there was, who had had a husband and children, who had taken lovers and been dissatisfied with them, and who loved him dearly as a writer, as a man, as a companion and as a proud possession; it was strange that when he did not love her at all and was lying, that he should be able to give her more for her money than when he had really loved.

We must all be cut out for what we do, he thought. However you make your living is where your talent lies. He had sold vitality, in one form or another, all his life and when your affections are not too involved you give much better value for the money. He had found that out but he would never write that, now, either. No, he would not write that, although it was well worth writing.

Now she came in sight, walking across the open toward the camp. She was wearing jodhpurs and carrying her rifle. The two boys had a Tommie slung and they were coming along behind her. She was still a good-looking woman, he thought, and she had a pleasant body. She had a great talent and appreciation for the bed, she was not pretty, but he liked her face, she read enormously, she liked to ride and shoot and, certainly, she drank too much. Her husband had died when she was still a comparatively young woman and for a while she had devoted herself to her two just-grown children, who did not need her and were embarrassed at having her about, to her stable of horses, to books, and to bottles. She liked to read in the evening before dinner and she drank Scotch and soda while she read. By dinner she was fairly drunk and after a bottle of wine at dinner she was usually drunk enough to sleep.

That was before the lovers. After she had the lovers she did not drink so much because she did not have to be drunk to sleep.

But the lovers bored her. She had been married to a man who had never bored her and these people bored her very much.

Then one of her two children was killed in a plane crash and after that was over she did not want the lovers, and drink being no anaesthetic she had to make another life. Suddenly, she had been acutely frightened of being alone. But she wanted some one that she respected with her.

It had begun very simply. She liked what he wrote and she had always envied the life he led. She thought he did exactly what he wanted to. The steps by which she had acquired him and the way in which she had finally fallen in love with him were all part of a regular progression in which she had built herself a new life and he had traded away what remained of his old life.

He had traded it for security, for comfort too, there was no denying that, and for what else? He did not know. She would have bought him anything he wanted. He knew that. She was a damned nice woman too. He would as soon be in bed with her as any one; rather with her, because she was richer, because she was very pleasant and appreciative and because she never made scenes. And now this life that she had built again was coming to a term because he had not used iodine two weeks ago when a thorn had scratched his knee as they moved forward trying to photograph a herd of waterbuck standing, their heads up, peering while their nostrils searched the air, their ears spread wide to hear the first noise that would send them rushing into the bush. They had bolted, too, before he got the picture.

Here she came now.

He turned his head on the cot to look toward her, "Hello," he said.

"I shot a Tommy ram," she told him. "He'll make you good broth and I'll have them mash some potatoes with the Klim. How do you feel?"

"Much better."

"Isn't that lovely? You know I thought perhaps you would. You were sleeping when I left."

"I had a good sleep. Did you walk far?"

"No. Just around behind the hill. I made quite a good shot on the Tommy."

"You shoot marvellously, you know."

"I love it. I've loved Africa. Really. If *you're* all right it's the most fun that I've ever had. You don't know the fun it's been to shoot with you. I've loved the country."

"I love it too."

"Darling, you don't know how marvellous it is to see you feeling better. I couldn't stand it when you felt that way. You won't talk to me like that again, will you? Promise me?"

"No," he said. "I don't remember what I said."

"You don't have to destroy me. Do you? I'm only a middle-aged woman who loves you and wants to do what you want to do. I've been destroyed two or three times already. You wouldn't want to destroy me again, would you?"

"I'd like to destroy you a few times in bed," he said.

"Yes. That's the good destruction. That's the way we're made to be destroyed. The plane will be here tomorrow."

"How do you know?"

"I'm sure. It's bound to come. The boys have the wood all ready and the grass to make the smudge. I went down and looked at it again today. There's plenty of room to land and we have the smudges ready at both ends."

"What makes you think it will come tomorrow?"

"I'm sure it will. It's overdue now. Then, in town, they will fix up your leg and then we will have some good destruction. Not that dreadful talking kind."

"Should we have a drink? The sun is down."

"Do you think you should?"

"I'm having one."

"We'll have one together. *Molo, letti dui whiskey-soda!*" she called.

"You'd better put on your mosquito boots," he told her.

"I'll wait till I bathe . . ."

While it grew dark they drank and just before it was dark and there was no longer enough light to shoot, a hyena crossed the open on his way around the hill.

"That bastard crosses there every night," the man said. "Every night for two weeks."

"He's the one makes the noise at night. I don't mind it. They're a filthy animal though."

Drinking together, with no pain now except the discomfort of lying in the one position, the boys lighting a fire, its shadow jumping on the tents, he could feel the return of acquiescence in this life of pleasant surrender. She *was* very good to him. He had been cruel and unjust in the afternoon. She was a fine woman, marvellous really. And just then it occurred to him that he was going to die.

It came with a rush; not as a rush of water nor of wind; but of a sudden evil-smelling emptiness and the odd thing was that the hyena slipped lightly along the edge of it.

"What is it, Harry?" she asked him.

"Nothing," he said. "You had better move over to the other side. To windward."

"Did Molo change the dressing?"

"Yes. I'm just using the boric now."

"How do you feel?"

"A little wobbly."

"I'm going in to bathe," she said. "I'll be right out. I'll eat with you and then we'll put the cot in."

So, he said to himself, we did well to stop the quarrelling. He had never quarrelled much with this woman, while with the women that he loved he had quarrelled so much they had finally, always, with the corrosion of the quarrelling, killed what they had together. He had loved too much, demanded too much, and he wore it all out.

He thought about alone in Constantinople that time, having quarrelled in Paris before he had gone out. He had whored the whole time and then, when that was over, and he had failed to kill his loneliness, but only made it worse, he had written her, *the first one, the one who left him a letter telling her how he had never been able to kill it. . . . How when he thought he saw her outside the Regence one time it made him go all faint and sick inside, and that he would follow a woman who looked like her in some way, along the Boulevard, afraid to see it was not she, afraid to lose the feeling it gave him. How every one he had slept with had only made him miss her more. How what she had done could never matter since he knew he could not cure himself of loving her. He wrote this letter at the Club, cold sober, and mailed it to New York asking her to write him at the office in Paris. That seemed safe. And that night missing her so much it made him feel hollow sick inside, he wandered up past Taxim's, picked a girl up and took her out to supper. He had gone to a place to dance with her afterward, she danced badly, and left her for a hot Armenian slut, that swung her belly against him so it almost scalded. He took her away from a British gunner subaltern after a row. The gunner asked him outside and they fought in the street on the cobbles in the dark. He'd hit him twice, hard, on the side of the jaw and when he didn't go down he knew he was in for a fight. The gunner hit him in the body, then beside his eye. He swung with his left again and landed and the gunner fell on him and grabbed his coat and tore the sleeve off and he clubbed him twice behind the ear and then smashed him with his right as he pushed him away. When the gunner went down his head hit first and he ran with the girl because they heard the M.P.'s coming. They got into a taxi and drove out to Rimmily Hissa along the Bosphorus, and around, and back in the cool night and went to bed and she felt as overripe as she looked but smooth, rose-petal, syrupy, smooth-bellied, big-breasted and needed no pillow under her buttocks, and he left her before she was awake looking blowsy enough in the first daylight and turned up at the Pera Palace with a black eye, carrying his coat because one sleeve was missing.*

That same night he left for Anatolia and he remembered, later on that trip, riding all day through fields of the poppies that they raised for opium and how strange it made you feel, finally, and all the distances seemed wrong, to where they had made the attack with the newly arrived Constantine officers, that did not know a goddamned thing, and the artillery had fired into the troops and the British observer had cried like a child.

That was the day he'd first seen dead men wearing white ballet skirts and upturned shoes with pompons on them. The Turks had come steadily and lumpily and he had seen the skirted men running and the officers shooting into them and running then themselves and he and the British observer had run too until his lungs ached and his mouth was full of the taste of pennies and they stopped behind some rocks and there were the Turks coming as lumpily as ever. Later he had seen the things that he could never think of and later still he had seen much worse. So when he got back to Paris that time he could not talk about it or stand to have it mentioned. And there in the café as he passed was that American poet with a pile of saucers in front of him and a stupid look on his potato face talking about the Dada movement with a Roumanian who said his name was Tristan Tzara, who always wore a monocle and had a headache, and, back at the apartment with his wife that now he loved again, the quarrel all over, the madness all over, glad to be home, the office sent his mail up to the flat. So then the letter in answer to the one he'd written came in on a platter one morning and when he saw the handwriting he went cold all over and tried to slip the letter underneath another. But his wife said, "Who is that letter from, dear?" and that was the end of the beginning of that.

He remembered the good times with them all, and the quarrels. They always picked the finest places to have the quarrels. And why had they always quarrelled when he was feeling best? He had never written any of that because at first, he never wanted to hurt any one and then it seemed as though there was enough to write without it. But he had always thought that he would write it finally. There was so much to write. He had seen the world change; not just the events; although he had seen many of them and had watched the people, but he had seen the subtler change and he could remember how the people were at different times. He had been in it and he had watched it and it was his duty to write of it; but now he never would.

"How do you feel?" she said. She had come out from the tent now after her bath.

"All right."

"Could you eat now?" He saw Molo behind her with the folding table and the other boy with the dishes.

"I want to write," he said.

"You ought to take some broth to keep your strength up."

"I'm going to die tonight," he said. "I don't need my strength up."

"Don't be melodramatic, Harry, please," she said.

"Why don't you use your nose? I'm rotted half way up my thigh now. What the hell should I fool with broth for? Molo bring whiskey-soda."

"Please take the broth," she said gently.

"All right."

The broth was too hot. He had to hold it in the cup until it cooled enough to take it and then he just got it down without gagging.

"You're a fine woman," he said. "Don't pay any attention to me."

She looked at him with her well-known, well-loved face from *Spur* and *Town and Country,* only a little the worse for drink, only a little the worse for bed, but *Town and Country* never showed those good breasts and those useful thighs and those lightly small-of-back-caressing hands, and as he looked and saw her well-known pleasant smile, he felt death come again. This time there was no rush. It was a puff, as of a wind that makes a candle flicker and the flame go tall.

"They can bring my net out later and hang it from the tree and build the fire up. I'm not going in the tent tonight. It's not worth moving. It's a clear night. There won't be any rain."

So this was how you died, in whispers that you did not hear.

Well, there would be no more quarrelling. He could promise that. The one experience that he had never had he was not going to spoil now. He probably would. You spoiled everything. But perhaps he wouldn't.

"You can't take dictation, can you?"

"I never learned," she told him.

"That's all right."

There wasn't time, of course, although it seemed as though it telescoped so that you might put it all into one paragraph if you could get it right.

There was a log house, chinked white with mortar, on a hill above the lake. There was a bell on a pole by the door to call the people in to meals. Behind the house were fields and behind the fields was the timber. A line of lombardy poplars ran from the house to the dock. Other poplars ran along the point. A road went up to the hills along the edge of the timber and along that road he picked blackberries. Then that log house was burned down and all the guns that had been on deer foot racks above the open fire place were burned and afterwards their barrels, with the lead melted in the magazines, and the stocks burned away, lay out on the heap of ashes that were used to make lye for the big iron soap kettles, and you asked Grandfather if you could have them to play with, and he said, no. You see they were his guns still and he never bought any others. Nor did he hunt any more. The house was rebuilt in the same place out of lumber now and painted white and from its porch you saw the poplars and the lake beyond; but there were never any more guns. The barrels of the guns that had hung on the deer feet on the wall of the log house lay out there on the heap of ashes and no one ever touched them.

In the Black Forest, after the war, we rented a trout stream and there were two ways to walk to it. One was down the valley from Triberg and around the valley road in the shade of the trees that bordered the white road, and then up a side road that went up through the hills past many small farms, with the big

*Schwarzwald houses, until that road crossed the stream. That
was where our fishing began.*

*The other way was to climb steeply up to the edge of the
woods and then go across the top of the hills through the pine
woods, and then out to the edge of a meadow and down across
this meadow to the bridge. There were birches along the stream
and it was not big, but narrow, clear and fast, with pools where
it had cut under the roots of the birches. At the Hotel in Triberg
the proprietor had a fine season. It was very pleasant and we
were all great friends. The next year came the inflation and the
money he had made the year before was not enough to buy supplies to open the hotel and he hanged himself.*

*You could dictate that, but you could not dictate the Place
Contrescarpe where the flower sellers dyed their flowers in the
street and the dye ran over the paving where the autobus started
and the old men and the women, always drunk on wine and
bad marc; and the children with their noses running in the cold;
the smell of dirty sweat and poverty and drunkenness at the
Café des Amateurs and the whores at the Bal Musette they
lived above. The Concierge who entertained the trooper of the
Garde Republicaine in her loge, his horsehair-plumed helmet
on a chair. The locataire across the hall whose husband was a
bicycle racer and her joy that morning at the Cremerie when she
had opened L'Auto and seen where he placed third in Paris-
Tours, his first big race. She had blushed and laughed and then
gone upstairs crying with the yellow sporting paper in her hand.
The husband of the woman who ran the Bal Musette drove a
taxi and when he, Harry, had to take an early plane the husband knocked upon the door to wake him and they each drank
a glass of white wine at the zinc of the bar before they started.
He knew his neighbors in that quarter then because they all
were poor.*

*Around that Place there were two kinds; the drunkards and
the sportifs. The drunkards killed their poverty that way; the
sportifs took it out in exercise. They were the descendants of the
Communards and it was no struggle for them to know their poli-*

tics. They knew who had shot their fathers, their relatives, their brothers, and their friends when the Versailles troops came in and took the town after the Commune and executed any one they could catch with calloused hands, or who wore a cap, or carried any other sign he was a working man. And in that poverty, and in that quarter across the street from a Boucherie Chevaline and a wine co-operative he had written the start of all he was to do. There never was another part of Paris that he loved like that, the sprawling trees, the old white plastered houses painted brown below, the long green of the autobus in that round square, the purple flower dye upon the paving, the sudden drop down the hill of the rue Cardinal Lemoine to the River, and the other way the narrow crowded world of the rue Mouffetard. The street that ran up toward the Pantheon and the other that he always took with the bicycle, the only asphalted street in all that quarter, smooth under the tires, with the high narrow houses and the cheap tall hotel where Paul Verlaine had died. There were only two rooms in the apartments where they lived and he had a room on the top floor of that hotel that cost him sixty francs a month where he did his writing, and from it he could see the roofs and chimney pots and all the hills of Paris.

From the apartment you could only see the wood and coal man's place. He sold wine too, bad wine. The golden horse's head outside the Boucherie Chevaline where the carcasses hung yellow gold and red in the open window, and the green painted co-operative where they bought their wine; good wine and cheap. The rest was plaster walls and the windows of the neighbors. The neighbors who, at night, when some one lay drunk in the street, moaning and groaning in that typical French ivresse that you were propaganded to believe did not exist, would open their windows and then the murmur of talk.

"Where is the policeman? When you don't want him the bugger is always there. He's sleeping with some concierge. Get the Agent." Till some one threw a bucket of water from a window and the moaning stopped. "What's that? Water. Ah, that's in-

telligent." And the windows shutting. Marie, his femme de mé-
nage, protesting against the eight-hour day saying, "If a husband
works until six he gets only a little drunk on the way home and
does not waste too much. If he works only until five he is drunk
every night and one has no money. It is the wife of the working
man who suffers from this shortening of hours."

"Wouldn't you like some more broth?" the woman asked him
now.

"No, thank you very much. It is awfully good."

"Try just a little."

"I would like a whiskey-soda."

"It's not good for you."

"No. It's bad for me. Cole Porter wrote the words and the
music. This knowledge that you're going mad for me."

"You know I like you to drink."

"Oh yes. Only it's bad for me."

When she goes, he thought. I'll have all I want. Not all I want
but all there is. Ayee he was tired. Too tired. He was going to
sleep a little while. He lay still and death was not there. It must
have gone around another street. It went in pairs, on bicycles,
and moved absolutely silently on the pavements.

No, he had never written about Paris. Not the Paris that he
cared about. But what about the rest that he had never written?

What about the ranch and the silvered gray of the sage brush,
the quick, clear water in the irrigation ditches, and the heavy
green of the alfalfa. The trail went up into the hills and the cat-
tle in the summer were shy as deer. The bawling and the steady
noise and slow moving mass raising a dust as you brought them
down in the fall. And behind the mountains, the clear sharpness
of the peak in the evening light and, riding down along the trail
in the moonlight, bright across the valley. Now he remembered
coming down through the timber in the dark holding the horse's
tail when you could not see and all the stories that he meant to
write.

About the half-wit chore boy who was left at the ranch that time and told not to let any one get any hay, and that old bastard from the Forks who had beaten the boy when he had worked for him stopping to get some feed. The boy refusing and the old man saying he would beat him again. The boy got the rifle from the kitchen and shot him when he tried to come into the barn and when they came back to the ranch he'd been dead a week, frozen in the corral, and the dogs had eaten part of him. But what was left you packed on a sled wrapped in a blanket and roped on and you got the boy to help you haul it, and the two of you took it out over the road on skis, and sixty miles down to town to turn the boy over. He having no idea that he would be arrested. Thinking he had done his duty and that you were his friend and he would be rewarded. He'd helped to haul the old man in so everybody could know how bad the old man had been and how he'd tried to steal some feed that didn't belong to him, and when the sheriff put the handcuffs on the boy he couldn't believe it. Then he'd started to cry. That was one story he had saved to write. He knew at least twenty good stories from out there and he had never written one. Why?

"You tell them why," he said.
"Why what, dear?"
"Why nothing."
She didn't drink so much, now, since she had him. But if he lived he would never write about her, he knew that now. Nor about any of them. The rich were dull and they drank too much, or they played too much backgammon. They were dull and they were repetitious. He remembered poor Julian and his romantic awe of them and how he had started a story once that began, "The very rich are different from you and me." And how some one had said to Julian, Yes, they have more money. But that was not humorous to Julian. He thought they were a special glamorous race and when he found they weren't it wrecked him just as much as any other thing that wrecked him.

He had been contemptuous of those who wrecked. You did

not have to like it because you understood it. He could beat anything, he thought, because nothing could hurt him if he did not care.

All right. Now he would not care for death. One thing he had always dreaded was the pain. He could stand pain as well as any man, until it went on too long, and wore him out, but here he had something that had hurt frightfully and just when he had felt it breaking him, the pain had stopped.

He remembered long ago when Williamson, the bombing officer, had been hit by a stick bomb some one in a German patrol had thrown as he was coming in through the wire that night and, screaming, had begged every one to kill him. He was a fat man, very brave, and a good officer, although addicted to fantastic shows. But that night he was caught in the wire, and a flare lighting him up and his bowels spilled out into the wire, so when they brought him in, alive, they had to cut him loose. Shoot me, Harry. For Christ sake shoot me. They had had an argument one time about our Lord never sending you anything you could not bear and some one's theory had been that meant that at a certain time the pain passed you out automatically. But he had always remembered Williamson, that night. Nothing passed out Williamson until he gave him all his morphine tablets that he had always saved to use himself and then they did not work right away.

Still this now, that he had, was very easy; and if it was no worse as it went on there was nothing to worry about. Except that he would rather be in better company.

He thought a little about the company that he would like to have.

No, he thought, when everything you do, you do too long, and do too late, you can't expect to find the people still there. The people all are gone. The party's over and you are with your hostess now.

I'm getting as bored with dying as with everything else, he thought.

"It's a bore," he said out loud.

"What is, my dear?"

"Anything you do too bloody long."

He looked at her face between him and the fire. She was leaning back in the chair and the firelight shone on her pleasantly lined face and he could see that she was sleepy. He heard the hyena make a noise just outside the range of the fire.

"I've been writing," he said. "But I got tired."

"Do you think you will be able to sleep?"

"Pretty sure. Why don't you turn in?"

"I like to sit here with you."

"Do you feel anything strange?" he asked her.

"No. Just a little sleepy."

"I do," he said.

He had just felt death come by again.

"You know the only thing I've never lost is curiosity," he said to her.

"You've never lost anything. You're the most complete man I've ever known."

"Christ," he said. "How little a woman knows. What is that? Your intuition?"

Because, just then, death had come and rested its head on the foot of the cot and he could smell its breath.

"Never believe any of that about a scythe and a skull," he told her. "It can be two bicycle policemen as easily, or be a bird. Or it can have a wide snout like a hyena."

It had moved up on him now, but it had no shape any more. It simply occupied space.

"Tell it to go away."

It did not go away but moved a little closer.

"You've got a hell of a breath," he told it. "You stinking bastard."

It moved up closer to him still and now he could not speak to it, and when it saw he could not speak it came a little closer, and now he tried to send it away without speaking, but it moved in on him so its weight was all upon his chest, and while it crouched there and he could not move, or speak, he heard the woman say, "Bwana is asleep now. Take the cot up very gently and carry it into the tent."

He could not speak to tell her to make it go away and it crouched now, heavier, so he could not breathe. And then, while they lifted the cot, suddenly it was all right and the weight went from his chest.

It was morning and had been morning for some time and he heard the plane. It showed very tiny and then made a wide circle and the boys ran out and lit the fires, using kerosene, and piled on grass so there were two big smudges at each end of the level place and the morning breeze blew them toward the camp and the plane circled twice more, low this time, and then glided down and levelled off and landed smoothly and, coming walking toward him, was old Compton in slacks, a tweed jacket and a brown felt hat.

"What's the matter, old cock?" Compton said.

"Bad leg," he told him. "Will you have some breakfast?"

"Thanks. I'll just have some tea. It's the Puss Moth you know. I won't be able to take the Memsahib. There's only room for one. Your lorry is on the way."

Helen had taken Compton aside and was speaking to him. Compton came back more cheery than ever.

"We'll get you right in," he said. "I'll be back for the Mem. Now I'm afraid I'll have to stop at Arusha to refuel. We'd better get going."

"What about the tea?"

"I don't really care about it you know."

The boys had picked up the cot and carried it around the green tents and down along the rock and out onto the plain and along past the smudges that were burning brightly now, the grass all consumed, and the wind fanning the fire, to the little plane. It was difficult getting him in, but once in he lay back in the leather seat, and the leg was stuck straight out to one side of the seat, where Compton sat. Compton started the motor and got in. He waved to Helen and to the boys and, as the clatter moved into the old familiar roar, they swung around with Compie watching for wart-hog holes and roared, bumping, along the stretch between the fires and with the last bump rose and he saw them all standing below, waving, and the camp beside the hill, flattening now, and the plain spreading, clumps of trees, and the bush flattening, while the game trails ran now smoothly to the dry waterholes, and there was new water that he had never known of. The zebra, small rounded backs now, and the wildebeeste, big-headed dots seeming to climb as they moved in long fingers across the plain, now scattering as the shadow came toward them, they were tiny now, and the movement had no gallop, and the plain as far as you could see, gray-yellow now and ahead old Compie's tweed back and the brown felt hat. Then they were over the first hills and the wildebeeste were trailing up them, and then they were over the mountains with sudden depths of green-rising forest and the solid bamboo slopes, and then the heavy forest again, sculptured into peaks and hollows until they crossed, and hills sloped down and then another plain, hot now, and purple brown, bumpy with heat and Compie looking back to see how he was riding. Then there were other mountains dark ahead.

And then instead of going on to Arusha they turned left, he evidently figured that they had the gas, and looking down he saw a pink sifting cloud, moving over the ground, and in the air, like the first snow in a blizzard, that comes from nowhere, and he knew the locusts were coming up from the South. Then they began to climb and they were going to the East it seemed, and then it darkened and they were in a storm, the rain so thick it seemed like flying through a waterfall, and then they were out and Compie turned his head and grinned and pointed and there, ahead, all he could see, as wide as all the world, great, high, and unbelievably white in the sun, was the square top of Kilimanjaro. And then he knew that there was where he was going.

Just then the hyena stopped whimpering in the night and started to make a strange, human, almost crying sound. The woman heard it and stirred uneasily. She did not wake. In her dream she was at the house on Long Island and it was the night before her daughter's début. Somehow her father was there and he had been very rude. Then the noise the hyena made was so loud she woke and for a moment she did not know where she was and she was very afraid. Then she took the flashlight and shone it on the other cot that they had carried in after Harry had gone to sleep. She could see his bulk under the mosquito bar but somehow he had gotten his leg out and it hung down alongside the cot. The dressings had all come down and she could not look at it.

"Molo," she called, "Molo! Molo!"

Then she said, "Harry, Harry!" Then her voice rising, "Harry! Please, Oh Harry!"

There was no answer and she could not hear him breathing.

Outside the tent the hyena made the same strange noise that had awakened her. But she did not hear him for the beating of her heart.

Ben Compton

JOHN DOS PASSOS

———

The history of all hitherto existing society is the history of class struggles. . . .

The old people were Jews but at school Benny always said no he wasn't a Jew he was an American because he'd been born in Brooklyn and lived at 2531 25th Avenue in Flatbush and they owned their home. The teacher in the seventh grade said he squinted and sent him home with a note, so Pop took an afternoon off from the jewelry store where he worked with a lens in his eye repairing watches, to take Benny to an optician who put drops in his eyes and made him read little teeny letters on a white card. Pop seemed tickled when the optician said Benny had to wear glasses, "Vatchmaker's eyes . . . takes after his old man," he said and patted his cheek. The steel eyeglasses were heavy on Benny's nose and cut into him behind the ears. It made him feel funny to have Pop telling the optician that a boy with glasses wouldn't be a bum and a baseball player like Sam and Isidore but would attend to his studies and be a lawyer and a scholar like the men of old. "A rabbi maybe," said the optician, but Pop said rabbis were loafers and lived on the blood of the poor, he and the old woman still ate kosher and kept the sabbath like their fathers but synagogue and the rabbis . . . he made a spitting sound with his lips. The optician laughed and said as for himself he was a freethinker but religion was good for the commonpeople. When they got home momma said the glasses made Benny look awful old. Sam and Izzy yelled, "Hello, foureyes," when they came in from selling papers, but at school next day they told the other kids it was a statesprison offence to roughhouse a feller with glasses. Once he had the glasses Benny got to be very good at his lessons.

In highschool he made the debating team. When he was thirteen Pop had a long illness and had to give up work for a year. They lost the house that was almost paid for and went to live in a flat on Myrtle Avenue. Benny got work in a drugstore evenings. Sam and Izzy left home, Sam to work in a furrier's in Newark; Izzy had gotten to loafing in poolparlors so Pop threw him out. He'd always been a good athlete and palled around with an Irishman named Pug Riley who was going to get him into the ring. Momma cried and Pop forbade any of the kids to mention his name; still they all knew that Gladys, the oldest one, who was working as a stenographer over in Manhattan, sent Izzy a five dollar bill now and then. Benny looked much older than he was and hardly ever thought of anything except making money so the old people could have a house of their own again. When he grew up he'd be a lawyer and a business man and make a pile quick so that Gladys could quit work and get married and the old people could buy a big house and live in the country. Momma used to tell him about how when she was a young maiden in the old country they used to go out in the woods after strawberries and mushrooms and stop by a farmhouse and drink milk all warm and foamy from the cow. Benny was going to get rich and take them all out in the country for a trip to a summer resort.

When Pop was well enough to work again he rented half a twofamily house in Flatbush where at least they'd be away from the noise of the elevated. The same year Benny graduated from highschool and won a prize for an essay on The American Government. He'd gotten very tall and thin and had terrible headaches. The old people said he'd outgrown himself and took him to see Dr. Cohen who lived on the same block but had his office downtown near Borough Hall. The doctor said he'd have to give up night work and studying too hard, what he needed was something that would keep him outdoors and develop his body. "All work and no play makes Jack a dull boy," he said, scratching the grizzled beard under his chin. Benny said he had to make some money this summer because he wanted to go to New York University in the fall. Dr. Cohen said he ought to eat plenty of milkdishes and fresh eggs and go somewhere where he could be out in the sun and take it easy all summer. He charged two dollars. Walking home the old man kept striking his forehead with the flat of his hand and saying he was a failure, thirty years he had worked in America and now he was a sick old man all used up and couldn't provide for his children. Momma cried. Gladys told them not to be silly, Benny was a clever boy and a bright student and what was the use of all his booklearning if he couldn't think up some way of getting a job in the country. Benny went to bed without saying anything.

A few days later Izzy came home. He rang the doorbell as

soon as the old man had gone to work one morning. "You almost met Pop," said Benny who opened the door. "Nutten doin'. I waited round the corner till I seen him go. . . . How's everybody?" Izzy had on a light grey suit and a green necktie and wore a fedora hat to match the suit. He said he had to get to Lancaster, Pennsylvania, to fight a Filipino featherweight on Saturday. "Take me with you," said Benny. "You ain't tough enough, kid . . . too much the momma's boy." In the end Benny went with him. They rode on the L to Brooklyn Bridge and then walked across New York to the ferry. They bought tickets to Elizabeth. When the train stopped in a freightyard they sneaked forward into the blind baggage. At West Philadelphia they dropped off and got chased by the yard detective. A brewery wagon picked them up and carried them along the road as far as West Chester. They had to walk the rest of the way. A Mennonite farmer let them spend the night in his barn, but in the morning he wouldn't let them have any breakfast until they'd chopped wood for two hours. By the time they got to Lancaster Benny was all in. He went to sleep in the lockerroom at the Athletic Club and didn't wake up until the fight was over. Izzy had knocked out the Filipino featherweight in the third round and won a purse of twentyfive dollars. He sent Benny over to a lodginghouse with the shine who took care of the lockerroom and went out with the boys to paint the town red. Next morning he turned up with his face green and his eyes bloodshot; he'd spent all his money, but he'd gotten Benny a job helping a feller who did a little smalltime fightpromoting and ran a canteen in a construction camp up near Mauch Chunk.

It was a road job. Ben stayed there for two months earning ten dollars a week and his keep. He learned to drive a team and to keep books. The boss of the canteen, Hiram Volle, gypped the construction workers in their accounts, but Benny didn't think much about it because they were most of 'em wops, until he got to be friends with a young fellow named Nick Gigli who worked with the gang at the gravelpit. Nick used to hang around the canteen before closingtime in the evening; then they'd go out and smoke a cigarette together and talk. Sunday's they'd walk out in the country with the Sunday paper and fool around all afternoon lying in the sun and talking about the articles in the magazine section. Nick was from north Italy and all the men in the gang were Sicilians, so he was lonely. His father and elder brothers were anarchists and he was too; he told Benny about Bakunin and Malatesta and said Benny ought to be ashamed of himself for wanting to get to be a rich business man; sure he ought to study and learn, maybe he ought to get to be a lawyer, but he ought to work for the revolution and the working class, to be a business man was to be a shark and a robber like that son of a bitch Volle. He taught Benny to roll cigarettes and told him about all the girls that were in love with him; that girl in the boxoffice of the movie in Mauch Chunk; he could have her anytime he wanted, but a revolutionist ought to be careful about the girls he went with, women took a classconscious working man's mind off his aims, they were the main seduction of capitalist society. Ben asked him if he thought he ought to throw up his job with Volle, because Volle was such a crook, but Nick said any other capitalist would be the same, all they could do was wait for the Day. Nick was eighteen with bitter brown eyes and a skin almost as dark as a mulatto's. Ben thought he was great on account of all he'd done; he'd shined shoes, been a sailor, a miner, a dishwasher and had worked in textile mills, shoefactories and a cement factory and had had all kinds of women and been in jail for three weeks in the Paterson strike. Round the camp if any of the wops saw Ben going anywhere alone he'd yell at him, "Hey, kid, where's Nick?"

On Friday evening there was an argument in front of the window where the construction boss was paying the men off. That night, when Ben was getting into his bunk in the back of the tarpaper shack the canteen was in, Nick came around and whispered in his ear that the bosses had been gypping the men on time and that they were going on strike tomorrow. Ben said if they went out he'd go out too. Nick called him a brave comrade in Italian and hauled off and kissed him on both cheeks.

Next morning only a few of the pick and shovel men turned out when the whistle blew. Ben hung around the door of the cook-shack not knowing what to do with himself. Volle noticed him and told him to hitch up the team to go down to the station after a box of tobacco. Ben looked at his feet and said he couldn't because he was on strike. Volle burst out laughing and told him to quit his kidding, funniest thing he'd ever heard of a kike walking out with a lot of wops. Ben felt himself go cold and stiff all over: "I'm not a kike any more'n you are. . . . I'm an American born . . . and I'm goin' to stick with my class, you dirty crook." Volle turned white and stepped up and shook a big fist under Ben's nose and said he was fired and that if he wasn't a little f—g shrimp of a foureyed kike he'd knock his goddam block off, anyway his brother sure would give him a whaling when he heard about it.

Ben went to his bunk and rolled his things into a bundle and went off to find Nick. Nick was a little down the road where the bunkhouses were, in the center of a bunch of wops all yelling and waving their arms. The superintendent and the gangbosses all turned out with revolvers in black holsters strapped around their waists and one of them made a speech in English and another one Sicilian saying that this was a square-shooting concern that had always treated laborers square and if they didn't like it they could get the hell out. They'd never had a strike and didn't propose to begin now. There was big money involved in this job and the company wasn't going to work and see it tied up by any goddam foolishness. Any man who wasn't on his job next time the whistle blew was fired and would have to get a move on and remember that the State of Pennsylvania had vagrancy laws. When the whistle blew again everybody went back to work except Ben and Nick. They walked off down the road with their bundles. Nick had tears in his eyes and was saying, "Too much gentle, too much patient . . . we do not know our strength yet."

That night they found a brokendown schoolhouse a little off the road on a hill above a river. They'd bought some bread and peanut butter at a store and sat out in front eating it and talking about what they'd do. By the time they'd finished eating it was dark. Ben had never been out in the country alone like that at night. The wind rustled the woods all around and the rapid river seethed down in the valley. It was a chilly August night with a heavy dew. They didn't have any covering so Nick showed Ben how to take his jacket off and put it over his head and how to sleep against the wall to keep from getting sore lying on the bare boards. He'd hardly gotten to sleep when he woke up icycold and shaking. There was a window broken; he could see the frame and the jagged bits of glass against the cloudy moonlight. He lay back, musta been dreaming. Something banged on the roof and rolled down the shingles over his head and dropped to the ground. "Hay, Ben, for chrissake wassat?" came Nick's voice in a hoarse whisper. They both got up and stared out through the broken windowframe.

"That was busted before," said Nick. He walked over and opened the outside door. They both shivered in the chilly wind up the valley that rustled the trees like rain, the river down below made a creaking grinding noise like a string of carts and wagons.

A stone hit the roof above them and rolled off. The next one went between their heads and hit the cracked plaster of the wall behind. Ben heard the click of the blade as Nick opened his pocketknife. He strained his eyes till the tears came but he couldn't make out anything but the leaves stirring in the wind.

"You come outa there . . . come up here . . . talk . . . you son of a bitch," yelled Nick.

There was no answer.

"What you think?" whispered Nick over his shoulder to Ben.

Ben didn't say anything; he was trying to keep his teeth from chattering. Nick pushed him back in and pulled the door to. They piled the dusty benches against the door and blocked up the lower part of the window with boards out of the floor.

"Break in. I keell one of him anyhow," said Nick. "You don't believe in speerits?"

"Naw, no such thing," said Ben. They sat down side by side on the floor with their backs to the cracked plaster and listened. Nick had put the knife down between them. He took Ben's fingers and made him feel the catch that held the blade steady. "Good knife . . . sailor knife," he whispered. Ben strained his ears. Only the spattering sound of the wind in the trees and the steady grind of the river. No more stones came.

Next morning they left the schoolhouse at first day. Neither of them had had any sleep. Ben's eyes were stinging. When the sun came up they found a man who was patching up a broken spring on a truck. They helped him jack it up with a block of wood and he gave them a lift into Scranton where they got jobs washing dishes in a hashjoint run by a Greek.

. . . all fixed fastfrozen relations, with their train of ancient and venerable prejudices and opinions, are swept away, all newformed ones become antiquated before they can ossify. . . .

Pearldiving wan't much to Ben's taste, so at the end of a couple of weeks, as he'd saved up the price of the ticket, he said he was going back home to see the old people. Nick stayed on because a girl in a candystore had fallen for him. Later he'd go up to Allentown, where a brother of his had a job in a steelmill and was making big money. The last thing he said when he went down and put Ben on the train for New York was, "Benny, you learn and study . . . be great man for workingclass and remember too much girls bad business."

Ben hated leaving Nick but he had to get home to find a job for the winter that would give him time to study. He took the exams and matriculated at the College of the City of New York. The old man borrowed a hundred dollars from the Morris Plan to get him started and Sam sent him twentyfive from Newark to buy books with. Then he made a little money himself working in Kahn's drugstore evenings. Sunday afternoons he went to the library and read Marx's *Capital.* He joined the Socialist Party and went to lectures at the Rand School whenever he got a chance. He was working to be a wellsharpened instrument.

The next spring he got sick with scarlet fever and was ten weeks in the hospital. When he got out his eyes were so bad it gave him a headache to read for an hour. The old man owed the Morris Plan another hundred dollars besides the first hundred dollars and the interest and the investigation fees.

Ben had met a girl at a lecture at Cooper Union who had worked in a textile mill over in Jersey. She'd been arrested during the Paterson strike and had been blacklisted. Now she was a salesgirl at Wanamaker's, but her folks still worked in the Botany Mill at Passaic. Her name was Helen Mauer; she was five years older than Ben, a pale blonde and already had lines in her face. She said there was nothing in the socialist movement; it was the syndicalists had the right idea. After the lecture she took him to the Cosmopolitan Café on 2nd Avenue to have a glass of tea and introduced him to some people she said were real rebels; when Ben told Gladys and the old people about them the old man said, "Pfooy . . . radical jews," and made a spitting sound with his lips. He said Benny ought to cut out these monkeyshines and get to work. He was getting old and now he was in debt, and if he got sick it would be up to Benny to support him and the old woman. Ben said he was working all the time but that your folks didn't count, it was the working-class that he was working for. The old man got red in the face and said his family was sacred and next to that his own people. Momma and Gladys cried. The old man got to his feet; choking and coughing, he raised his hands above his head and cursed Ben and Ben left the house.

He had no money on him and was still weak from the scarlet fever. He walked across Brooklyn and across the Manhattan Bridge and up through the East Side, all full of ruddy lights and crowds and pushcarts with vegetables that smelt of the spring, to the house where Helen lived on East 6th Street. The landlady said he couldn't go up to her room. Helen said it wasn't any of her business but while they were arguing about it his ears began to ring and he fainted on the hall settee. When he came to with water running down his neck Helen helped him up the

four flights and made him lie down on her bed. She yelled
down to the landlady who was screaming about the police, that
she would leave first thing in the morning and nothing in the
world could make her leave sooner. She made Ben some tea
and they sat up all night talking on her bed. They decided that
they'd live in free union together and spent the rest of the night
packing her things. She had mostly books and pamphlets.

Next morning they went out at six o'clock, because she had to
be at Wanamaker's at eight, to look for a room. They didn't exactly tell the next landlady they weren't married, but when she
said, "So you're bride and groom?" they nodded and smiled.
Fortunately Helen had enough money in her purse to pay the
week in advance. Then she had to run off to work. Ben didn't
have any money to buy anything to eat so he lay on the bed
reading *Progress and Poverty* all day. When she came back in
the evening she brought in some supper from a delicatessen.
Eating the rye bread and salami they were very happy. She had
such large breasts for such a slender little girl. He had to go out
to the drugstore to buy some safeties because she said how could
she have a baby just now when they had to give all their strength
to the movement. There were bedbugs in the bed, but they told
each other that they were as happy as they could be under the
capitalist system, that some day they'd have a free society where
workers wouldn't have to huddle in filthy lodginghouses full of
bedbugs or row with landladies and lovers could have babies
if they wanted to.

A few days later Helen was laid off from Wanamaker's because they were cutting down their personnel for the slack summer season. They went over to Jersey where she went to live
with her folks and Ben got a job in the shipping department of
a worsted mill. They rented a room together in Passaic. When
a strike came he and Helen were both on the committee. Ben
got to be quite a speechmaker. He was arrested several times
and almost had his skull cracked by a policeman's billy and got
six months in jail out of it. But he'd found out that when he
got up on a soapbox to talk he could make people listen to him,

that he could talk and say what he thought and get a laugh or a cheer out of the massed upturned faces. When he stood up in court to take his sentence he started to talk about surplus value. The strikers in the audience cheered and the judge had the attendants clear the courtroom. Ben could see the reporters busily taking down what he said; he was glad to be a living example of the injustice and brutality of the capitalist system. The judge shut him up by saying he'd give him another six months for contempt of court if he didn't keep quiet, and Ben was taken to the county jail in an automobile full of special deputies with riot guns. The papers spoke of him as a wellknown socialist agitator.

In jail Ben got to be friends with a wobbly named Bram Hicks, a tall youngster from Frisco with light hair and blue eyes who told him if he wanted to know the labormovement he ought to get him a red card and go out to the Coast. Bram was a boilermaker by profession but had shipped as a sailor for a change and landed in Perth Amboy broke. He'd been working on the repairshift of one of the mills and had gone out with the rest. He'd pushed a cop in the face when they'd broken up a picketline and been sent up for six months for assault and battery. Meeting him once a day in the prison yard was the one thing kept Ben going in jail.

They were both released on the same day. They walked along the street together. The strike was over. The mills were running. The streets where there'd been picketlines, the hall where Ben had made speeches looked quiet and ordinary. He took Bram around to Helen's. She wasn't there, but after a while she came in with a little redfaced ferretnosed Englishman whom she introduced as Billy, an English comrade. First thing Ben guessed that he was sleeping with her. He left Bram in the room with the Englishman and beckoned her outside. The narrow upper hall of the old frame house smelt of vinegar. "You're through with me?" he asked in a shaky voice.

"Oh, Ben, don't act so conventional."

"You mighta waited till I got outa jail."

"But can't you see that we're all comrades? You're a brave fighter and oughtn't to be so conventional, Ben. . . . Billy doesn't mean anything to me. He's a steward on a liner. He'll be going away soon."

"Then I don't mean anything to you either." He grabbed Helen's wrist and squeezed it as hard as he could. "I guess I'm all wrong, but I'm crazy about you. . . . I thought you . . ."

"Ouch, Ben . . . you're talkin' silly, you know how much I like you." They went back in the room and talked about the movement. Ben said he was going west with Bram Hicks.

. . . he becomes an appendage of the machine and it is only the most simple, most monotonous, most easily required knack that is required of him. . . .

Bram knew all the ropes. Walking, riding blind baggage or on empty gondolas, hopping rides on delivery wagons and trucks, they got to Buffalo. In a flophouse there Bram found a guy he knew who got them signed on as deckhands on a whaleback going back light to Duluth. In Duluth they joined a gang being shipped up to harvest wheat for an outfit in Saskatchewan. At first the work was very heavy for Ben and Bram was scared he'd cave in, but the fourteen hour days out in the sun and the dust, the copious grub, the dead sleep in the lofts of the big barns began to toughen him up. Lying flat on the straw in his sweaty clothes he'd still feel through his sleep the tingle of the sun on his face and neck, the strain in his muscles, the whir of the reapers and binders along the horizon, the roar of the thresher, and grind of gears of the trucks carrying the red wheat to the elevators. He began to talk like a harvest stiff. After the harvest they worked in a fruitcannery on the Columbia River, a lousy steamy job full of the sour stench of rotting fruitpeelings. There they read in *Solidarity* about the shingleweavers' strike and the free speech fight in Everett, and decided they'd go down and see what they could do to help out. The last day they worked there Bram lost the forefinger of his right hand repairing the slicing and peeling machinery. The company doctor said he couldn't get any compensation because he'd already given notice, and, besides, not being a Canadian . . . A little shyster lawyer came around to the boarding house where Bram was lying on the bed in a fever, with his hand in a big wad of bandage, and tried to get him to sue, but Bram yelled at the lawyer to get the hell out. Ben said he was wrong, the working class ought to have its lawyers too.

When the hand had healed a little they went down on the boat from Vancouver to Seattle. I.W.W. headquarters there was like a picnic ground, crowded with young men coming in from every part of the U.S. and Canada. One day a big bunch went down to Everett on the boat to try to hold a meeting at the corner of Wetmore and Hewitt Avenues. The dock was full of deputies with rifles, and revolvers. "The Commercial Club boys are waiting for us," some guy's voice tittered nervously. The deputies had white handkerchiefs around their necks. "There's Sheriff McRae," said somebody. Bram edged up to Ben. "We better stick together. . . . Looks to me like we was goin' to get tamped up some." The wobblies were arrested as fast as they stepped off the boat and herded down to the end of the dock. The deputies were drunk most of them, Ben could smell the whiskey on the breath of the redfaced guy who grabbed him by the arm. "Get a move on there, you son of a bitch . . ." He got a blow from a riflebutt in the small of the back. He could hear the crack of saps on men's skulls. Anybody who resisted had his face beaten to a jelly with a club. The wobblies were made to climb up into a truck. With the dusk a cold drizzle had come on. "Boys, we got to show 'em we got guts," a redhaired boy said. A deputy who was holding on to the back of the truck aimed a blow at him with his sap but lost his balance and fell off. The wobblies laughed. The deputy climbed on again, purple in the face. "You'll be laughin' outa the other side of your dirty mugs when we get through with you," he yelled.

Out in the woods where the county road crossed the railroad track they were made to get out of the trucks. The deputies stood around them with their guns leveled while the sheriff who was reeling drunk, and two well-dressed middleaged men talked over what they'd do. Ben heard the word gauntlet. "Look here, sheriff," somebody said, "we're not here to make any kind of disturbance. All we want's our constitutional rights of free speech." The sheriff turned towards them waving the butt of his revolver, "Oh, you do, do you, you c——s. Well, this is Snohomish county and you ain't goin' to forget it . . . if you come here again some of you fellers is goin' to die, that's all there is about it. . . . All right, boys, let's go."

The deputies made two lines down towards the railroad track. They grabbed the wobblies one by one and beat them up. Three of them grabbed Ben. "You a wobbly?" "Sure I am, you dirty yellow . . ." he began. The sheriff came up and hauled off to hit him. "Look out, he's got glasses on." A big hand pulled the glasses off. "We'll fix that." Then the sheriff punched him in the nose with his fist. "Say you ain't." Ben's mouth was full of blood. He set his jaw. "He's a kike, hit him again for me." "Say, you ain't a wobbly." Somebody whacked a riflebarrel against his shins and he fell forward. "Run for it," they were yelling. Blows with clubs and riflebutts were splitting his ears.

He tried to walk forward without running. He tripped on a rail and fell, cutting his arm on something sharp. There was so much blood in his eyes he couldn't see. A heavy boot was kicking him again and again in the side. He was passing out. Somehow he staggered forward. Somebody was holding him up under the arms and was dragging him free of the cattleguard on the track. Another fellow began to wipe his face off with a handkerchief. He heard Bram's voice way off somewhere, "We're over the county line, boys." What with losing his glasses and the rain and the night and the shooting pain all up and down his back Ben couldn't see anything. He heard shots behind them and yells from where other guys were running the gauntlet. He was the center of a little straggling group of wobblies making their way down the railroad track. "Fellow workers," Bram was saying in his deep quiet voice, "we must never forget this night."

At the interurban trolley station they took up a collection

among the ragged and bloody group to buy tickets to Seattle for the guys most hurt. Ben was so dazed and sick he could hardly hold the ticket when somebody pushed it into his hand. Bram and the rest of them set off to walk the thirty miles back to Seattle.

· Ben was in hospital three weeks. The kicks in the back had affected his kidneys and he was in frightful pain most of the time. The morphine they gave him made him so dopey he barely knew what was happening when they brought in the boys wounded in the shooting on the Everett dock on November 5th. When he was discharged he could just walk. Everybody he knew was in jail. At General Delivery he found a letter from Gladys enclosing fifty dollars and saying his father wanted him to come home.

The Defense Committee told him to go ahead; he was just the man to raise funds for them in the east. An enormous amount of money would be needed for the defense of the seventyfour wobblies held in the Everett jail charged with murder. Ben hung around Seattle for a couple of weeks doing odd jobs for the Defense Committee, trying to figure out a way to get home. A sympathizer who worked in a shipping office finally got him a berth as supercargo on a freighter that was going to New York through the Panama canal. The sea trip and the detailed clerical work helped him to pull himself together. Still there wasn't a night he didn't wake up with a nightmare scream in his throat sitting up in his bunk dreaming the deputies were coming to get him to make him run the gauntlet. When he got to sleep again he'd dream he was caught in the cattleguard and the teeth were tearing his arms and heavy boots were kicking him in the back. It got so it took all his nerve to lie down in his bunk to go to sleep. The men on the ship thought he was a hophead and steered clear of him. It was a great day when he saw the tall buildings of New York shining in the brown morning haze.

. . . when in the course of development class distinctions have disappeared and all production has been concentrated in

the hands of a vast association of the whole nation, the public power will lose its political character. . . .

Ben lived at home that winter because it was cheaper. When he told Pop he was going to study law in the office of a radical lawyer named Morris Stein whom he'd met in connection with raising money for the Everett boys, the old man was delighted. "A clever lawyer can protect the workers and the poor Jews and make money too," he said, rubbing his hands. "Benny, I always knew you were a good boy." Momma nodded and smiled. "Because in this country it's not like over there under the warlords, even a lazy bum's got constitootional rights, that's why they wrote the constitootion for." It made Ben feel sick talking to them about it.

He worked as a clerk in Stein's office on lower Broadway and in the evenings addressed protest meetings about the Everett massacre. Morris Stein's sister Fanya, who was a thin dark wealthy woman about thirtyfive, was an ardent pacifist and made him read Tolstoy and Kropotkin. She believed that Wilson would keep the country out of the European war and sent money to all the women's peace organizations. She had a car and used to run him around town sometimes when he had several meetings in one evening. His heart would always be thumping when he went into the hall where the meeting was and began to hear the babble and rustle of the audience filing in, garment workers on the East Side, waterfront workers in Brooklyn, workers in chemical and metalproducts plants in Newark, parlor socialists and pinks at the Rand School or on lower Fifth Avenue, the vast anonymous mass of all classes, races, trades in Madison Square Garden. His hands would always be cold when he shook hands with the chairman and other speakers on the platform. When his turn came to speak there'd be a moment when all the faces looking up at him would blur into a mass of pink, the hum of the hall would deafen him, he'd be in a panic for fear he'd forgotten what he wanted to say. Then all at once he'd hear his own voice enunciating clearly and firmly, feel its reverberance along the walls and ceiling, feel ears growing tense, men and women leaning forward in their chairs, see the rows of faces quite clearly, the groups of people who couldn't find seats crowding at the doors. Phrases like *protest, massaction, united workingclass of this country and the world, revolution,* would light up the eyes and faces under him like the glare of a bonfire.

After the speech he'd feel shaky, his glasses would be so misted he'd have to wipe them, he'd feel all the awkwardness of his tall gangling frame. Fanya would get him away as soon as she could, tell him with shining eyes that he'd spoken magnificently, take him downtown, if the meeting had been in Manhattan, to have some supper in the Brevoort basement or at the Cosmopolitan Café before he went home on the subway to Brooklyn. He knew that she was in love with him, but they rarely talked about anything outside of the movement.

When the Russian revolution came in February, Ben and the Steins bought every edition of the papers for weeks, read all the correspondents' reports with desperate intentness; it was the dawning of The Day. There was a feeling of carnival all down the East Side and in the Jewish sections of Brooklyn. The old people cried whenever they spoke of it. "Next Austria, then the Reich, then England . . . freed peoples everywhere," Pop would say. "And last, Uncle Sam." Ben would add, grimly setting his jaw.

The April day Woodrow Wilson declared war, Fanya went to bed with a hysterical crying fit. Ben went up to see her at the apartment Morris Stein and his wife had on Riverside Drive. She'd come back from Washington the day before. She'd been up there with a women's peace delegation trying to see the President. The detectives had run them off the White House lawn and several girls had been arrested. "What did you expect? . . . of course the capitalists want war. They'll think a little different when they find what they're getting's a revolution." She begged him to stay with her, but he left saying he had to go see them down at *The Call*. As he left the house, he found himself making a spitting noise with his lips like his father. He told himself he'd never go there again.

He registered for the draft on Stein's advice, though he wrote *conscientious objector* on the card. Soon after that he and Stein quarrelled. Stein said there was nothing to it but to bow before the storm; Ben said he was going to agitate against it until he was put in jail. That meant he was out of a job and it was the end of his studying law. Kahn wouldn't take him back in his drugstore because he was afraid the cops would raid him if it got to be known he had a radical working for him. Ben's brother Sam was working in a munition factory at Perth Amboy and making big money; he kept writing Ben to stop his foolishness and get a job there too. Even Gladys told him it was silly to ram his head against a stone wall. In July he left home and went back to live with Helen Mauer over in Passaic. His number hadn't been called yet, so it was easy to get a job in the shipping department of one of the mills. They were working overtime and losing hands fast by the draft.

The Rand School had been closed up, *The Call* suspended, every day new friends were going around to Wilson's way of looking at things. Helen's folks and their friends were making good money, working overtime; they laughed or got sore at any talk of protest strikes or revolutionary movements; people were buying washing machines, liberty bonds, vacuum cleaners, making first payments on houses. The girls were buying fur coats and silk stockings. Helen and Ben began to plan to go out to Chicago, where the wobblies were putting up a fight. September 2nd came the roundup of I.W.W. officials by government agents. Ben and Helen expected to be arrested, but they were passed over. They spent a rainy Sunday huddled on the bed in their dank room, trying to decide what they ought to do. Everything they trusted was giving way under their feet. "I feel like a rat in a trap," Helen kept saying. Every now and then Ben would jump up and walk up and down hitting his forehead with the palm of his hand. "We gotta do something here, look what they're doing in Russia."

One day a warworker came around to the shipping department to sign everybody up for a Liberty Bond. He was a cocky-looking young man in a yellow slicker. Ben wasn't much given to arguments during working hours, so he just shook his head and went back to the manifest he was making out. "You don't want to spoil the record of your department, do you? It's one hundred percent perfect so far." Ben tried to smile. "It seems too bad, but I guess it'll have to be." Ben could feel the eyes of the other men in the office on him. The young man in the slicker was balancing uneasily from one foot to the other. "I don't suppose you want people to think you're a pro-German or a pacifist, do you?" "They can suppose what they damn like, for all I care." "Let's see your registration card, I bet you're a slacker." "Look here, get me," said Ben, getting to his feet, "I don't believe in capitalist war and I'm not going to do anything I can help to support it." The young man in the slicker turned his back, "Oh, if you're one of them yellow bastards I won't even talk to you." Ben went back to work. That evening when he was punching the timeclock a cop stepped up to him. "Let's see your registration card, buddy." Ben brought the card out from his inside pocket. The cop read it over carefully, "Looks all right to me," he said reluctantly. At the end of the week Ben found he was fired; no reason given.

He went to the room in a panic. When Helen came back he said he was going to Mexico. "They could get me under the espionage act for what I told that guy about fighting capitalism." Helen tried to calm him down, but he said he wouldn't sleep in that room another night, so they packed their bags and went over to New York on the train. They had about a hundred dollars saved up between them. They got a room on East 8th Street under the name of Mr. and Mrs. Gold. It was the next morning that they read in the *Times* that the Maximalists had taken over the government in Petrograd with the slogan All

Power to the Soviets. They were sitting in a small pastry shop on 2nd Avenue drinking their morning coffee, when Ben, who had run around to the newsstand for a paper, came back with the news. Helen began to cry: "Oh, darling, it's too good to be true. It's the world revolution. . . . Now the workers'll see that they were being deceived by false good times, that the war's really aimed at them. Now the other armies'll start to mutiny." Ben took her hand under the table and squeezed it hard. "We gotto work now, darling. . . . I'll go to jail here before I'll run away to Mexico. I'd acted like a yellow bastard if it hadn't been for you, Helen. . . . A man's no good alone."

They gulped their coffee and walked around to the Ferbers' house on 17th Street. Al Ferber was a doctor, a short stout man with a big paunch; he was just leaving the house to go to his office. He went back into the hall with them and yelled upstairs to his wife: "Molly, come down . . . Kerensky's run out of Petrograd with a flea in his ear . . . dressed as a woman he ran." Then he said in Yiddish to Ben that if the comrades were going to hold a meeting to send greetings to the soldiers' and peasants' government, he'd give a hundred dollars towards expenses, but his name would have to be kept out of it or else he'd lose his practice. Molly Ferber came downstairs in a quilted dressing gown and said she'd sell something and add another hundred. They spent the day going around to find comrades they had the addresses of; they didn't dare use the phone for fear of the wires being tapped.

The meeting was held at the Empire Casino in the Bronx a week later. Two Federal agents with beefsteak faces sat in the front row with a stenographer who took down everything that was said. The police closed the doors after the first couple of hundred people had come in. The speakers on the platform could hear them breaking up the crowd outside with motorcycles. Soldiers and sailors in uniform were sneaking into the gallery by ones and twos and trying to stare the speakers out of countenance.

When the old whitehaired man who was chairman of the

meeting walked to the front of the stage and said, "Comrades,
gentlemen of the Department of Justice and not forgetting
our young well wishers up in the gallery, we have met to send
a resolution of greetings from the oppressed workers of America
to the triumphant workers of Russia," everybody stood up and
cheered. The crowd milling around outside cheered too. Somewhere they could hear a bunch singing the *International*. They
could hear policewhistles and the dang dang of a patrol wagon.
Ben noticed that Fanya Stein was in the audience; she looked
pale and her eyes held onto him with a fixed feverish stare.
When his turn came to speak he began by saying that on account
of the kind sympathizers from Washington in the audience, he
couldn't say what he wanted to say but that every man and
woman in the audience who was not a traitor to their class
knew what he wanted to say. . . . "The capitalist govern-
ments are digging their own graves by driving their people to
slaughter in a crazy unnecessary war that nobody can benefit
from except bankers and munition makers. . . . The American
working class, like the working classes of the rest of the world,
will learn their lesson. The profiteers are giving us instruction in
the use of guns; the day will come when we will use it." "That's
enough, let's go, boys," yelled a voice from the gallery. The soldiers and sailors started hustling the people out of the seats. The
police from the entrances converged on the speakers. Ben and a
couple of others were arrested. The men in the audience who
were of conscription age were made to show their registration
cards before they could leave. Ben was hustled out into a closed
limousine with the blinds drawn before he could speak to
Helen. He'd hardly noticed who it was had clicked the handcuffs on his wrists.

They kept him for three days without anything to eat or drink
in a disused office in the Federal building on Park Row. Every
few hours a new bunch of detectives would stamp into the room
and question him. His head throbbing, and ready to faint with
thirst, he'd face the ring of long yellow faces, jowly red faces,
pimply faces, boozers' and hopheads' faces, feel the eyes boring

into him; sometimes they kidded and cajoled him, and sometimes they bullied and threatened; one bunch brought in pieces of rubber hose to beat him up with. He jumped up and faced them. For some reason they didn't beat him up, but instead brought him some water and a couple of stale ham sandwiches. After that he was able to sleep a little.

An agent yanked him off his bench and led him out into a wellappointed office where he was questioned almost kindly by an elderly man at a mahogany desk with a bunch of roses on the corner of it. The smell of the roses made him feel sick. The elderly man said he could see his lawyer and Morris Stein came into the room.

"Benny," he said, "leave everything to me . . . Mr. Watkins has consented to quash all charges if you'll promise to report for military training. It seems your number's been called."

"If you let me out," Ben said in a low trembling voice, "I'll do my best to oppose capitalist war until you arrest me again." Morris Stein and Mr. Watkins looked at each other and shook their heads indulgently. "Well," said Mr. Watkins, "I can't help but admire your spirit and wish it was in a better cause." It ended by his being let out on fifteen thousand dollars bail on Morris Stein's assurance that he would do no agitating until the date of his trial. The Steins wouldn't tell him who put up the bail.

Morris and Edna Stein gave him a room in their apartment; Fanya was there all the time. They fed him good food and tried to make him drink wine with his meals and a glass of milk before going to bed. He didn't have any interest in anything, slept as much as he could, read all the books he found on the place. When Morris would try to talk to him about his case he'd shut him up, "You're doing this, Morris . . . do anything . . . why should I care. I might as well be in jail as like this." "Well, I must say that's a compliment," Fanya said laughing.

Helen Mauer called up several times to tell him how things were going. She'd always say she had no news to tell that she could say over the telephone, but he never asked her to come up to see him. About as far as he went from the Steins' apartment was to go out every day to sit for a while on a bench on the Drive and look out over the grey Hudson at the rows of frame houses on the Jersey side and the grey palisades.

The day his case came up for trial the press was full of hints of German victories. It was spring and sunny outside the broad grimy windows of the courtroom. Ben sat sleepily in the stuffy gloom. Everything seemed very simple. Stein and the judge had their little jokes together and the Assistant District Attorney was positively genial. The jury reported "guilty" and the judge sentenced him to twenty years' imprisonment. Morris Stein filed an appeal and the judge let him stay out on bail. The only moment Ben came to life was when he was allowed to address the court before being sentenced. He made a speech about the revolutionary movement he'd been preparing all these weeks. Even as he said it it seemed silly and weak. He almost stopped in the middle. His voice strengthened and filled the courtroom as he got to the end. Even the judge and the old snuffling attendants sat up when he recited for his peroration, the last words of the communist manifesto:

In place of the old bourgeois society, with its classes and class antagonisms, we shall have an association, in which the free development of each is the condition for the free development of all.

The appeal dragged and dragged. Ben started studying law again. He wanted to work in Stein's office to pay for his keep, but Stein said it would be risky, he said the war would be over soon and the red scare would die down, so that he could get him off with a light sentence. He brought lawbooks up for him to study and promised to take him into partnership if he passed his bar exam, once he could get his citizenship restored. Edna Stein was a fat spiteful woman and rarely spoke to him; Fanya fussed over him with nervous doting attentions that made him feel sick. He slept badly and his kidneys bothered him. One night he got up and dressed and was tiptoeing down the carpeted hall towards the door with his shoes in his hand, when Fanya with her black hair down her back came out of the door of her room. She was in a nightdress that showed her skinny figure and flat breasts. "Benny, where are you going?"

"I'm going crazy here . . . I've got to get out." His teeth were chattering. "I've got to get back into the movement. . . . They'll catch me and send me to jail right away . . . it will be better like that."

"You poor boy, you're in no condition." She threw her arms round his neck and pulled him into her room.

"Fanya, you gotto let me go. . . . I might make it across the Mexican border . . . other guys have."

"You're crazy . . . and what about your bail?"

"What do I care . . . don't you see we gotto do something."

She'd pulled him down on her bed and was stroking his forehead. "Poor boy . . . I love you so, Benny, couldn't you think of me a little bit . . . just a little teeny bit . . . I could help you so much in the movement. . . . Tomorrow we'll talk about it . . . I want to help you, Benny." He let her untie his necktie.

The armistice came, and news of the peace conference, revolutionary movements all over Europe, Trotsky's armies driving the whites out of Russia. Fanya Stein told everybody she and Ben were married and took him to live with her at her studio apartment on 8th Street, where she nursed him through the flu and double pneumonia. The first day the doctor said he could go out she drove up the Hudson in her Buick sedan. They came back in the early summer gloaming to find a special delivery letter from Morris. The circuit court had denied the appeal, but reduced the sentence to ten years. The next day at noon he'd have to report to be delivered by his bondsmen to the custody of the U.S. District Court. He'd probably go to Atlanta. Soon after the letter Morris himself turned up. Fanya had broken down and was crying hysterically. Morris looked pale. "Ben," he said, "we're beaten . . . You'll have to go to Atlanta for a while . . . you'll have good company down there . . . but don't worry. We'll take your case to the President. Now that the war's over they can't keep the liberal press muzzled any more."

"That's all right," said Ben, "it's better to know the worst."

Fanya jumped up from the couch where she'd been sobbing and started screaming at her brother. When Ben went out to walk around the block he left them quarreling bitterly. He found himself looking carefully at the houses, the taxicabs, the streetlights, people's faces, a funny hydrant that had a torso like a woman's, some bottles of mineral oil stacked in a drugstore window, Nujol. He decided he'd better go over to Brooklyn to say goodby to the old people. At the subway station he stopped. He hadn't the strength; he'd write them.

Next morning at nine he went down to Morris Stein's office with his suitcase in his hand. He'd made Fanya promise not to come. He had to tell himself several times he was going to jail, he felt as if he was going on a business trip of some kind. He had on a new suit of English tweed Fanya had bought him.

Lower Broadway was all streaked red, white and blue with flags; there were crowds of clerks and stenographers and office-boys lining both pavements where he came up out of the subway. Cops on motorcycles were keeping the street clear. From down towards the Battery came the sound of a military band playing *Keep the Home Fires Burning*. Everybody looked flushed and happy. It was hard to keep from walking in step to the music in the fresh summer morning that smelt of the harbor and ships. He had to keep telling himself: those are the people who sent Debs to jail, those are the people who shot Joe Hill, who murdered Frank Little, those are the people who beat us up in Everett, who want me to rot for ten years in jail.

The colored elevatorboy grinned at him when he took him up in the elevator, "Is they startin' to go past yet, mister?" Ben shook his head and frowned.

The lawoffice looked clean and shiny. The telephone girl had red hair and wore a gold star. There was an American flag draped over the door of Stein's private office. Stein was at his desk talking to an upperclasslooking young man in a tweed suit. "Ben," Stein said cheerily, "meet Stevens Warner . . . He's just gotten out of Charlestown, served a year for refusing to register."

"Not quite a year," said the young man, getting up and shaking hands. "I'm out on good behavior."

Ben didn't like him, in his tweed suit and his expensive looking necktie; all at once he remembered that he was wearing the same kind of suit himself. The thought made him sore. "How was it?" he asked coldly.

"Not so bad, they had me working in the greenhouse . . . They treated me fairly well when they found out I'd already been to the front."

"How was that?"

"Oh, in the ambulance service. . . . They just thought I was mildly insane. . . . It was a damned instructive experience."

"They treat the workers different," said Ben angrily.

"And now we're going to start a nationwide campaign to get all the other boys out," said Stein, getting to his feet and rubbing his hands, "starting with Debs . . . you'll see, Ben, you won't be down there long . . . people are coming to their senses already."

A burst of brassy music came up from Broadway, and the regular tramp of soldiers marching. They all looked out of the window. All down the long grey canyon flags were streaming out, uncoiling tickertape and papers glinted all through the ruddy sunlight, squirmed in the shadows; people were yelling themselves hoarse.

"Damn fools," said Warner, "it won't make the doughboys forget about K.P."

Morris Stein came back into the room with a funny brightness in his eyes. "Makes me feel maybe I missed something."

"Well, I've got to be going," said Warner, shaking hands again. "You certainly got a rotten break, Compton . . . don't think for a minute we won't be working night and day to get you out . . . I'm sure public sentiment will change. We have great hopes of President Wilson . . . after all, his labor record was fairly good before the war."

"I guess it'll be the workers will get me out, if I'm gotten out," said Ben.

Warner's eyes were searching his face. Ben didn't smile. Warner stood before him uneasily for a moment and then took his hand again. Ben didn't return the pressure. "Good luck," said Warner and walked out of the office.

"What's that, one of these liberalminded college boys?" Ben asked of Stein. Stein nodded. He'd gotten interested in some papers on his desk. "Yes . . . great boy, Steve Warner . . . you'll find some books or magazines in the library . . . I'll be with you in a few minutes."

Ben went into the library and took down a book on Torts. He read and read the fine print. When Stein came to get him he didn't know what he'd been reading or how much time had passed. Walking up Broadway the going was slow on account of the crowds and the bands and the steady files of marching soldiers in khaki with tin hats on their heads. Stein nudged him to take his hat off as a regimental flag passed them in the middle of a fife and drum corps. He kept it in his hand so as not to have to take it off again. He took a deep breath of the dusty sunny air of the street, full of girls' perfumerysmells and gasoline from the exhaust of the trucks hauling the big guns, full of laughing and shouting and shuffle and tramp of feet; then the dark doorway of the Federal Building gulped them.

It was a relief to have it all over, alone with the deputy on the train for Atlanta. The deputy was a big morose man with bluish sacks under his eyes. As the handcuffs cut Ben's wrist he unlocked them except when the train was in a station. Ben remembered it was his birthday; he was twentythree years old.

Flight

JOHN STEINBECK

About fifteen miles below Monterey, on the wild coast, the Torres family had their farm, a few sloping acres above a cliff that dropped to the brown reefs and to the hissing white waters of the ocean. Behind the farm the stone mountains stood up against the sky. The farm buildings huddled like little clinging aphids on the mountain skirts, crouched low to the ground as though the wind might blow them into the sea. The little shack, the rattling, rotting barn were grey-bitten with sea salt, beaten by the damp wind until they had taken on the color of the granite hills. Two horses, a red cow and a red calf, half a dozen pigs and a flock of lean, multi-colored chickens stocked the place. A little corn was raised on the sterile slope, and it grew short and thick under the wind, and all the cobs formed on the landward sides of the stalks.

Mama Torres, a lean, dry woman with ancient eyes, had ruled the farm for ten years, ever since her husband tripped over a stone in the field one day and fell full length on a rattlesnake. When one is bitten on the chest there is not much that can be done.

Mama Torres had three children, two undersized black ones of twelve and fourteen, Emilio and Rosy, whom Mama kept fishing on the rocks below the farm when the sea was kind and when the truant officer was in some distant part of Monterey County. And there was Pepé, the tall smiling son of nineteen, a gentle, affectionate boy, but very lazy. Pepé had a tall head, pointed at the top, and from its peak, coarse black hair grew down like a thatch all around. Over his smiling little eyes Mama cut a straight bang so he could see. Pepé had sharp Indian cheek bones and an eagle nose, but his mouth was as sweet and shapely as a girl's mouth, and his chin was fragile and chiseled. He was loose and gangling, all legs and feet and wrists, and he was very lazy. Mama thought him fine and brave, but she never told him so. She said, "Some lazy cow must have got into thy. father's family, else how could I have a son like thee." And she said, "When I carried thee, a sneaking lazy coyote came out of the brush and looked at me one day. That must have made thee so."

Pepé smiled sheepishly and stabbed at the ground with his knife to keep the blade sharp and free from rust. It was his inheritance, that knife, his father's knife. The long heavy blade folded back into the black handle. There was a button on the handle. When Pepé pressed the button, the blade leaped out ready for use. The knife was with Pepé always, for it had been his father's knife.

One sunny morning when the sea below the cliff was glinting and blue and the white surf creamed on the reef, when even the stone mountains looked kindly, Mama Torres called out the door of the shack, "Pepé, I have a labor for thee."

There was no answer. Mama listened. From behind the barn she heard a burst of laughter. She lifted her full long skirt and walked in the direction of the noise.

Pepé was sitting on the ground with his back against a box. His white teeth glistened. On either side of him stood the two black ones, tense and expectant. Fifteen feet away a redwood post was set in the ground. Pepé's right hand lay limply in his lap, and in the palm the big black knife rested. The blade was closed back into the handle. Pepé looked smiling at the sky.

Suddenly Emilio cried, "Ya!"

Pepé's wrist flicked like the head of a snake. The blade seemed to fly open in mid-air, and with a thump the point dug into the redwood post, and the black handle quivered. The three burst into excited laughter. Rosy ran to the post and pulled out the knife and brought it back to Pepé. He closed the blade and settled the knife carefully in his listless palm again. He grinned self-consciously at the sky.

"Ya!"

The heavy knife lanced out and sunk into the post again. Mama moved forward like a ship and scattered the play.

"All day you do foolish things with the knife, like a toy-baby," she stormed. "Get up on thy huge feet that eat up shoes. Get up!" She took him by one loose shoulder and hoisted at him. Pepé grinned sheepishly and came half-heartedly to his feet. "Look!" Mama cried. "Big lazy, you must catch the horse and put on him thy father's saddle. You must ride to Monterey. The medicine bottle is empty. There is no salt. Go thou now, Peanut! Catch the horse."

A revolution took place in the relaxed figure of Pepé. "To Monterey, me? Alone? Sí, Mama."

She scowled at him. "Do not think, big sheep, that you will buy candy. No, I will give you only enough for the medicine and the salt."

Pepé smiled. "Mama, you will put the hatband on the hat?"

She relented then. "Yes, Pepé. You may wear the hatband."

His voice grew insinuating, "And the green handkerchief, Mama?"

"Yes, if you go quickly and return with no trouble, the silk green handkerchief will go. If you make sure to take off the handkerchief when you eat so no spot may fall on it. . . ."

"Sí, Mama. I will be careful. I am a man."

"Thou? A man? Thou art a peanut."

He went into the rickety barn and brought out a rope, and he walked agilely enough up the hill to catch the horse.

When he was ready and mounted before the door, mounted on his father's saddle that was so old that the oaken frame showed through torn leather in many places, then Mama brought out the round black hat with the tooled leather band, and she reached up and knotted the green silk handkerchief about his neck. Pepé's blue denim coat was much darker than his jeans, for it had been washed much less often.

Mama handed up the big medicine bottle and the silver coins. "That for the medicine," she said, "and that for the salt. That for a candle to burn for the papa. That for *dulces* for the little ones. Our friend Mrs. Rodriguez will give you dinner and maybe a bed for the night. When you go to the church say only ten Paternosters and only twenty-five Ave Marias. Oh! I know, big coyote. You would sit there flapping your mouth over Aves all day while you looked at the candles and the holy pictures. That is not good devotion to stare at the pretty things."

The black hat, covering the high pointed head and black thatched hair of Pepé, gave him dignity and age. He sat the rangy horse well. Mama thought how handsome he was, dark and lean and tall. "I would not send thee now alone, thou little one, except for the medicine," she said softly. "It is not good to have no medicine, for who knows when the toothache will come, or the sadness of the stomach. These things are."

"*Adios*, Mama," Pepé cried. "I will come back soon. You may send me often alone. I am a man."

"Thou art a foolish chicken."

He straightened his shoulders, flipped the reins against the horse's shoulder and rode away. He turned once and saw that they still watched him, Emilio and Rosy and Mama. Pepé grinned with pride and gladness and lifted the tough buckskin horse to a trot.

When he had dropped out of sight over a little dip in the road, Mama turned to the black ones, but she spoke to herself. "He is nearly a man now," she said. "It will be a nice thing to have a man in the house again." Her eyes sharpened on the children. "Go to the rocks now. The tide is going out. There will be abalones to be found." She put the iron hooks into their hands and saw them down the steep trail to the reefs. She brought the smooth stone *metate* to the doorway and sat grinding her corn to flour and looking occasionally at the road over which Pepé had gone. The noonday came and then the afternoon, when the little ones beat the abalones on a rock to make them tender and Mama patted the tortillas to make them thin. They ate their dinner as the red sun was plunging down toward the ocean. They sat on the doorsteps and watched the big white moon come over the mountain tops.

Mama said, "He is now at the house of our friend Mrs. Rodriguez. She will give him nice things to eat and maybe a present."

Emilio said, "Some day I too will ride to Monterey for medicine. Did Pepé come to be a man today?"

Mama said wisely, "A boy gets to be a man when a man is needed. Remember this thing. I have known boys forty years old because there was no need for a man."

Soon afterwards they retired, Mama in her big oak bed on one side of the room, Emilio and Rosy in their boxes full of straw and sheepskins on the other side of the room.

The moon went over the sky and the surf roared on the rocks. The roosters crowed the first call. The surf subsided to a whispering surge against the reef. The moon dropped toward the sea. The roosters crowed again.

The moon was near down to the water when Pepé rode on a winded horse to his home flat. His dog bounced out and circled the horse yelping the pleasure. Pepé slid off the saddle to the ground. The weathered little shack was silver in the moonlight and the square shadow of it was black to the north and east. Against the east the piling mountains were misty with light; their tops melted into the sky.

Pepé walked wearily up the three steps and into the house. It was dark inside. There was a rustle in the corner.

Mama cried out from her bed. "Who comes? Pepé, is it thou?"

"Sí, Mama."

"Did you get the medicine?"

"Sí, Mama."

"Well, go to sleep, then. I thought you would be sleeping at the house of Mrs. Rodriguez." Pepé stood silently in the dark room. "Why do you stand there, Pepé? Did you drink wine?"

"Sí, Mama."

"Well, go to bed then and sleep out the wine."

His voice was tired and patient, but very firm. "Light the candle, Mama. I must go away into the mountains."

"What is this, Pepé? You are crazy." Mama struck a sulphur match and held the little blue burr until the flame spread up the stick. She set light to the candle on the floor beside her bed. "Now, Pepé, what is this you say?" She looked anxiously into his face.

He was changed. The fragile quality seemed to have gone from his chin. His mouth was less full than it had been, the lines of the lips were straighter, but in his eyes the greatest change had taken place. There was no laughter in them any more, nor any bashfulness. They were sharp and bright and purposeful.

He told her in a tired monotone, told her everything just as it had happened. A few people came into the kitchen of Mrs. Rodriguez. There was wine to drink. Pepé drank wine. The little quarrel—the man started toward Pepé and then the knife—it went almost by itself. It flew, it darted before Pepé knew it. As he talked, Mama's face grew stern, and it seemed to grow more lean. Pepé finished. "I am a man now, Mama. The man said names to me I could not allow."

Mama nodded. "Yes, thou art a man, my poor little Pepé. Thou art a man. I have seen it coming on thee. I have watched you throwing the knife into the post, and I have been afraid." For a moment her face had softened, but now it grew stern again. "Come! We must get you ready. Go. Awaken Emilio and Rosy. Go quickly."

Pepé stepped over to the corner where his brother and sister slept among the sheepskins. He leaned down and shook them gently. "Come, Rosy! Come, Emilio! The mama says you must arise."

The little black ones sat up and rubbed their eyes in the candlelight. Mama was out of bed now, her long black skirt over her nightgown. "Emilio," she cried. "Go up and catch the other horse for Pepé. Quickly, now! Quickly." Emilio put his legs in his overalls and stumbled sleepily out the door.

"You heard no one behind you on the road?" Mama demanded.

"No, Mama. I listened carefully. No one was on the road."

Mama darted like a bird about the room. From a nail on the wall she took a canvas water bag and threw it on the floor. She stripped a blanket from her bed and rolled it into a tight tube and tied the ends with string. From a box beside the stove she lifted a flour sack half full of black stringy jerky. "Your father's black coat, Pepé. Here, put it on."

Pepé stood in the middle of the floor watching her activity. She reached behind the door and brought out the rifle, a long 38-56, worn shiny the whole length of the barrel. Pepé took it from her and held it in the crook of his elbow. Mama brought a little leather bag and counted the cartridges into his hand. "Only ten left," she warned. "You must not waste them."

Emilio put his head in the door. " '*Qui 'st 'l caballo*, Mama."

"Put on the saddle from the other horse. Tie on the blanket. Here, tie the jerky to the saddle horn."

Still Pepé stood silently watching his mother's frantic activity. His chin looked hard, and his sweet mouth was drawn and thin. His little eyes followed Mama about the room almost suspiciously.

Rosy asked softly, "Where goes Pepé?"

Mama's eyes were fierce. "Pepé goes on a journey. Pepé is a man now. He has a man's thing to do."

Pepé straightened his shoulders. His mouth changed until he looked very much like Mama.

At last the preparation was finished. The loaded horse stood outside the door. The water bag dripped a line of moisture down the bay shoulder.

The moonlight was being thinned by the dawn and the big white moon was near down to the sea. The family stood by the shack. Mama confronted Pepé. "Look, my son! Do not stop until it is dark again. Do not sleep even though you are tired. Take care of the horse in order that he may not stop of weariness. Remember to be careful with the bullets—there are only ten. Do not fill they stomach with jerky or it will make thee sick. Eat a little jerky and fill thy stomach with grass. When thou comest to the high mountains, if thou seest any of the dark watching men, go not near to them nor try to speak to them. And forget not thy prayers." She put her lean hands on Pepé's shoulders, stood on her toes and kissed him formally on both cheeks, and Pepé kissed her on both cheeks. Then he went to Emilio and Rosy and kissed both of their cheeks.

Pepé turned back to Mama. He seemed to look for a little softness, a little weakness in her. His eyes were searching, but Mama's face remained fierce. "Go now," she said. "Do not wait to be caught like a chicken."

Pepé pulled himself into the saddle. "I am a man," he said.

It was the first dawn when he rode up the hill toward the little canyon which let a trail into the mountains. Moonlight and daylight fought with each other, and the two warring qualities made it difficult to see. Before Pepé had gone a hundred yards, the outlines of his figure were misty; and long before he entered the canyon, he had become a grey, indefinite shadow.

Mama stood stiffly in front of her doorstep, and on either side of her stood Emilio and Rosy. They cast furtive glances at Mama now and then.

When the grey shape of Pepé melted into the hillside and disappeared, Mama relaxed. She began the high, whining keen of the death wail. "Our beautiful—our brave," she cried. "Our protector, our son is gone." Emilio and Rosy moaned beside her. "Our beautiful—our brave, he is gone." It was the formal wail. It rose to a high piercing whine and subsided to a moan. Mama raised it three times and then she turned and went into the house and shut the door.

Emilio and Rosy stood wondering in the dawn. They heard Mama whimpering in the house. They went out to sit on the cliff above the ocean. They touched shoulders. "When did Pepé come to be a man?" Emilio asked.

"Last night," said Rosy. "Last night in Monterey." The ocean clouds turned red with the sun that was behind the mountains.

"We will have no breakfast," said Emilio. "Mama will not want to cook." Rosy did not answer him. "Where is Pepé gone?" he asked.

Rosy looked around at him. She drew her knowledge from the quiet air. "He has gone on a journey. He will never come back."

"Is he dead? Do you think he is dead?"

Rosy looked back at the ocean again. A little steamer, drawing a line of smoke sat on the edge of the horizon. "He is not dead," Rosy explained. "Not yet."

Pepé rested the big rifle across the saddle in front of him. He let the horse walk up the hill and he didn't look back. The stony slope took on a coat of short brush so that Pepé found the entrance to a trail and entered it.

When he came to the canyon opening, he swung once in his saddle and looked back, but the houses were swallowed in the misty light. Pepé jerked forward again. The high shoulder of the canyon closed in on him. His horse stretched out its neck and sighed and settled to the trail.

It was a well-worn path, dark soft leaf-mould earth strewn with broken pieces of sandstone. The trail rounded the shoulder of the canyon and dropped steeply into the bed of the stream. In the shallows the water ran smoothly, glinting in the first morning sun. Small round stones on the bottom were as brown as rust with sun moss. In the sand along the edges of the stream the tall, rich wild mint grew, while in the water itself the cress, old and tough, had gone to heavy seed.

The path went into the stream and emerged on the other side. The horse sloshed into the water and stopped. Pepé dropped his bridle and let the beast drink of the running water.

Soon the canyon sides became steep and the first giant sentinel redwoods guarded the trail, great round red trunks bearing foliage as green and lacy as ferns. Once Pepé was among the trees, the sun was lost. A perfumed and purple light lay in the pale green of the underbrush. Gooseberry bushes and blackberries and tall ferns lined the stream, and overhead the branches of the redwoods met and cut off the sky.

Pepé drank from the water bag, and he reached into the flour sack and brought out a black string of jerky. His white teeth gnawed at the string until the tough meat parted. He chewed slowly and drank occasionally from the water bag. His little eyes were slumberous and tired, but the muscles of his face were hard set. The earth of the trail was black now. It gave up a hollow sound under the walking hoofbeats.

The stream fell more sharply. Little waterfalls splashed on the stones. Five-fingered ferns hung over the water and dripped spray from their fingertips. Pepé rode half over in his saddle, dangling one leg loosely. He picked a bay leaf from a tree beside the way and put it into his mouth for a moment to flavor the dry jerky. He held the gun loosely across the pommel.

Suddenly he squared in his saddle, swung the horse from the trail and kicked it hurriedly up behind a big redwood tree. He pulled up the reins tight against the bit to keep the horse from whinnying. His face was intent and his nostrils quivered a little.

A hollow pounding came down the trail, and a horseman rode by, a fat man with red cheeks and a white stubble beard. His horse put down its head and blubbered at the trail when it came to the place where Pepé had turned off. "Hold up!" said the man and he pulled up his horse's head.

When the last sound of the hoofs died away, Pepé came back into the trail again. He did not relax in the saddle any more. He lifted the big rifle and swung the lever to throw a shell into the chamber, and then he let down the hammer to half cock.

The trail grew very steep. Now the redwood trees were smaller and their tops were dead, bitten dead where the wind reached them. The horse plodded on; the sun went slowly overhead and started down toward the afternoon.

Where the stream came out of a side canyon, the trail left it.
Pepé dismounted and watered his horse and filled up his water
bag. As soon as the trail had parted from the stream, the trees
were gone and only the thick brittle sage and manzanita and
chaparral edged the trail. And the soft black earth was gone,
too, leaving only the light tan broken rock for the trail bed.
Lizards scampered away into the brush as the horse rattled
over the little stones.

Pepé turned in his saddle and looked back. He was in the
open now: he could be seen from a distance. As he ascended
the trail the country grew more rough and terrible and dry. The
way wound about the bases of great square rocks. Little grey
rabbits skittered in the brush. A bird made a monotonous high
creaking. Eastward the bare rock mountaintops were pale and
powder-dry under the dropping sun. The horse plodded up
and up the trail toward a little V in the ridge which was the
pass.

Pepé looked suspiciously back every minute or so, and his
eyes sought the tops of the ridges ahead. Once, on a white barren spur, he saw a black figure for a moment, but he looked
quickly away, for it was one of the dark watchers. No one knew
who the watchers were, nor where they lived, but it was better
to ignore them and never to show interest in them. They did
not bother one who stayed on the trail and minded his own
business.

The air was parched and full of light dust blown by the
breeze from the eroding mountains. Pepé drank sparingly from
his bag and corked it tightly and hung it on the horn again. The
trail moved up the dry shale hillside, avoiding rocks, dropping
under clefts, climbing in and out of old water scars. When he
arrived at the little pass he stopped and looked back for a long
time. No dark watchers were to be seen now. The trail behind
was empty. Only the high tops of the redwoods indicated where
the stream flowed.

Pepé rode on through the pass. His little eyes were nearly
closed with weariness, but his face was stern, relentless and

manly. The high mountain wind coasted sighing through the pass and whistled on the edges of the big blocks of broken granite. In the air, a red-tailed hawk sailed over close to the ridge and screamed angrily. Pepé went slowly through the broken jagged pass and looked down on the other side.

The trail dropped quickly, staggering among broken rock. At the bottom of the slope there was a dark crease, thick with brush, and on the other side of the crease a little flat, in which a grove of oak trees grew. A scar of green grass cut across the flat. And behind the flat another mountain rose, desolate with dead rocks and starving little black bushes. Pepé drank from the bag again for the air was so dry that it encrusted his nostrils and burned his lips. He put the horse down the trail. The hooves slipped and struggled on the steep way, starting little stones that rolled off into the brush. The sun was gone behind the westward mountain now, but still it glowed brilliantly on the oaks and on the grassy flat. The rocks and the hillsides still sent up waves of the heat they had gathered from the day's sun.

Pepé looked up to the top of the next dry withered ridge. He saw a dark form against the sky, a man's figure standing on top of a rock, and he glanced away quickly not to appear curious. When a moment later he looked up again, the figure was gone.

Downward the trail was quickly covered. Sometimes the horse floundered for footing, sometimes set his feet and slid a little way. They came at last to the bottom where the dark chaparral was higher than Pepé's head. He held up his rifle on one side and his arm on the other to shield his face from the sharp brittle fingers of the brush.

Up and out of the crease he rode, and up a little cliff. The grassy flat was before him, and the round comfortable oaks. For a moment he studied the trail down which he had come, but there was no movement and no sound from it. Finally he rode out over the flat, to the green streak, and at the upper end of the damp he found a little spring welling out of the earth and dropping into a dug basin before it seeped out over the flat.

Pepé filled his bag first, and then he let the thirsty horse drink out of the pool. He led the horse to the clump of oaks, and in the middle of the grove, fairly protected from sight on all sides, he took off the saddle and the bridle and laid them on the ground. The horse stretched his jaws sideways and yawned. Pepé knotted the lead rope about the horse's neck and tied him to a sapling among the oaks, where he could graze in a fairly large circle.

When the horse was gnawing hungrily at the dry grass, Pepé went to the saddle and took a black string of jerky from the sack and strolled to an oak tree on the edge of the grove, from under which he could watch the trail. He sat down in the crisp dry oak leaves and automatically felt for his big black knife to cut the jerky, but he had no knife. He leaned back on his elbow and gnawed at the tough strong meat. His face was blank, but it was a man's face.

The bright evening light washed the eastern ridge, but the valley was darkening. Doves flew down from the hills to the spring, and the quail came running out of the brush and joined them, calling clearly to one another.

Out of the corner of his eye Pepé saw a shadow grow out of the bushy crease. He turned his head slowly. A big spotted wild-cat was creeping toward the spring, belly to the ground, moving like thought.

Pepé cocked his rifle and edged the muzzle slowly around. Then he looked apprehensively up the trail and dropped the hammer again. From the ground beside him he picked an oak twig and threw it toward the spring. The quail flew up with a roar and the doves whistled away. The big cat stood up: for a long moment he looked at Pepé with cold yellow eyes, and then fearlessly walked back into the gulch.

The dusk gathered quickly in the deep valley. Pepé muttered his prayers, put his head down on his arm and went instantly to sleep.

The moon came up and filled the valley with cold blue light, and the wind swept rustling down from the peaks. The owls worked up and down the slopes looking for rabbits. Down in the brush of the gulch a coyote gabbled. The oak trees whispered softly in the night breeze.

Pepé started up, listening. His horse had whinnied. The moon was just slipping behind the western ridge, leaving the valley in darkness behind it. Pepé sat tensely gripping his rifle. From far up the trail he heard an answering whinny and the crash of shod hooves on the broken rock. He jumped to his feet, ran to his horse and led it under the trees. He threw on the saddle and cinched it tight for the steep trail, caught the unwilling head and forced the bit into the mouth. He felt the saddle to make sure the water bag and the sack of jerky were there. Then he mounted and turned up the hill.

It was velvet dark. The horse found the entrance to the trail where it left the flat, and started up, stumbling and slipping on the rocks. Pepé's hand rose up to his head. His hat was gone. He had left it under the oak tree.

The horse had struggled far up the trail when the first change of dawn came into the air, a steel greyness as light mixed thoroughly with dark. Gradually the sharp snaggled edge of the ridge stood out above them, rotten granite tortured and eaten by the winds of time. Pepé had dropped his reins on the horn, leaving direction to the horse. The brush grabbed at his legs in the dark until one knee of his jeans was ripped.

Gradually the light flowed down over the ridge. The starved brush and rocks stood out in the half light, strange and lonely in high perspective. Then there came warmth into the light. Pepé drew up and looked back, but he could see nothing in the darker valley below. The sky turned blue over the coming sun. In the waste of the mountainside, the poor dry brush grew only three feet high. Here and there, big outcroppings of unrotted granite stood up like mouldering houses. Pepé relaxed a little. He drank from his water bag and bit off a piece of jerky. A single eagle flew over, high in the light.

Without warning Pepé's horse screamed and fell on its side. He was almost down before the rifle crash echoed up from the valley. From a hole behind the struggling shoulder, a stream of bright crimson blood pumped and stopped and pumped and stopped. The hooves threshed on the ground. Pepé lay half stunned beside the horse. He looked slowly down the hill. A piece of sage clipped off beside his head and another crash echoed up from side to side of the canyon. Pepé flung himself frantically behind a bush.

He crawled up the hill on his knees and one hand. His right hand held the rifle up off the ground and pushed it ahead of him. He moved with the instinctive care of an animal. Rapidly he wormed his way toward one of the big outcroppings of granite on the hill above him. Where the brush was high he doubled up and ran, but where the cover was slight he wriggled forward on his stomach, pushing the rifle ahead of him. In the last little distance there was no cover at all. Pepé poised and then he darted across the space and flashed around the corner of the rock.

He leaned panting against the stone. When his breath came easier he moved along behind the big rock until he came to a narrow split that offered a thin section of vision down the hill. Pepé lay on his stomach and pushed the rifle barrel through the slit and waited.

The sun reddened the western ridges now. Already the buzzards were settling down toward the place where the horse lay. A small brown bird scratched in the dead sage leaves directly in front of the rifle muzzle. The coasting eagle flew back toward the rising sun.

Pepé saw a little movement in the brush far below. His grip tightened on the gun. A little brown doe stepped daintily out on the trail and crossed it and disappeared into the brush again. For a long time Pepé waited. Far below he could see the little flat and the oak trees and the slash of green. Suddenly his eyes flashed back at the trail again. A quarter of a mile down there had been a quick movement in the chaparral. The rifle swung over. The front sight nestled in the V of the rear sight. Pepé studied for a moment and then raised the rear sight a notch. The little movement in the brush came again. The sight settled on it. Pepé squeezed the trigger. The explosion crashed down the mountain and up the other side, and came rattling back. The whole side of the slope grew still. No more movement. And then a white streak cut into the granite of the slit and a bullet whined away and a crash sounded up from below. Pepé felt a sharp pain in his right hand. A sliver of granite was sticking out from between his first and second knuckles and the point protruded from his palm. Carefully he pulled out the sliver of stone. The wound bled evenly and gently. No vein nor artery was cut.

Pepé looked into a little dusty cave in the rock and gathered a handful of spider web, and he pressed the mass into the cut, plastering the soft web into the blood. The flow stopped almost at once.

The rifle was on the ground. Pepé picked it up, levered a new shell into the chamber. And then he slid into the brush on his stomach. Far to the right he crawled, and then up the hill, moving slowly and carefully, crawling to cover and resting and then crawling again.

In the mountains the sun is high in its arc before it penetrates the gorges. The hot face looked over the hill and brought instant heat with it. The white light beat on the rocks and reflected from them and rose up quivering from the earth again, and the rocks and bushes seemed to quiver behind the air.

Pepé crawled in the general direction of the ridge peak, zigzagging for cover. The deep cut between his knuckles began to throb. He crawled close to a rattlesnake before he saw it, and when it raised its dry head and made a soft beginning whirr, he backed up and took another way. The quick grey lizards flashed in front of him, raising a tiny line of dust. He found another mass of spider web and pressed it against his throbbing hand.

Pepé was pushing the rifle with his left hand now. Little drops of sweat ran to the ends of his coarse black hair and rolled down his cheeks. His lips and tongue were growing thick and heavy. His lips writhed to draw saliva into his mouth. His little dark eyes were uneasy and suspicious. Once when a grey lizard paused in front of him on the parched ground and turned its head sideways he crushed it flat with a stone.

When the sun slid past noon he had not gone a mile. He crawled exhaustedly a last hundred yards to a patch of high sharp manzanita, crawled desperately, and when the patch was reached he wriggled in among the tough gnarly trunks and dropped his head on his left arm. There was little shade in the meager brush, but there was cover and safety. Pepé went to sleep as he lay and the sun beat on his back. A few little birds hopped close to him and peered and hopped away. Pepé squirmed in his sleep and he raised and dropped his wounded hand again and again.

The sun went down behind the peaks and the cool evening came, and then the dark. A coyote yelled from the hillside, Pepé started awake and looked about with misty eyes. His hand was swollen and heavy; a little thread of pain ran up the inside of his arm and settled in a pocket in his armpit. He peered about and then stood up, for the mountains were black and the moon had not yet risen. Pepé stood up in the dark. The coat of his father pressed on his arm. His tongue was swollen until it nearly filled his mouth. He wriggled out of the coat and dropped it in the brush, and then he struggled up the hill, falling over rocks and tearing his way through the brush. The rifle knocked against stones as he went. Little dry avalanches of gravel and shattered stone went whispering down the hill behind him.

After a while the old moon came up and showed the jagged ridge top ahead of him. By moonlight Pepé traveled more easily. He bent forward so that his throbbing arm hung away from his body. The journey uphill was made in dashes and rests, a frantic rush up a few yards and then a rest. The wind coasted down the slope rattling the dry stems of the bushes.

The moon was at meridian when Pepé came at last to the sharp backbone of the ridge top. On the last hundred yards of the rise no soil had clung under the wearing winds. The way was on solid rock. He clambered to the top and looked down on the other side. There was a draw like the last below him, misty with moonlight, brushed with dry struggling sage and chaparral. On the other side the hill rose up sharply and at the top the jagged rotten teeth of the mountain showed against the sky. At the bottom of the cut the brush was thick and dark.

Pepé stumbled down the hill. His throat was almost closed with thirst. At first he tried to run, but immediately he fell and rolled. After that he went more carefully. The moon was just disappearing behind the mountains when he came to the bottom. He crawled into the heavy brush feeling with his fingers for water. There was no water in the bed of the stream, only damp earth. Pepé laid his gun down and scooped up a handful of mud and put it in his mouth, and then he spluttered and scraped the earth from his tongue with his finger, for the mud drew at his mouth like a poultice. He dug a hole in the stream bed with his fingers, dug a little basin to catch water; but before it was very deep his head fell forward on the damp ground and he slept.

The dawn came and the heat of the day fell on the earth, and still Pepé slept. Late in the afternoon his head jerked up. He looked slowly around. His eyes were slits of wariness. Twenty feet away in the heavy brush a big tawny mountain lion stood looking at him. Its long thick tail waved gracefully, its ears were erect with interest, not laid back dangerously. The lion squatted down on its stomach and watched him.

Pepé looked at the hole he had dug in the earth. A half inch of muddy water had collected in the bottom. He tore the sleeve from his hurt arm, with his teeth ripped out a little square, soaked it in the water and put it in his mouth. Over and over he filled the cloth and sucked it.

Still the lion sat and watched him. The evening came down but there was no movement on the hills. No birds visited the dry bottom of the cut. Pepé looked occasionally at the lion. The eyes of the yellow beast drooped as though he were about to sleep. He yawned and his long thin red tongue curled out. Suddenly his head jerked around and his nostrils quivered. His big tail lashed. He stood up and slunk like a tawny shadow into the thick brush.

A moment later Pepé heard the sound, the faint far crash of horses' hooves on gravel. And he heard something else, a high whining yelp of a dog.

Pepé took his rifle in his left hand and he glided into the brush almost as quietly as the lion had. In the darkening evening he crouched up the hill toward the next ridge. Only when the dark came did he stand up. His energy was short. Once it was dark he fell over the rocks and slipped to his knees on the steep slope, but he moved on and on up the hill, climbing and scrabbling over the broken hillside.

When he was far up toward the top, he lay down and slept for a little while. The withered moon, shining on his face, awakened him. He stood up and moved up the hill. Fifty yards away he stopped and turned back, for he had forgotten his rifle. He walked heavily down and poked about in the brush, but he could not find his gun. At last he lay down to rest. The pocket of pain in his armpit had grown more sharp. His arm seemed to swell out and fall with every heartbeat. There was no position lying down where the heavy arm did not press against his armpit.

With the effort of a hurt beast, Pepé got up and moved again toward the top of the ridge. He held his swollen arm away from his body with his left hand. Up the steep hill he dragged himself, a few steps and a rest, and a few more steps. At last he was nearing the top. The moon showed the uneven sharp back of it against the sky.

Pepé's brain spun in a big spiral up and away from him. He slumped to the ground and lay still. The rock ridge top was only a hundred feet above him.

The moon moved over the sky. Pepé half turned on his back. His tongue tried to make words, but only a thick hissing came from between his lips.

When the dawn came, Pepé pulled himself up. His eyes were

sane again. He drew his great puffed arm in front of him and looked at the angry wound. The black line ran up from his wrist to his armpit. Automatically he reached in his pocket for the big black knife, but it was not there. His eyes searched the ground. He picked up a sharp blade of stone and scraped at the wound, sawed at the proud flesh and then squeezed the green juice out in big drops. Instantly he threw back his head and whined like a dog. His whole right side shuddered at the pain, but the pain cleared his head.

In the grey light he struggled up the last slope to the ridge and crawled over and lay down behind a line of rocks. Below him lay a deep canyon exactly like the last, waterless and desolate. There was no flat, no oak trees, not even heavy brush in the bottom of it. And on the other side a sharp ridge stood up, thinly brushed with starving sage, littered with broken granite. Strewn over the hill there were giant outcroppings, and on the top the granite teeth stood out against the sky.

The new day was light now. The flame of the sun came over the ridge and fell on Pepé where he lay on the ground. His course black hair was littered with twigs and bits of spider web. His eyes had retreated back into his head. Between his lips the tip of his black tongue showed.

He sat up and dragged his great arm into his lap and nursed it, rocking his body and moaning in his throat. He threw back his head and looked up into the pale sky. A big black bird circled nearly out of sight, and far to the left another was sailing near.

He lifted his head to listen, for a familiar sound had come to him from the valley he had climbed out of; it was the crying yelp of hounds, excited and feverish, on a trail.

Pepé bowed his head quickly. He tried to speak rapid words but only a thick hiss came from his lips. He drew a shaky cross on his breast with his left hand. It was a long struggle to get to his feet. He crawled slowly and mechanically to the top of a big rock on the ridge peak. Once there, he arose slowly, swaying to

his feet, and stood erect. Far below he could see the dark brush
where he had slept. He braced his feet and stood there, black
against the morning sky.

There came a ripping sound at his feet. A piece of stone flew
up and a bullet droned off into the next gorge. The hollow crash
echoed up from below. Pepé looked down for a moment and
then pulled himself straight again.

His body jarred back. His left hand fluttered helplessly toward his breast. The second crash sounded from below. Pepé
swung forward and toppled from the rock. His body struck and
rolled over and over, starting a little avalanche. And when at
last he stopped against a bush, the avalanche slid slowly down
and covered up his head.

The Four Lost Men

THOMAS WOLFE

———

Suddenly, at the green heart of June, I heard my father's voice
again. That year I was sixteen; the week before I had come
home from my first year at college, and the huge thrill and menace of the war, which we had entered just two months before,
had filled our hearts. And war gives life to men as well as death.
It fills the hearts of young men with wild song and jubilation.
It wells up in their throats in great-starred night, the savage cry
of all their pain and joy. And it fills them with a wild and wordless prophecy not of death, but life, for it speaks to them of new
lands, triumph, and discovery, of heroic deeds, the fame and
fellowship of heroes, and the love of glorious unknown women
—of a shining triumph and a grand success in a heroic world,

and of a life more fortunate and happy than they have ever known.

So was it with us all that year. Over the immense and waiting earth, the single pulse and promise of the war impended. One felt it in the little towns at dawn, with all their quiet, casual, utterly familiar acts of life beginning. One felt it in the route-boy deftly flinging the light folded block of paper on a porch, a man in shirt-sleeves coming out upon the porch and bending for the paper, the slow-clopping hoofs of the milk horse in a quiet street, the bottle-clinking wagon, and the sudden pause, the rapid footsteps of the milkman and the clinking bottles, then clopping hoof and wheel, and morning, stillness, the purity of light, and the dew-sweet bird-song rising in the street again.

In all these ancient, ever-new, unchanging, always magic acts of life and light and morning one felt the huge impending presence of the war. And one felt it in the brooding hush of noon, in the ring of the ice-tongs in the street, the cool whine of the ice-saws droning through the smoking block, in leaf, and blade and flower, in smell of tar, and the sudden haunting green-gold summer absence of a street-car after it had gone.

The war had got in everything: it was in things that moved, and in things that were still, in the animate red silence of an old brick wall as well as in all the thronging life and traffic in the streets. It was in the faces of the people passing, and in ten thousand familiar moments of man's daily life and business.

And lonely, wild, and haunting, calling us on forever with the winding of its far lost horn, it had got into the time-enchanted loneliness of the magic hills around us, in all the sudden, wild, and lonely lights that came and passed and vanished on the massed green of the wilderness.

The war was in far cries and broken sounds and cow-bells tinkling in the gusty wind, and in the far, wild, wailing joy and sorrow of a departing train, as it rushed eastward, seaward, war-ward through a valley of the South in the green spell and golden magic of full June, and in the houses where men lived, the brief flame and fire of sheeted window panes.

And it was in field and gulch and hollow, in the sweet green mountain valleys fading into dusk, and in the hill-flanks reddened with the ancient light, and slanting fast into steep cool shade and lilac silence. It was in the whole huge mystery of earth that, after all the dusty tumult of the day, could lapse with such immortal stillness to the hush, the joy, the sorrow of oncoming night.

The war had got into all sounds and secrecies, the sorrow, longing, and delight, the mystery, hunger and wild joy that came from the deep-breasted heart of fragrant, all-engulfing night. It was in the sweet and secret rustling of the leaves in summer streets, in footsteps coming quiet, slow, and lonely along the darkness of a leafy street, in screen doors slammed, and silence, the distant barking of a dog, far voices, laughter, faint pulsing music at a dance, and in all the casual voices of the night, far, strangely near, most intimate and familiar.

And suddenly, as I sat there under the proud and secret mystery of huge-starred, velvet-breasted night, hearing my father's great voice sounding from the porch again, the war, with a wild and intolerable loneliness of ecstasy and desire, came to me in the sudden throbbing of a racing motor, far-away silence, an image of the cool sweet darkness of the mountainside, the white flesh and yielding tenderness of women. And even as I thought of this I heard the rich, sensual welling of a woman's voice, voluptuous, low, and tender, from the darkness of a summer porch across the street.

What had the war changed? What had it done to us? What miracle of transformation had it wrought upon our lives? It had changed nothing; it had heightened, intensified, and made glorious all the ancient and familiar things of life. It had added hope to hope, joy to joy, and life to life; and from that vital wizardry it had rescued all our lives from hopelessness and despair, and made us live again who thought that we were lost.

The war seemed to have collected in a single image of joy, and power, and proud compacted might all of the thousand images of joy and power and all-exulting life which we had al-

ways had, and for which we had never had a word before. Over
the fields of silent and mysterious night it seemed that we could
hear the nation marching, that we could hear, soft and thunderous in the night, the million-footed unison of marching men.
And that single glorious image of all-collected joy and unity
and might had given new life and new hope to all of us.

My father was old, he was sick with a cancer that flowered
and fed forever at his entrails, eating from day to day the gaunt
sinew of his life away beyond a hope or remedy, and we knew
that he was dying. Yet, under the magic life and hope the war
had brought to us, his life seemed to have revived again out of
its grief of pain, its death of joy, its sorrow of irrevocable memory.

For a moment he seemed to live again in his full prime. And
instantly we were all released from the black horror of death
and time that hung above him, from the nightmare terror that
had menaced us for years. Instantly we were freed from the evil
spell of sorrowful time and memory that had made his living
death more horrible than his real one could ever be.

And instantly the good life, the golden and jubilant life of
childhood, in whose full magic we had been sustained by the
power of his life, and which had seemed so lost and irrecover-
able that it had a dreamlike strangeness when we thought of it,
had, under this sudden flare of life and joy and war, returned in
all its various and triumphant colors. And for a moment we believed that all would be again for us as it had been, that he
never could grow old and die, but that he must live forever, and
that the summertime, the orchard and bright morning, would be
ours again, could never die.

I could hear him talking now about old wars and ancient
troubles, hurling against the present and its leaders the full
indictment of his soaring rhetoric that howled, rose, fell, and
swept out into the night, piercing all quarters of the darkness
with the naked penetration which his voice had in the old days
when he sat talking on his porch in summer darkness, and the
neighborhood attended and was still.

Now as my father talked, I could hear the boarders on the porch attending in the same way, the stealthy creak of a rocker now and then, a low word spoken, a question, protest or agreement, and then their hungry, feeding, and attentive silence as my father talked. He spoke of all the wars and troubles he had known, told how he had stood, "a bare-foot country boy," beside a dusty road twelve miles from Gettysburg, and had watched the ragged rebels march past upon the road that led to death and battle and the shipwreck of their hopes.

He spoke of the faint and ominous trembling of the guns across the hot brooding silence of the countryside, and how silence, wonder, and unspoken questions filled the hearts of all the people, and how they had gone about their work upon the farm as usual. He spoke of the years that had followed on the war when he was a stone-cutter's apprentice in Baltimore, and he spoke of ancient joys and labors, forgotten acts and histories, and he spoke then with familiar memory of the lost Americans —the strange, lost, time-far, dead Americans, the remote, voiceless, and bewhiskered faces of the great Americans, who were more lost to me than Egypt, more far from me than the Tartarian coasts, more haunting strange than Cipango or the lost faces of the first dynastic kings that built the Pyramids—and whom he had seen, heard, known, found familiar in the full pulse, and passion, and proud glory of his youth: the lost, time-far, voiceless faces of Buchanan, Johnson, Douglas, Blaine—the proud, vacant, time-strange and bewhiskered visages of Garfield, Arthur, Harrison, and Hayes.

"Ah, Lord!" he said—his voice rang out in darkness like a gong, "Ah, Lord!—I've known all of 'em since James Buchanan's time—for I was a boy of six when he took office!" Here he paused a moment, lunged forward violently in his rocking chair, and spat cleanly out a spurt of strong tobacco juice across the porch-rail into the loamy earth, the night-sweet fragrance of the geranium beds. "Yes, sir," he said gravely, lunging back again, while the attentive, hungry boarders waited in the living dark-

ness and were still, "I remember all of them since James Buchanan's time, and I've seen most of them that came since Lincoln!
—Ah, Lord!" he paused briefly for another waiting moment,
shaking his grave head sadly in the dark. "Well do I remember
the day when I stood on a street in Baltimore—poor friendless
orphan that I was!" my father went on sorrowfully, but somewhat illogically, since at this time his mother was alive and in
good health, upon her little farm in Pennsylvania, and would
continue so for almost fifty years—"a poor friendless country
boy of sixteen years, alone in the great city where I had come to
learn my trade as an apprentice—and heard Andrew Johnson,
then the President of this *great* nation," said my father, "speak
from the platform of a horse-car—and he was so drunk—so
drunk—" he howled, "the President of this country was so
drunk that they had to stand on each side of him, and hold him
as he spoke—or he'd a-gone head over heels into the gutter!"
Here he paused, wet his great thumb briefly, cleared his throat
with considerable satisfaction, lunged forward violently again
in his rocking chair and spat strongly a wad of bright tobacco
juice into the loamy fragance of the dark geranium bed.

"The first vote I ever cast for President," my father continued
presently, as he lunged back again, "I cast in 1872, in Baltimore,
for that *great* man—that brave and noble soldier—U. S. Grant!
And I have voted for every Republican nominee for President
ever since. I voted for Rutherford Hayes of Ohio in 1876—that
was the year, as you well know, of the great Hayes-Tilden con-
troversy, in 1880 for James Abram Garfield—that *great* good
man," he said passionately, "who was so foully and brutally
done to death by the cowardly assault of a murderous assassin."
He paused, wet his thumb, breathing heavily, lunged forward
in his rocking chair, and spat again. "In 1884, I cast my vote for
James G. Blaine in the year that Grover Cleveland defeated
him," he said shortly, "for Benjamin Harrison in 1888, and for
Harrison again in 1892, the time that Cleveland got in for his
second term—a time we will all remember to our dying days,"
my father said grimly, "for the Democrats were in and we had

soup kitchens. And, you can mark my words," he howled, "you'll have them again, before these next four years are over— your guts will grease your backbone, as sure as there's a God in heaven, before that fearful, that awful, that cruel, inhuman and bloodthirsty Monster who kept us out of war," my father jeered derisively, "is done with you—for hell, ruin, misery, and damnation commence every time the Democrats get in. You can rest assured of that!" he said shortly, cleared his throat, wet his thumb, lunged forward violently and spat again. And for a moment there was silence and the boarders waited.

"Ah, Lord!" my father said at length sadly, gravely, in a low, almost inaudible tone. And suddenly, all the old life and howling fury of his rhetoric had gone from him: he was an old man again, sick, indifferent, dying, and his voice had grown old, worn, weary, sad.

"Ah, Lord!" he muttered, shaking his head sadly, thinly, wearily in the dark. "I've seen them all. . . . I've seen them come and go . . . Garfield, Arthur, Harrison, and Hayes . . . and all . . . all . . . all of them are dead. . . . I'm the only one that's left," he said illogically, "and soon I'll be gone, too." And for a moment he was silent. "It's pretty strange when you come to think of it," he muttered. "By God it is!" And he was silent, and darkness, mystery, and night were all about us.

Garfield, Arthur, Harrison, and Hayes—time of my father's time, blood of his blood, life of his life, had been living, real, and actual people in all the passion, power, and feeling of my father's youth. And for me they were the lost Americans: their gravely vacant and bewhiskered faces mixed, melted, swam together in the sea-depths of a past intangible, immeasurable, and unknowable as the buried city of Persepolis.

And they were lost.

For who was Garfield, martyred man, and who had seen him in the streets of life? Who could believe his footfalls ever sounded on a lonely pavement? Who had heard the casual and familiar tones of Chester Arthur? And where was Harrison?

Where was Hayes? Which had the whiskers, which the burnsides: which was which?

Were they not lost?

Into their ears, as ours, the tumults of forgotten crowds, upon their brains the million printings of lost time, and suddenly upon their dying sight the brief bitter pain and joy of a few death-bright, fixed and fading memories: the twisting of a leaf upon a bough, the grinding felloe-rim against the curb, the long, distant and retreating thunder of a train upon the rails.

Garfield, Hayes, and Harrison were Ohio men; but only the name of Garfield had been brightened by his blood. But at night had they not heard the howlings of demented wind, the sharp, clean, windy raining to the earth of acorns? Had all of them not walked down lonely roads at night in winter and seen a light and known it was theirs? Had all of them not known the wilderness?

Had they not known the smell of old bound calf and well-worn leathers, the Yankee lawyer's smell of strong tobacco spit and courthouse urinals, the smell of horses, harness, hay, and sweating country men, of jury rooms and court rooms—the strong male smell of Justice at the county seat, and heard a tap along dark corridors where fell a drop in darkness with a punctual crescent monotone of time, dark time?

Had not Garfield, Hayes, and Harrison studied law in offices with a dark brown smell? Had not the horses trotted past below their windows in wreaths of dust along a straggling street of shacks and buildings with false fronts? Had they not heard below them the voices of men talking, loitering up in drawling heat? Had they not heard the casual, rich-fibered, faintly howling country voices, and heard the rustling of a woman's skirt, and waiting silence, slyly lowered tones of bawdry and then huge guffaws, slapped meaty thighs, and high fat choking laughter? And in the dusty dozing heat, while time buzzed slowly, like a fly, had not Garfield, Arthur, Harrison, and Hayes then smelled the river, the humid, subtly fresh, half-rotten river, and thought of the white flesh of the women then beside the river, and felt a slow impending passion in their entrails, a heavy rending power in their hands?

Then Garfield, Arthur, Harrison, and Hayes had gone to war, and each became a brigadier or major-general. All were bearded men: they saw a spattering of bright blood upon the leaves, and they heard the soldiers talking in the dark of food and women. They held the bridge-head in bright dust at places with such names as Wilson's Mill and Spangler's Run, and their men smashed cautiously through dense undergrowth. And they had heard the surgeons cursing after battles, and the little rasp of saws. They had seen boys standing awkwardly holding their entrails in their hands, and pleading pitifully with fear-bright eyes: "Is it bad, General? Do you think it's bad?"

When the canister came through it made a ragged hole. It smashed through tangled leaves and boughs, sometimes it plunked solidly into the fiber of a tree. Sometimes when it struck a man it tore away the roof of his brain, the wall of his skull, raggedly, so that his brains seethed out upon a foot of wilderness, and the blood blackened and congealed, and he lay there in his thick clumsy uniform, with a smell of urine in the wool, in the casual, awkward, and incompleted attitude of sudden death. And when Garfield, Arthur, Harrison, and Hayes saw these things they saw that it was not like the picture they had had, as children, it was not like the works of Walter Scott and William Gilmore Simms. They saw that the hole was not clean and small and in the central front, and the field was not green, nor fenced, nor mown. Over the vast and immemorable earth the quivering heated light of afternoon was shining, a field swept rudely upward to a lift of rugged wood, and field by field, gully by gulch by fold, the earth advanced in rude, sweet, limitless convolutions.

Then Garfield, Arthur, Harrison, and Hayes had paused by the bridge-head for a moment and were still, seeing the bright blood at noon upon the trampled wheat, feeling the brooding hush of six o'clock across the fields where all the storming feet had passed at dawn, seeing the way the rough field hedge

leaned out across the dusty road, the casual intrusions of the
coarse field grasses and the hot dry daisies to the edges of the
road, seeing the rock-bright shallows of the creek, the sweet
cool shade and lean of river trees across the water.

They paused then by the bridge-head looking at the water.
They saw the stark blank flatness of the old red mill that somehow was like sunset, coolness, sorrow, and delight, and looking
at the faces of dead boys among the wheat, the most-oh-most-
familiar-plain, the death-strange faces of the dead Americans,
they stood there for a moment, thinking, feeling, thinking, with
strong wordless wonder in their hearts:

"As we leaned on the sills of evening, as we stood in the frames
of the marvellous doors, as we were received into silence, the
flanks of the slope and the slanted light, as we saw the strange
hushed shapes upon the land, the muted distances, knowing
all things then—what could we say except that all our comrades were spread quietly around us and that noon was far?

"What can we say now of the lonely land—what can we say
now of the deathless shapes and substances—what can we say
who have lived here with our lives, bone, blood, and brain, and
all our tongueless languages, hearing on many a casual road
the plain-familiar voices of Americans, and who to-morrow will
be buried in the earth, knowing the fields will steep to silence
after us, the slant light deepen on the slopes, and peace and
evening will come back again—at one now with the million
shapes and single substance of our land, at one with evening,
peace, the huge-stride of the undulant oncoming night, at one,
also, with morning?

"Silence, receive us, and the field of peace, hush of the meas-
ureless land, the unabated distances; shape of the one and
single substance and the million forms, replenish us, restore us,
and unite us with your vast images of quietness and joy. Stride
of the undulant night, come swiftly now; engulf us, silence, in
your great-starred secrecy; speak to our hearts of stillness, for
we have, save this, no speech.

"There is the bridge we crossed, the mill we slept in, and the creek. There is a field of wheat, a hedge, a dusty road, an apple orchard, and the sweet wild tangle of a wood upon that hill. And there is six o'clock across the fields again, now and always, as it was and will be to world's end forever. And some of us have died this morning coming through the field—and that was time—time—time. We shall not come again, we never shall come back again, we never shall come back along this road again as we did once at morning—so, brothers, let us look again before we go. . . . There is the mill, and there the hedge, and there the shallows of the rock-bright waters of the creek, and there the sweet and most familiar coolness of the trees—and surely we have been this way before!" they cried.

"Oh, surely, brothers, we have sat upon the bridge, before the mill, and sung together by the rock-bright waters of the creek at evening, and come across the wheatfield in the morning and heard the dew-sweet birdsong rising from the hedge before! You plain, oh-most-familiar and most homely earth, proud earth of this huge land unutterable, proud nobly swelling earth, in all your delicacy, wildness, savagery, and terror—grand earth in all your loneliness, beauty and wild joy, terrific earth in all your limitless fecundities, swelling with infinite fold and convolution into the reaches of the West forever—American earth!—bridge, hedge, and creek and dusty road—you plain tremendous poetry of Wilson's Mill, where boys died in the wheat this morning—you unutterable far-near, strange-familiar, homely earth of magic, for which a word would do if we could find it, for which a word would do if we could call it by its name, for which a word would do that never can be spoken, that can never be forgotten, and that will never be revealed—oh, proud, familiar, nobly swelling earth, it seems we must have known you before it! It seems we must have known you forever, but all we know for certain is that we came along this road one time at morning, and now our blood is painted on the wheat, and you are ours now, we are yours forever—and there is something here we never shall remember—there is something here we never shall forget!"

Had Garfield, Arthur, Harrison, and Hayes been young? Or had they all been born with flowing whiskers, sideburns, and wing collars, speaking gravely from the cradle of their mother's arms the noble vacant sonorities of far-seeing statesmanship? It could not be. Had they not all been young men in the 'Thirties, the 'Forties, and the 'Fifties? Did they not, as we, cry out at night along deserted roads into demented winds? Did they not, as we, cry out in ecstasy and exultancy, as the full measure of their hunger, their potent and inchoate hope, went out into that single wordless cry?

Did they not, as we, when young, prowl softly up and down in the dark hours of the night, seeing the gaslamps flare and flutter on the corner, falling with livid light upon the corners of old cobbled streets of brownstone houses? Had they not heard the lonely rhythmic clopping of a horse, the jounting wheels of a hansom cab, upon those barren cobbles? And had they not waited, trembling in the darkness till the horse and cab had passed, had vanished with the lonely recession of shod hoofs, and then were heard no more?

And then had Garfield, Arthur, Harrison, and Hayes not waited, waited in the silence of the night, prowling up and down the lonely cobbled street, with trembling lips, numb entrails, pounding hearts? Had they not set their jaws, made sudden indecisive movements, felt terror, joy, a numb impending ecstasy, and waited, waited then—for what? Had they not waited, hearing sounds of shifting engines in the yards at night, hearing the hoarse, gaseous breaths of little engines through the grimy fan-flare of their funnels? Had they not waited there in that dark street with the fierce lone hunger of a boy, feeling around them the immense and moving quietness of sleep, the heartbeats of ten thousand sleeping men, as they waited, waited in the night?

Had they not, as we, then turned their eyes up and seen the huge starred visage of the night, the immense and lilac darkness of America in April? Had they not heard the sudden, shrill, and piping whistle of a departing engine? Had they not waited, thinking, feeling, seeing then the immense mysterious continent of night, the wild and lyric earth, so casual, sweet, and strange-familiar, in all its space and savagery and terror, its mystery and joy, its limitless sweep and rudeness, its delicate and savage fecundity? Had they not had a vision of the plains, the mountains, and the rivers flowing in the darkness, the huge pattern of the everlasting earth and the all-engulfing wilderness of America?

Had they not felt, as we have felt, as they waited in the night, the huge, lonely earth of night-time and America, on which ten thousand lonely sleeping little towns were strewn? Had they not seen the fragile network of light, racketing, ill-joined little rails across the land, over which the lonely little trains rushed on in darkness, flinging a handful of lost echoes at the river's edge, leaving an echo in the cut's resounding cliff, and being engulfed then in huge lonely night, in all-brooding, all-engulfing night? Had they not known, as we have known, the wild secret joy and mystery of the everlasting earth, the lilac dark, the savage, silent, all-possessing wilderness that gathered in around ten thousand lonely little towns, ten million lost and lonely sleepers, and waited, and abode forever, and was still?

Had not Garfield, Arthur, Harrison, and Hayes then waited, feeling wild joy and sorrow in their hearts, and a savage hunger and desire—a flame, a fire, a fury—burning fierce and lean and lonely in the night, burning forever while the sleepers slept? Were they not burning, burning, burning, even as the rest of us have burned? Were Garfield, Arthur, Harrison, and Hayes not burning in the night? Were they not burning forever in the silence of the little towns, with all the fierce hunger, savage passion, limitless desire that young men in this land have known in the darkness?

Had Garfield, Arthur, Harrison, and Hayes not waited then, as we have waited, with numb lips and pounding hearts and fear, delight, strong joy and terror stirring in their entrails as they stood in the silent street before a house, proud, evil, lavish, lighted—certain, secret, and alone? And as they heard the hoof,

the wheel, the sudden whistle and the immense and sleeping
silence of the town, did they not wait there in the darkness,
thinking:

"Oh, there are new lands, morning, and a shining city. Soon,
soon, soon!"

Did not Garfield, Arthur, Harrison, and Hayes, those fierce
and jubilant young men, who waited there, as we have waited,
in the silent barren street, with trembling lips, numb hands,
with terror, savage joy, fierce rapture alive and stirring in their
entrails—did they not feel, as we have felt, when they heard
the shrill departing warning of the whistle in the dark, the
sound of great wheels pounding at the river's edge? Did they
not feel, as we have felt, as they waited there in the intolerable
sweetness, wildness, mystery, and terror of the great earth in
the month of April, and knew themselves alone, alive and
young and mad and secret with desire and hunger in the great
sleep-silence of the night, the impending, cruel, all-promise of
this land? Were they not torn, as we have been, by sharp pain
and wordless lust, the asp of time, the thorn of spring, the sharp,
the tongueless cry? Did they not say:

"Oh, there are women in the East—and new lands, morning,
and a shining city! There are forgotten fume-flaws of bright
smoke above Manhattan, the forest of masts about the crowded
isle, the proud cleavages of departing ships, the soaring web, the
wing-like swoop and joy of the great bridge, and men with
derby hats who come across the Bridge to greet us—come,
brothers, let us go to find them all! For the huge murmur of the
city's million-footed life, far, bee-like, drowsy, strange as time,
has come to haunt our ears with all its golden prophecy of joy
and triumph, fortune, happiness and love such as no men before
have ever known. Oh, brothers, in the city, in the far-shining,
glorious, time-enchanted spell of that enfabled city we shall find
great men and lovely women, and unceasingly ten thousand
new delights, a thousand magical adventures! We shall wake at
morning in our rooms of lavish brown to hear the hoof and
wheel upon the city street again, and smell the harbor, fresh,

half-rotten, with its bracelet of bright tides, its traffic of proud seaborne ships, its purity and joy of dancing morning-gold.

"Street of the day, with the unceasing promise of your million-footed life, we come to you!" they cried. "Street of the thunderous wheels at noon, street of the great parades of marching men, the band's bright oncoming blare, the brave stick-candy whippings of a flag, street of the cries and shouts, the swarming feet,—street of the jounting cabs, the ringing hooves, the horse-cars and the jingling bells, the in-horse ever bending its sad nodding head toward its lean and patient comrade on the right—great street of furious life and movement, noon, and joyful labors, your image blazes in our hearts forever, and we come!

"Street of the morning, street of hope!" they cried. "Street of coolness, slanted light, the frontal cliff and gulch of steep blue shade, street of the dancing morning-gold of waters on the flashing tides, street of the rusty weathered slips, the blunt-nosed ferry foaming in with its packed wall of small white staring faces, all silent and intent, all turned toward *you*—proud street! Street of the pungent sultry smells of new-ground coffee, the good green smell of money, the fresh half-rotten harbor smells with all its evocation of your mast-bound harbor and its tide of ships, great street!—Street of the old buildings grimed richly with the warm and mellow dinginess of trade—street of the million morning feet forever hurrying onward in the same direction—proud street of hope and joy and morning, in your steep canyon we shall win the wealth, the fame, the power and the esteem which our lives and talents merit!

"Street of the night!" they cried, "great street of mystery and suspense, terror and delight, eagerness and hope, street edged forever with the dark menace of impending joy, and unknown happiness and fulfilment, street of gaiety, warmth, and evil, street of the great hotels, the lavish bars and restaurants, and the softly golden glow, the fading lights and empetalled whiteness of a thousand hushed white thirsty faces in the crowded theatres, street of the tidal flood of faces, lighted with your million lights and all thronging, tireless and unquenched in their insatiate searching after pleasure, street of the lovers coming along with slow steps, their faces turned toward each other, lost in the oblivion of love among the everlasting web and weaving of the crowd, street of the white face, the painted mouth, the shining and inviting eye—oh, street of night, with all your mystery, joy, and terror—we have thought of you, proud street.

"And we shall move at evening in the noiseless depths of sumptuous carpets through all the gaiety, warmth, and brilliant happiness of great lighted chambers of the night, filled with the mellow thrum and languor of the violins, and where the love-liest and most desirable women in the world—the beloved daughters of great merchants, bankers, millionaires, or rich young widows, beautiful, loving, and alone—are moving with a slow proud undulance, a look of depthless tenderness in their fragile, lovely faces. And the loveliest of them all," they cried, "is ours, is ours forever, if we want her! For, brothers, in the city, in the far-shining, magic, golden city, we shall move among great men and glorious women and know nothing but strong joy and happiness forever, winning by our courage, talent, and deserving the highest and most honored place in the most fortunate and happy life that men have known, if only we will go and make it ours!"

So thinking, feeling, waiting as we have waited in the sleep-ing silence of the night in silent streets, hearing, as we have heard, the sharp blast of the warning whistle, the thunder of great wheels upon the river's edge, feeling, as we have felt, the mystery of night-time and of April, the huge impending pres-ence, the wild and secret promise, of the savage, lonely, ever-lasting earth, finding, as we have found, no doors to enter, and being torn, as we were torn, by the thorn of spring, the sharp, the wordless cry, did they not carry—these young men of the past, Garfield, Arthur, Harrison, and Hayes—even as we have carried, within their little tenements of bone, blood, sinew, sweat, and agony, the intolerable burden of all the pain, joy, hope and savage hunger that a man can suffer, that the world can know?

Were they not lost? Were they not lost, as all of us have been who have known youth and hunger in this land, and who have waited lean and mad and lonely in the night, and who have found no goal, no wall, no dwelling, and no door? .

The years flow by like water, and one day it is spring again. Shall we ever ride out of the gates of the East again, as we did once at morning, and seek again, as we did then, new lands, the promise of the war, and glory, joy, and triumph, and a shining city?

O youth, still wounded, living, feeling with a woe unutterable, still grieving with a grief intolerable, still thirsting with a thirst unquenchable—where are we to seek? For the wild tempest breaks above us, the wild fury beats about us, the wild hunger feeds upon us—and we are houseless, doorless, unassuaged, and driven on forever; and our brains are mad, our hearts are wild and wordless, and we cannot speak.

Wash

WILLIAM FAULKNER

Sutpen stood above the pallet bed on which the mother and child lay. Between the shrunken planking of the wall the early sunlight fell in long pencil strokes, breaking upon his straddled legs and upon the riding whip in his hand, and lay across the still shape of the mother, who lay looking up at him from still, inscrutable, sullen eyes, the child at her side wrapped in a piece of dingy though clean cloth. Behind them an old Negro woman squatted beside the rough hearth where a meager fire smoldered.

"Well, Milly," Sutpen said, "too bad you're not a mare. Then I could give you a decent stall in the stable."

Still the girl on the pallet did not move. She merely continued to look up at him without expression, with a young, sullen, inscrutable face still pale from recent travail. Sutpen moved, bringing into the splintered pencils of sunlight the face of a man of sixty. He said quietly to the squatting Negress, "Griselda foaled this morning."

"Horse or mare?" the Negress said.

"A horse. A damned fine colt. . . . What's this?" He indicated the pallet with the hand which held the whip.

"That un's a mare, I reckon."

"Hah," Sutpen said. "A damned fine colt. Going to be the spit and image of old Rob Roy when I rode him North in '61. Do you remember?"

"Yes, Marster."

"Hah." He glanced back towards the pallet. None could have said if the girl still watched him or not. Again his whip hand indicated the pallet. "Do whatever they need with whatever we've got to do it with." He went out, passing out the crazy doorway and stepping down into the rank weeds (there yet leaned rusting against the corner of the porch the scythe which Wash had borrowed from him three months ago to cut them with) where his horse waited, where Wash stood holding the reins.

When Colonel Sutpen rode away to fight the Yankees, Wash did not go. "I'm looking after the Kernel's place and niggers," he would tell all who asked him and some who had not asked— a gaunt, malaria-ridden man with pale, questioning eyes, who looked about thirty-five, though it was known that he had not only a daughter but an eight-year-old granddaughter as well. This was a lie, as most of them—the few remaining men between eighteen and fifty—to whom he told it, knew, though there were some who believed that he himself really believed it, though even these believed that he had better sense than to put it to the test with Mrs. Sutpen or the Sutpen slaves. Knew better or was just too lazy and shiftless to try it, they said, knowing that his sole connection with the Sutpen plantation lay in the fact that for years now Colonel Sutpen had allowed him to squat in a crazy shack on a slough in the river bottom on the Sutpen place, which Sutpen had built for a fishing lodge in his bachelor days and which had since fallen in dilapidation from disuse, so that now it looked like an aged or sick wild beast crawled terrifically there to drink in the act of dying.

The Sutpen slaves themselves heard of his statement. They laughed. It was not the first time they had laughed at him, calling him white trash behind his back. They began to ask him themselves, in groups, meeting him in the faint road which led up from the slough and the old fish camp, "Why ain't you at de war, white man?"

Pausing, he would look about the ring of black faces and white eyes and teeth behind which derision lurked. "Because I got a daughter and family to keep," he said. "Git out of my road, niggers."

"Niggers?" they repeated; "niggers?" laughing now. "Who him, calling us niggers?"

"Yes," he said. "I ain't got no niggers to look after my folks if I was gone."

"Nor nothing else but dat shack down yon dat Cunnel wouldn't *let* none of us live in."

"Now he cursed them; sometimes he rushed at them, snatching up a stick from the ground while they scattered before him, yet seeming to surround him still with that black laughing, derisive, evasive, inescapable, leaving him panting and impotent and raging. Once it happened in the very back yard of the big house itself. This was after bitter news had come down from the Tennessee mountains and from Vicksburg, and Sherman had passed through the plantation, and most of the Negroes had followed him. Almost everything else had gone with the Federal troops,

and Mrs. Sutpen had sent word to Wash that he could have the
scuppernongs ripening in the arbor in the back yard. This time
it was a house servant, one of the few Negroes who remained;
this time the Negress had to retreat up the kitchen steps, where
she turned. "Stop right dar, white man. Stop right whar you is.
You ain't never crossed dese steps whilst Cunnel here, and you
ain't ghy' do hit now."

This was true. But there was this of a kind of pride: he had
never tried to enter the big house, even though he believed that
if he had, Sutpen would have received him, permitted him.
"But I ain't going to give no black nigger the chance to tell me
I can't go nowhere," he said to himself. "I ain't even going to
give Kernel the chance to have to cuss a nigger on my account."
This, though he and Sutpen had spent more than one afternoon
together on those rare Sundays when there would be no company in the house. Perhaps his mind knew that it was because
Sutpen had nothing else to do, being a man who could not bear
his own company. Yet the fact remained that the two of them
would spend whole afternoons in the scuppernong arbor, Sutpen
in the hammock and Wash squatting against a post, a pail of
cistern water between them, taking drink for drink from the
same demijohn. Meanwhile on weekdays he would see the fine
figure of the man—they were the same age almost to a day,
though neither of them (perhaps because Wash had a grand-
child while Sutpen's son was a youth in school) ever thought
of himself as being so—on the fine figure of the black stallion,
galloping about the plantation. For that moment his heart
would be quiet and proud. It would seem to him that that
world in which Negroes, whom the Bible told him had been
created and cursed by God to be brute and vassal to all men of
white skin, were better found and housed and even clothed
than he and his; that world in which he sensed always about
him mocking echoes of black laughter was but a dream and an
illusion, and that the actual world was this one across which his
own lonely apotheosis seemed to gallop on the black thorough-
bred, thinking how the Book said also that all men were created

in the image of God and hence all men made the same image in God's eyes at least; so that he could say, as though speaking of himself, "A fine proud man. If God Himself was to come down and ride the natural earth, that's what He would aim to look like."

Sutpen returned in 1865, on the black stallion. He seemed to have aged ten years. His son had been killed in action the same winter in which his wife had died. He returned with his citation for gallantry from the hand of General Lee to a ruined plantation, where for a year now his daughter had subsisted partially on the meager bounty of the man to whom fifteen years ago he had granted permission to live in that tumbledown fishing camp whose very existence he had at the time forgotten. Wash was there to meet him, unchanged: still gaunt, still ageless, with his pale, questioning gaze, his air diffident, a little servile, a little familiar. "Well, Kernel," Wash said, "they kilt us but they ain't whupped us yit, air they?"

That was the tenor of their conversation for the next five years. It was inferior whisky which they drank now together from a stoneware jug, and it was not in the scuppernong arbor. It was in the rear of the little store which Sutpen managed to set up on the highroad: a frame shelved room where, with Wash for clerk and porter, he dispensed kerosene and staple foodstuffs and stale gaudy candy and cheap beads and ribbons to Negroes or poor whites of Wash's own kind, who came afoot or on gaunt mules to haggle tediously for dimes and quarters with a man who at one time could gallop (the black stallion was still alive; the stable in which his jealous get lived was in better repair than the house where the master himself lived) for ten miles across his own fertile land and who had led troops gallantly in battle; until Sutpen in fury would empty the store, close and lock the doors from the inside. Then he and Wash would repair to the rear and the jug. But the talk would not be quiet now, as when Sutpen lay in the hammock, delivering an arrogant monologue while Wash squatted guffawing against his post. They both sat now, though Sutpen had the single chair while Wash used whatever box or keg was handy, and even this for just a little while, because soon Sutpen would reach that stage of impotent and furious undefeat in which he would rise, swaying and plunging, and declare again that he would take his pistol and the black stallion and ride single-handed into Washington and kill Lincoln, dead now, and Sherman, now a private citizen. "Kill them!" he would shout. "Shoot them down like the dogs they are—"

"Sho, Kernel; sho, Kernel," Wash would say, catching Sutpen as he fell. Then he would commandeer the first passing wagon or, lacking that, he would walk the mile to the nearest neighbor and borrow one and return and carry Sutpen home. He entered the house now. He had been doing so for a long time, taking Sutpen home in whatever borrowed wagon might be, talking him into locomotion with cajoling murmurs as though he were a horse, a stallion himself. The daughter would meet them and hold open the door without a word. He would carry his burden through the once white formal entrance, surmounted by a fanlight imported piece by piece from Europe and with a board now nailed over a missing pane, across a velvet carpet from which all nap was now gone, and up a formal stairs, now but a fading ghost of bare boards between two strips of fading paint, and into the bedroom. It would be dusk by now, and he would let his burden sprawl onto the bed and undress it and then he would sit quietly in a chair beside. After a time the daughter would come to the door. "We're all right now," he would tell her. "Don't you worry none, Miss Judith."

Then it would become dark, and after a while he would lie down on the floor beside the bed, though not to sleep, because after a time—sometimes before midnight—the man on the bed would stir and groan and then speak. "Wash?"

"Hyer I am, Kernel. You go back to sleep. We ain't whupped yit, air we? Me and you kin do hit."

Even then he had already seen the ribbon about his granddaughter's waist. She was now fifteen, already mature, after the early way of her kind. He knew where the ribbon came from;

he had been seeing it and its kind daily for three years, even if she had lied about where she got it, which she did not, at once bold, sullen, and fearful. "Sho now," he said. "Ef Kernel wants to give hit to you, I hope you minded to thank him."

His heart was quiet, even when he saw the dress, watching her secret, defiant, frightened face when she told him that Miss Judith, the daughter, had helped her to make it. But he was quite grave when he approached Sutpen after they closed the store that afternoon, following the other to the rear.

"Get the jug," Sutpen directed.

"Wait," Wash said. "Not yit for a minute."

Neither did Sutpen deny the dress. "What about it?" he said.

But Wash met his arrogant stare; he spoke quietly. "I've knowed you for going on twenty years. I ain't never yit denied to do what you told me to do. And I'm a man nigh sixty. And she ain't nothing but a fifteen-year-old gal."

"Meaning that I'd harm a girl? I, a man as old as you are?"

"If you was ara other man, I'd say you was as old as me. And old or no old, I wouldn't let her keep that dress nor nothing else that come from your hand. But you are different."

"How different?" But Wash merely looked at him with his pale, questioning, sober eyes. "So that's why you are afraid of me?"

Now Wash's gaze no longer questioned. It was tranquil, serene. "I ain't afraid. Because you air brave. It ain't that you were a brave man at one minute or day of your life and got a paper to show hit from General Lee. But you air brave, the same as you air alive and breathing. That's where hit's different. Hit don't need no ticket from nobody to tell me that. And I know that whatever you handle or tech, whether hit's a regiment of men or a ignorant gal or just a hound dog, that you will make hit right."

Now it was Sutpen who looked away, turning suddenly, brusquely. "Get the jug," he said sharply.

"Sho, Kernel," Wash said.

So on that Sunday dawn two years later, having watched the Negro midwife, which he had walked three miles to fetch, enter the crazy door beyond which his granddaughter lay wailing, his heart was still quiet though concerned. He knew what they had been saying—the Negroes in cabins about the land, the white men who loafed all day long about the store, watching quietly the three of them: Sutpen, himself, his granddaughter with her air of brazen and shrinking defiance as her condition became daily more and more obvious, like three actors that came and went upon a stage. "I know what they say to one another," he thought. "I can almost hyear them: *Wash Jones has fixed old Sutpen at last. Hit taken him twenty years, but he has done hit at last.*"

It would be dawn after a while, though not yet. From the house, where the lamp shone dim beyond the warped doorframe, his granddaughter's voice came steadily as though run by a clock, while thinking went slowly and terrifically, fumbling, involved somehow with a sound of galloping hooves, until there broke suddenly free in mid-gallop the fine proud figure of the man on the fine proud stallion, galloping; and then that at which thinking fumbled, broke free too and quite clear, not in justification nor even explanation, but as the apotheosis, lonely, explicable, beyond all fouling by human touch: "He is bigger than all them Yankees that kilt his son and his wife and taken his niggers and ruined his land, bigger than this hyer durn country that he fit for and that has denied him into keeping a little country store; bigger than the denial which hit helt to his lips like the bitter cup in the Book. And how could I have lived this nigh to him for twenty years without being teched and changed by him? Maybe I ain't as big as him and maybe I ain't done none of the galloping. But at least I done been drug along. Me and him kin do hit, if so be he will show me what he aims for me to do."

Then it was dawn. Suddenly he could see the house, and the old Negress in the door looking at him. Then he realized that his granddaughter's voice had ceased. "It's a girl," the Negress said. "You can go tell him if you want to." She reëntered the house.

"A girl," he repeated; "a girl"; in astonishment, hearing the galloping hooves, seeing the proud galloping figure emerge again. He seemed to watch it pass, galloping through avatars which marked the accumulation of years, time, to the climax where it galloped beneath a brandished saber and a shot-torn flag rushing down a sky in color like thunderous sulphur, thinking for the first time in his life that perhaps Sutpen was an old man like himself. "Gittin a gal," he thought in that astonishment; then he thought with the pleased surprise of a child: "Yes, sir. Be dawg if I ain't lived to be a great-grandpaw after all."

He entered the house. He moved clumsily, on tiptoe, as if he no longer lived there, as if the infant which had just drawn breath and cried in light had dispossessed him, be it of his own blood too though it might. But even above the pallet he could see little save the blur of his granddaughter's exhausted face. Then the Negress squatting at the hearth spoke, "You better gawn tell him if you going to. Hit's daylight now."

But this was not necessary. He had no more than turned the corner of the porch where the scythe leaned which he had borrowed three months ago to clear away the weeds through which he walked, when Sutpen himself rode up on the old stallion. He did not wonder how Sutpen had got the word. He took it for granted that this was what had brought the other out at this hour on Sunday morning, and he stood while the other dismounted, and he took the reins from Sutpen's hand, an expression on his gaunt face almost imbecile with a kind of weary triumph, saying, "Hit's a gal, Kernel. I be dawg if you ain't as old as I am—" until Sutpen passed him and entered the house. He stood there with the reins in his hand and heard Sutpen cross the floor to the pallet. He heard what Sutpen said, and something seemed to stop dead in him before going on.

The sun was now up, the swift sun of Mississippi latitudes, and it seemed to him that he stood beneath a strange sky, in a strange scene, familiar only as things are familiar in dreams, like the dreams of falling to one who has never climbed. "I kain't have heard what I thought I heard," he thought quietly. "I know I kain't." Yet the voice, the familiar voice which had said the words was still speaking, talking now to the old Negress about a colt foaled that morning. "That's why he was up so early," he thought. "That was hit. Hit ain't me and mine. Hit ain't even hisn that got him outen bed."

Sutpen emerged. He descended into the weeds, moving with that heavy deliberation which would have been haste when he was younger. He had not yet looked full at Wash. He said, "Dicey will stay and tend to her. You better—" Then he seemed to see Wash facing him and paused. "What?" he said.

"You said—" To his own ears Wash's voice sounded flat and ducklike, like a deaf man's. "You said if she was a mare, you could give her a good stall in the stable."

"Well?" Sutpen said. His eyes widened and narrowed, almost like a man's fists flexing and shutting, as Wash began to advance towards him, stooping a little. Very astonishment kept Sutpen still for the moment, watching that man whom in twenty years he had no more known to make any motion save at command than he had the horse which he rode. Again his eyes narrowed and widened; without moving he seemed to rear suddenly upright. "Stand back," he said suddenly and sharply. "Don't you touch me."

"I'm going to tech you, Kernel," Wash said in that flat, quiet, almost soft voice, advancing.

Sutpen raised the hand which held the riding whip; the old Negress peered around the crazy door with her black gargoyle face of a worn gnome. "Stand back, Wash," Sutpen said. Then he struck. The old Negress leaped down into the weeds with the agility of a goat and fled. Sutpen slashed Wash again across the face with the whip, striking him to his knees. When Wash rose and advanced once more he held in his hands the scythe which he had borrowed from Sutpen three months ago and which Sutpen would never need again.

When he reëntered the house his granddaughter stirred on the pallet bed and called his name fretfully. "What was that?" she said.

"What was what, honey?"

"That ere racket out there."

" 'Twarn't nothing," he said gently. He knelt and touched her hot forehead clumsily. "Do you want ara thing?"

"I want a sup of water," she said querulously. "I been laying here wanting a sup of water a long time, but don't nobody care enough to pay me no mind."

"Sho now," he said soothingly. He rose stiffly and fetched the dipper of water and raised her head to drink and laid her back and watched her turn to the child with an absolutely stone-like face. But a moment later he saw that she was crying quietly. "Now, now," he said, "I wouldn't do that. Old Dicey says hit's a right fine gal. Hit's all right now. Hit's all over now. Hit ain't no need to cry now."

But she continued to cry quietly, almost sullenly, and he rose again and stood uncomfortably above the pallet for a time, thinking as he had thought when his own wife lay so and then his daughter in turn: "Women. Hit's a mystry to me. They seem to want em, and yit when they git em they cry about hit. Hit's a mystry to me. To ara man." Then he moved away and drew a chair up to the window and sat down.

Through all that long, bright, sunny forenoon he sat at the window, waiting. Now and then he rose and tiptoed to the pallet. But his granddaughter slept now, her face sullen and calm and weary, the child in the crook of her arm. Then he returned to the chair and sat again, waiting, wondering why it took them so long, until he remembered that is was Sunday. He was sitting there at mid-afternoon when a half-grown white boy came around the corner of the house upon the body and gave a choked cry and looked up and glared for a mesmerized instant at Wash in the window before he turned and fled. Then Wash rose and tiptoed again to the pallet.

The granddaughter was awake now, wakened perhaps by the boy's cry without hearing it. "Milly," he said, "air you hungry?" She didn't answer, turning her face away. He built up the fire on the hearth and cooked the food which he had brought home the day before: fatback it was, and cold corn pone; he poured water into the stale coffee pot and heated it. But she would not eat when he carried the plate to her, so he ate himself, quietly, alone, and left the dishes as they were and returned to the window.

Now he seemed to sense, feel, the men who would be gathering with horses and guns and dogs—the curious, and the vengeful: men of Sutpen's own kind, who had made the company about Sutpen's table in the time when Wash himself had yet to approach nearer to the house than the scuppernong arbor—men who had also shown the lesser ones how to fight in battle, who maybe also had signed papers from the generals saying that they were among the first of the brave; who had also galloped in the old days arrogant and proud on the fine horses across the fine plantations—symbols also of admiration and hope; instruments too of despair and grief.

That was whom they would expect him to run from. It seemed to him that he had no more to run from than he had to run to. If he ran, he would merely be fleeing one set of bragging and evil shadows for another just like them, since they were all of a kind throughout all the earth which he knew, and he was old, too old to flee far even if he were to flee. He could never escape them, no matter how much or how far he ran: a man going on sixty could not run that far. Not far enough to escape beyond the boundaries of earth where such men lived, set the order and the rule of living. It seemed to him that he now saw for the first time, after five years, how it was that Yankees or any other living armies had managed to whip them: the gallant, the proud, the brave; the acknowledged and chosen best among them all to carry courage and honor and pride. Maybe if he had gone to the war with them he would have discovered them sooner. But if he had discovered them sooner, what would he have done with his life since? How could he have borne to remember for five years what his life had been before?

Now it was getting toward sunset. The child had been crying; when he went to the pallet he saw his granddaughter nursing it, her face still bemused, sullen, inscrutable. "Air you hungry yit?" he said.

"I don't want nothing."

"You ought to eat."

This time she did not answer at all, looking down at the child. He returned to his chair and found that the sun had set. "Hit kain't be much longer," he thought. He could feel them quite near now, the curious and the vengeful. He could even seem to hear what they were saying about him, the undercurrent of believing beyond the immediate fury: *Old Wash Jones he come a tumble at last. He thought he had Sutpen, but Sutpen fooled him. He thought he had Kernel where he would have to marry the gal or pay up. And Kernel refused.* "But I never expected that, Kernel!" he cried aloud, catching himself at the sound of his own voice, glancing quickly back to find his granddaughter watching him.

"Who you talking to now?" she said.

"Hit ain't nothing. I was just thinking and talked out before I knowed hit."

Her face was becoming indistinct again, again a sullen blur in the twilight. "I reckon so. I reckon you'll have to holler louder than that before he'll hear you, up yonder at that house. And I reckon you'll need to do more than holler before you get him down here too."

"Sho now," he said. "Don't you worry none." But already thinking was going smoothly on: "You know I never. You know how I ain't never expected or asked nothing from ara living man but what I expected from you. And I never asked that. I didn't think hit would need. I said, *I don't need to. What need has a fellow like Wash Jones to question or doubt the man that General Lee himself says in a handwrote ticket that he was brave? Brave,*" he thought. "Better if nara one of them had never rid back home in '65"; thinking *Better if his kind and mine too had never drawn the breath of life on this earth. Better that all who remain of us be blasted from the face of earth than that another Wash Jones should see his whole life shredded from him and shrivel away like a dried shuck thrown onto the fire.*

He ceased, became still. He heard the horses, suddenly and plainly; presently he saw the lantern and the movement of men, the glint of gun barrels, in its moving light. Yet he did not stir. It was quite dark now, and he listened to the voices and the sounds of underbrush as they surrounded the house. The lantern itself came on; its light fell upon the quiet body in the weeds and stopped, the horses tall and shadowy. A man descended and stooped in the lantern light, above the body. He held a pistol; he rose and faced the house. "Jones," he said.

"I'm here," Wash said quietly from the window. "That you, Major?"

"Come out."

"Sho," he said quietly. "I just want to see to my grand-daughter."

"We'll see to her. Come on out."

"Sho, Major. Just a minute."

"Show a light. Light your lamp."

"Sho. In just a minute." They could hear his voice retreat into the house, though they could not see him as he went swiftly to the crack in the chimney where he kept the butcher knife: the one thing in his slovenly life and house in which he took pride, since it was razor sharp. He approached the pallet, his grand-daughter's voice:

"Who is it? Light the lamp, grandpaw."

"Hit won't need no light, honey. Hit won't take but a min-ute," he said, kneeling, fumbling toward her voice, whispering now. "Where air you?"

"Right here," she said fretfully. "Where would I be? What is . . ." His hand touched her face. "What is . . . Grandpaw! Grand. . . ."

"Jones!" the sheriff said. "Come out of there!"

"In just a minute, Major," he said. Now he rose and moved swiftly. He knew where in the dark the can of kerosene was, just as he knew that it was full, since it was not two days ago that he had filled it at the store and held it there until he got a ride home with it, since the five gallons were heavy. There were still coals on the hearth; besides, the crazy building itself was like tinder: the coals, the hearth, the walls exploding in a single blue glare. Against it the waiting men saw him in a wild instant springing toward them with the lifted scythe before the horses reared and whirled. They checked the horses and turned them back toward the glare, yet still in wild relief against it the gaunt figure ran toward them with the lifted scythe.

"Jones!" the sheriff shouted; "stop! Stop, or I'll shoot. Jones! *Jones!*" Yet still the gaunt, furious figure came on against the glare and roar of the flames. With the scythe lifted, it bore down upon them, upon the wild glaring eyes of the horses and the swinging glints of gun barrels, without any cry, any sound.

POETRY

EDWIN ARLINGTON ROBINSON

Credo

I cannot find my way: there is no star
In all the shrouded heavens anywhere;
And there is not a whisper in the air
Of any living voice but one so far
That I can hear it only as a bar
Of lost, imperial music, played when fair
And angel fingers wove, and unaware,
Dead leaves to garlands where no roses are.

No, there is not a glimmer, nor a call,
For one that welcomes, welcomes when he fears,
The black and awful chaos of the night;
For through it all—above, beyond it all—
I know the far-sent message of the years,
I feel the coming glory of the Light.

Mr. Flood's Party

Old Eben Flood, climbing alone one night
Over the hill between the town below
And the forsaken upland hermitage
That held as much as he should ever know
On earth again of home, paused warily.

The road was his with not a native near;
And Eben, having leisure, said aloud,
For no man else in Tilbury Town to hear:

"Well, Mr. Flood, we have the harvest moon
Again, and we may not have many more;   10
The bird is on the wing, the poet says,
And you and I have said it here before.
Drink to the bird." He raised up to the light
The jug that he had gone so far to fill,
And answered huskily: "Well, Mr. Flood,
Since you propose it, I believe I will."

Alone, as if enduring to the end
A valiant armor of scarred hopes outworn,
He stood there in the middle of the road
Like Roland's ghost winding a silent horn.   20
Below him, in the town among the trees,
Where friends of other days had honored him,
A phantom salutation of the dead
Rang thinly till old Eben's eyes were dim.

Then, as a mother lays her sleeping child
Down tenderly, fearing it may awake,
He set the jug down slowly at his feet
With trembling care, knowing that most things break;
And only when assured that on firm earth
It stood, as the uncertain lives of men   30
Assuredly did not, he paced away,
And with his hand extended paused again:

"Well, Mr. Flood, we have not met like this
In a long time; and many a change has come
To both of us, I fear, since last it was
We had a drop together. Welcome home!"
Convivially returning with himself,
Again he raised the jug up to the light;

And with an acquiescent quaver said:
"Well, Mr. Flood, if you insist, I might.

"Only a very little, Mr. Flood—
For auld lang syne. No more, sir; that will do."
So, for the time, apparently it did,
And Eben evidently thought so too;
For soon amid the silver loneliness
Of night he lifted up his voice and sang,
Secure, with only two moons listening,
Until the whole harmonious landscape rang—
"For auld lang syne." The weary throat gave out,
The last word wavered; and the song being done,   50
He raised again the jug regretfully
And shook his head, and was again alone.
There was not much that was ahead of him,
And there was nothing in the town below—
Where strangers would have shut the many doors
That many friends had opened long ago.

Eros Turannos

She fears him, and will always ask
   What fated her to choose him;
She meets in his engaging mask
   All reasons to refuse him;
But what she meets and what she fears
Are less than are the downward years,
Drawn slowly to the foamless weirs
   Of age, were she to lose him.

Between a blurred sagacity
   That once had power to sound him,   10

And Love, that will not let him be
  The Judas that she found him,
Her pride assuages her almost,
As if it were alone the cost.—
He sees that he will not be lost,
  And waits and looks around him.

A sense of ocean and old trees
  Envelops and allures him;
Tradition, touching all he sees,
  Beguiles and reassures him;   20
And all her doubts of what he says
Are dimmed with what she knows of days—
Till even prejudice delays
  And fades, and she secures him.

The falling leaf inaugurates
  The reign of her confusion;
The pounding wave reverberates
  The dirge of her illusion;
And home, where passion lived and died,
Becomes a place where she can hide,   30
While all the town and harbour side
  Vibrate with her seclusion.

We tell you, tapping on our brows,
  The story as it should be—
As if the story of a house
  Were told, or ever could be;
We'll have no kindly veil between
Her visions and those we have seen—
As if we guessed what hers have been,
  Or what they are or would be.   40

Meanwhile we do no harm; for they
  That with a god have striven,
Not hearing much of what we say,

Take what the god has given;
Though like waves breaking it may be,
Or like a changed familiar tree,
Or like a stairway to the sea
  Where down the blind are driven.

EZRA POUND

Hugh Selwyn Mauberley

(LIFE AND CONTACTS)

"VOCAT AESTUS IN UMBRAM"
                    Nemesianus, Ec. IV

I

E. P. ODE POUR L'ELECTION DE SON
SEPULCHRE

For three years, out of key with his time,
He strove to resuscitate the dead art
Of poetry; to maintain "the sublime"
In the old sense. Wrong from the start—

No hardly, but seeing he had been born
In a half savage country, out of date;
Bent resolutely on wringing lilies from the acorn;
Capaneus; trout for factitious bait;

Ἴδμεν γάρ τοι πάνζ', ὅσ' ἐνὶ Τροίη[1]
Caught in the unstopped ear;   10
Giving the rocks small lee-way
The chopped seas held him, therefore, that year.

All of Pound's poems reprinted here are from *Ezra Pound: Collected Poems*
by Ezra Pound; copyright, 1926, 1934, 1937, 1940, 1948, 1949, by Ezra
Pound. Used by permission of the publishers, New Directions.
[1] "For we know all the things that are in Troy"

His true Penelope was Flaubert,
He fished by obstinate isles;
Observed the elegance of Circe's hair
Rather than the mottoes on sun-dials.

Unaffected by "the march of events,"
He passed from men's memory in *l'an trentiesme*
De son eage;[2] the case presents
No adjunct to the Muses' diadem.   20

II

The age demanded an image
Of its accelerated grimace,
Something for the modern stage,
Not, at any rate, an Attic grace;

Not, not certainly, the obscure reveries
Of the inward gaze;
Better mendacities
Than the classics in paraphrase!

The "age demanded" chiefly a mould in plaster,
Made with no loss of time,   30
A prose kinema, not, not assuredly, alabaster
Or the "sculpture" of rhyme.

III

The tea-rose tea-gown, etc.
Supplants the mousseline of Cos,
The pianola "replaces"
Sappho's barbitos.

Christ follows Dionysus,
Phallic and ambrosial

---

[2] "In the thirtieth year of his age"

Made way for macerations;
Caliban casts out Ariel.   40

All things are a flowing,
Sage Heracleitus says;
But a tawdry cheapness
Shall outlast our days.

Even the Christian beauty
Defects—after Samothrace;
We see τὸ καλὸν[3]
Decreed in the market place.

Faun's flesh is not to us,
Nor the saint's vision.   50
We have the press for wafer;
Franchise for circumcision.

All men, in law, are equals.
Free of Pisistratus,
We choose a knave or an eunuch
To rule over us.

O bright Apollo,
τίν' ἄνδρα, τίν' ἤρωα, τίνα θεὸν,[4]
What god, man, or hero
Shall I place a tin wreath upon!   60

IV

These fought in any case,
and some believing,
                    pro domo,[5] in any case . . .

_____

[3] the beautiful
[4] "What man, what hero, what god"
[5] "For home"

Some quick to arm,
some for adventure,
some from fear of weakness,
some from fear of censure,
some for love of slaughter, in imagination,
learning later . . .
some in fear, learning love of slaughter;

Died some, pro patria,
                    non "dulce" non "et decor" [6] . . .   70
walked eye-deep in hell
believing in old men's lies, then unbelieving
came home, home to a lie,
home to many deceits,
home to old lies and new infamy;
usury age-old and age-thick
and liars in public places.
Daring as never before, wastage as never before.
Young blood and high blood,
fair cheeks, and fine bodies;   80

frankness as never before,

Frankness as never before,
disillusions as never told in the old days,
hysterias, trench confessions,
laughter out of dead bellies.

                              V

There died a myriad,
And of the best, among them,
For an old bitch gone in the teeth,
For a botched civilization,

---

[6] "For the homeland, not 'sweet' not 'and fitting' "

Charm, smiling at the good mouth,   90
Quick eyes gone under earth's lid,

For two gross of broken statues,
For a few thousand battered books.

Canto XLV

With *Usura*[1]
With usura hath no man a house of good stone
each block cut smooth and well fitting
that design might cover their face,
with usura
hath no man a painted paradise on his church wall
harpes et luthes[2]
or where virgin receiveth message
and halo projects from incision,
with usura   10
seeth no man Gonzaga his heirs and his concubines
no picture is made to endure nor to live with
but it is made to sell and sell quickly
with usura, sin against nature,
is thy bread ever more of stale rags
is thy bread dry as paper,
with no mountain wheat, no strong flour
with usura the line grows thick
with usura is no clear demarcation
and no man can find site for his dwelling.   20
Stone cutter is kept from his stone
weaver is kept from his loom
WITH USURA
wool comes not to market
sheep bringeth no gain with usura

---

[1] Money transactions at exorbitant rates of interest or profit.
[2] harps and lutes

Usura is a murrain, usura
blunteth the needle in the maid's hand
and stoppeth the spinner's cunning. Pietro Lombardo
Came not by usura
Duccio came not by usura   30
nor Pier della Francesca; Zuan Bellin' not by usura
nor was 'La Calunnia' painted.
Came not by usura Angelico; came not Ambrogio Praedis,
came no church of cut stone signed: *Adamo me fecit.*[3]
Not by usura St. Trophime
Not by usura Saint Hilaire,
Usura rusteth the chisel
It rusteth the craft and the craftsman
It gnaweth the thread in the loom
None learneth to weave gold in her pattern;   40
Azure hath a canker by usura; cramoisi is unbroidered
Emerald findeth no Memling
Usura slayeth the child in the womb
It stayeth the young man's courting
It hath brought palsey to bed, lyeth
between the young bride and her bridegroom

CONTRA NATURAM [4]

They have brought whores for Eleusis
Corpses are set to banquet
at behest of usura.

Na Audiart

Que be-m vols mal

NOTE: Anyone who has read anything of the troubadours knows well the
tale of Bertran of Born and My Lady Maent of Montaignac, and knows
also the song he made when she would none of him, the song wherein he,
seeking to find or make her equal, begs of each preëminent lady of Langue

---

[3] Adam made me
[4] Against nature

d'Oc some trait or some fair semblance: thus of Cembelins her "esgart amoros," to wit, her love-lit glance, of Aelis her speech free-running, of the Vicomtess of Chalais her throat and her two hands, at Roacoart of Anhes her hair golden as Iseult's; and even in this fashion of Lady Audiart "although she would that ill come unto him" he sought and praised the lineaments of the torse. And all this to make "Una dompna soiseubuda" a borrowed lady or as the Italians translated it "Una donna ideale."

Though thou well dost wish me ill
       Audiart, Audiart,
Where thy bodice laces start
As ivy fingers clutching through
Its crevices,
       Audiart, Audiart,
Stately, tall and lovely tender
Who shall render
       Audiart, Audiart,
Praises meet unto thy fashion?   10
Here a word kiss!
       Pass I on
Unto Lady "Miles-de-Ben,"
Having praised thy girdle's scope
How the stays ply back from it;
I breathe no hope
That thou shouldst . . .
       Nay no whit
Bespeak thyself for anything.
Just a word in thy praise, girl,   20
Just for the swirl
Thy satins make upon the stair,
'Cause never a flaw was there
Where thy torse and limbs are met
Though thou hate me, read it set
In rose and gold.
Or when the minstrel, tale half told,
Shall burst to lilting at the praise
       "Audiart, Audiart" . . .
Bertrans, master of his lays,   30

Bertrans of Aultaforte thy praise
Sets forth, and though thou hate me well,
Yea though thou wish me ill,
                Audiart, Audiart
Thy loveliness is here writ till,
                Audiart,
Oh, till thou come again.
And being bent and wrinkled, in a form
That hath no perfect limning, when the warm
Youth dew is cold   40
Upon thy hands, and thy old soul
Scorning a new, wry'd casement,
Churlish at seemed misplacement,
Finds the earth as bitter
As now seems it sweet,
Being so young and fair
As then only in dreams,
Being then young and wry'd,
Broken of ancient pride,
Thou shalt then soften,   50
Knowing, I know not how,
Thou wert once she
                Audiart, Audiart
For whose fairness one forgave
                Audiart,
Audiart
            Que be-m vols mal.

Erat Hora

"Thank you, whatever comes." And then she turned
And, as the ray of sun on hanging flowers
Fades when the wind hath lifted them aside,
Went swiftly from me. Nay, whatever comes
One hour was sunlit and the most high gods

May not make boast of any better thing
Than to have watched that hour as it passed.

The Garret

Come, let us pity those who are better off than we are.
Come, my friend, and remember
   that the rich have butlers and no friends,
And we have friends and no butlers.
Come, let us pity the married and the unmarried.

Dawn enters with little feet
   like a gilded Pavlova,
And I am near my desire.
Nor has life in it aught better
Than this hour of clear coolness,
   the hour of waking together.

Meditatio

When I carefully consider the curious habits of dogs
I am compelled to conclude
That man is the superior animal
When I consider the curious habits of man
I confess, my friend, I am puzzled.

Tame Cat

"It rests me to be among beautiful women.
Why should one always lie about such matters?
I repeat:
It rests me to converse with beautiful women
Even though we talk nothing but nonsense,

The purring of the invisible antennae
Is both stimulating and delightful."

CARL SANDBURG

Skyscraper

By day the skyscraper looms in the smoke and sun and has a
soul.

Prairie and valley, streets of the city, pour people into it and
they mingle among its twenty floors and are poured out
again back to the streets, prairies and valleys.

It is the men and women, boys and girls so poured in and out all
day that give the building a soul of dreams and thoughts
and memories.

(Dumped in the sea or fixed in a desert, who would care for the
building or speak its name or ask a policeman the way to
it?)

Elevators slide on their cables and tubes catch letters and par-
cels and iron pipes carry gas and water in and sewage out.

Wires climb with secrets, carry light and carry words, and tell
terrors and profits and loves—curses of men grappling plans
of business and questions of women in plots of love.

Hour by hour the caissons reach down to the rock of the earth
and hold the building to a turning planet.

Hour by hour the girders play as ribs and reach out and hold
together the stone walls and floors.

Hour by hour the hand of the mason and the stuff of the mortar
clinch the pieces and parts to the shape an architect voted.

Hour by hour the sun and the rain, the air and the rust, and the
press of time running into centuries, play on the building
inside and out and use it.

Men who sunk the pilings and mixed the mortar are laid in
graves where the wind whistles a wild song without words.

And so are men who strung the wires and fixed the pipes and
tubes and those who saw it rise floor by floor.

Souls of them all are here, even the hod carrier begging at back
doors hundreds of miles away and the bricklayer who went
to state's prison for shooting another man while drunk.

(One man fell from a girder and broke his neck at the end of a
straight plunge—he is here—his soul has gone into the
stones of the building.)

On the office doors from tier to tier—hundreds of names and
each name standing for a face written across with a dead
child, a passionate lover, a driving ambition for a million
dollar business or a lobster's ease of life.

Behind the signs on the doors they work and the walls tell nothing from room to room.

Ten-dollar-a-week stenographers take letters from corporation
officers, lawyers, efficiency engineers, and tons of letters go
bundled from the building to all ends of the earth.

Smiles and tears of each office girl go into the soul of the building just the same as the master-men who rule the building.

Hands of clocks turn to noon hours and each floor empties its
men and women who go away and eat and come back to
work.

Toward the end of the afternoon all work slackens and all jobs
go slower as the people feel day closing on them.

One by one the floors are emptied . . . The uniformed elevator men are gone. Pails clang . . . Scrubbers work, talking
foreign tongues. Broom and water and mop clean from the
floors human dust and spit, and machine grime of the day.

Spelled in electric fire on the roof are words telling miles of
houses and people where to buy a thing for money. The
sign speaks till midnight.

Darkness on the hallways. Voices echo. Silence holds . . .
Watchmen walk slow from floor to floor and try the doors.
Revolvers bulge from their hip pockets . . . Steel safes
stand in corners. Money is stacked in them.

A young watchman leans at a window and sees the lights of
barges butting their way across a harbor, nets of red and
white lanterns in a railroad yard, and a span of glooms
splashed with lines of white and blurs of crosses and clus-
ters over the sleeping city.

By night the skyscraper looms in the smoke and the stars and
has a soul.

From the Shore

A lone gray bird,
Dim-dipping, far-flying,
Alone in the shadows and grandeurs and tumults
Of night and the sea
And the stars and storms.

Out over the darkness it wavers and hovers,
Out into the gloom it swings and batters,
Out into the wind and the rain and the vast,
Out into the pit of a great black world,
Where fogs are at battle, sky-driven, sea-blown,
Love mist and rapture of flight,
Glories of chance and hazards of death
On its eager and palpitant wings.

Out into the deep of the great dark world,
Beyond the long borders where foam and drift
Of the sundering waves are lost and gone
On the tides that plunge and rear and crumble.

T. S. ELIOT

Gerontion

Thou hast nor youth nor age
But as it were an after dinner sleep
Dreaming of both.

Here I am, an old man in a dry month,
Being read to by a boy, waiting for rain.
I was neither at the hot gates
Nor fought in the warm rain
Nor knee deep in the salt marsh, heaving a cutlass,
Bitten by flies, fought.
My house is a decayed house,
And the jew squats on the window sill, the owner,
Spawned in some estaminet of Antwerp,
Blistered in Brussels, patched and peeled in London.   10
The goat coughs at night in the field overhead;
Rocks, moss, stonecrop, iron, merds.
The woman keeps the kitchen, makes tea,
Sneezes at evening, poking the peevish gutter.
                              I an old man,
A dull head among windy spaces.

Signs are taken for wonders. "We would see a sign!"
The word within a word, unable to speak a word,
Swaddled with darkness. In the juvescence of the year
Came Christ the tiger
In depraved May, dogwood and chestnut, flowering judas,   20
To be eaten, to be divided, to be drunk
Among whispers; by Mr. Silvero

With caressing hands, at Limoges
Who walked all night in the next room;

By Hakagawa, bowing among the Titians;
By Madame de Tornquist, in the dark room
Shifting the candles; Fräulein von Kulp
Who turned in the hall, one hand on the door. Vacant shuttles
Weave the wind. I have no ghosts,
An old man in a draughty house   30
Under a windy knob.

After such knowledge, what forgiveness? Think now
History has many cunning passages, contrived corridors
And issues, deceives with whispering ambitions,
Guides us by vanities. Think now
She gives when our attention is distracted
And what she gives, gives with such supple confusions
That the giving famishes the craving. Gives too late
What's not believed in, or if still believed,
In memory only, reconsidered passion. Gives too soon   40
Into weak hands, what's thought can be dispensed with
Till the refusal propagates a fear. Think
Neither fear nor courage saves us. Unnatural vices
Are fathered by our heroism. Virtues
Are forced upon us by our impudent crimes.
These tears are shaken from the wrath-bearing tree.
The tiger springs in the new year. Us he devours. Think at last
We have not reached conclusion, when I
Stiffen in a rented house. Think at last
I have not made this show purposelessly   50
And it is not by any concitation
Of the backward devils
I would meet you upon this honestly.
I that was near your heart was removed therefrom
To lose beauty in terror, terror in inquisition.
I have lost my passion: why should I need to keep it

Since what is kept must be adulterated?
I have lost my sight, smell, hearing, taste and touch:
How should I use them for your closer contact?

These with a thousand small deliberations   60
Protract the profit of their chilled delirium,
Excite the membrane, when the sense has cooled,
With pungent sauces, multiply variety
In a wilderness of mirrors. What will the spider do,
Suspend its operations, will the weevil
Delay? De Bailhache, Fresca, Mrs. Cammell, whirled
Beyond the circuit of the shuddering Bear
In fractured atoms. Gull against the wind, in the windy straits
Of Belle Isle, or running on the Horn,
White feathers in the snow, the Gulf claims,   70
And an old man driven by the Trades
To a sleepy corner.
                              Tenants of the house,
Thoughts of a dry brain in a dry season.

The Dry Salvages

(The Dry Salvages—presumably *les trois sauvages*—is a small group of
rocks, with a beacon, off the N.E. coast of Cape Ann, Massachusetts. *Salvages*
is pronounced to rhyme with *assuages*. *Groaner:* a whistling buoy.)

I

I do not know much about gods; but I think that the river
Is a strong brown god—sullen, untamed and intractable,
Patient to some degree, at first recognised as a frontier;
Useful, untrustworthy, as a conveyor of commerce;
Then only a problem confronting the builder of bridges.
The problem once solved, the brown god is almost forgotten
By the dwellers in cities—ever, however, implacable,

From *Four Quartets*, copyright, 1943, by T. S. Eliot. Reprinted by permission of Harcourt, Brace and Company, Inc.

Keeping his seasons and rages, destroyer, reminder
Of what men choose to forget. Unhonoured, unpropitiated
By worshippers of the machine, but waiting, watching and
    waiting.   10
His rhythm was present in the nursery bedroom,
In the rank ailanthus of the April dooryard,
In the smell of grapes on the autumn table,
And the evening circle in the winter gaslight.

The river is within us, the sea is all about us;
The sea is the land's edge also, the granite
Into which it reaches, the beaches where it tosses
Its hints of earlier and other creation:
The starfish, the hermit crab, the whale's backbone;
The pools where it offers to our curiosity   20
The more delicate algae and the sea anemone.
It tosses up our losses, the torn seine,
The shattered lobsterpot, the broken oar
And the gear of foreign dead men. The sea has many voices,
Many gods and many voices.
                        The salt is on the briar rose,
The fog is in the fir trees.
                The sea howl
And the sea yelp, are different voices
Often together heard; the whine in the rigging,
The menace and caress of wave that breaks on water,
The distant rote in the granite teeth,   30
And the wailing warning from the approaching headland
Are all sea voices, and the heaving groaner
Rounded homewards, and the seagull:
And under the oppression of the silent fog
The tolling bell
Measures time not our time, rung by the unhurried
Ground swell, a time
Older than the time of chronometers, older
Than time counted by anxious worried women

Lying awake, calculating the future,   40
Trying to unweave, unwind, unravel
And piece together the past and the future,
Between midnight and dawn, when the past is all deception,
The future futureless, before the morning watch
When time stops and time is never ending;
And the ground swell, that is and was from the beginning,
Clangs
The bell.

II

Where is there an end of it, the soundless wailing,
The silent withering of autumn flowers   50
Dropping their petals and remaining motionless;
Where is there an end to the drifting wreckage,
The prayer of the bone on the beach, the unprayable
Prayer at the calamitous annunciation?

There is no end, but addition: the trailing
Consequence of further days and hours,
While emotion takes to itself the emotionless
Years of living among the breakage
Of what was believed in as the most reliable—
And therefore the fittest for renunciation.   60

There is the final addition, the failing
Pride or resentment at failing powers,
The unattached devotion which might pass for devotionless,
In a drifting boat with a slow leakage,
The silent listening to the undeniable
Clamour of the bell of the last annunciation.

Where is the end of them, the fishermen sailing
Into the wind's tail, where the fog cowers?
We cannot think of a time that is oceanless
Or of an ocean not littered with wastage   70

Or of a future that is not liable
Like the past, to have no destination.

We have to think of them as forever bailing,
Setting and hauling, while the North East lowers
Over shallow banks unchanging and erosionless
Or drawing their money, drying sails at dockage;
Not as making a trip that will be unpayable
For a haul that will not bear examination.

There is no end of it, the voiceless wailing,
No end to the withering of withered flowers,   80
To the movement of pain that is painless and motionless,
To the drift of the sea and the drifting wreckage,
The bone's prayer to Death its God. Only the hardly, barely
    prayable
Prayer of the one Annunciation.

It seems, as one becomes older,
That the past has another pattern, and ceases to be a mere
    sequence—
Or even development: the latter a partial fallacy,
Encouraged by superficial notions of evolution,
Which becomes, in the popular mind, a means of disowning the
    past.
The moments of happiness—not the sense of well-being,   90
Fruition, fulfilment, security or affection,
Or even a very good dinner, but the sudden illumination—
We had the experience but missed the meaning,
And approach to the meaning restores the experience
In a different form, beyond any meaning
We can assign to happiness. I have said before
That the past experience revived in the meaning
Is not the experience of one life only
But of many generations—not forgetting
Something that is probably quite ineffable: 100

The backward look behind the assurance
Of recorded history, the backward half-look
Over the shoulder, towards the primitive terror.
Now, we come to discover that the moments of agony
(Whether, or not, due to misunderstanding,
Having hoped for the wrong things or dreaded the wrong things,
Is not in question) are likewise permanent
With such permanence as time has. We appreciate this better
In the agony of others, nearly experienced,
Involving ourselves, than in our own.   110
For our own past is covered by the currents of action,
But the torment of others remains an experience
Unqualified, unworn by subsequent attrition.
People change, and smile: but the agony abides.
Time the destroyer is time the preserver,
Like the river with its cargo of dead Negroes, cows and chicken
    coops,
The bitter apple and the bite in the apple.
And the ragged rock in the restless waters,
Waves wash over it, fogs conceal it;
On a halcyon day it is merely a monument,   120
In navigable weather it is always a seamark
To lay a course by: but in the sombre season
Or the sudden fury, is what it always was.

III

I sometimes wonder if that is what Krishna meant—
Among other things—or one way of putting the same thing:
That the future is a faded song, a Royal Rose or a lavender spray
Of wistful regret for those who are not yet here to regret,
Pressed between yellow leaves of a book that has never been
    opened.
And the way up is the way down, the way forward is the way
    back.
You cannot face it steadily, but this thing is sure,   130
That time is no healer: the patient is no longer here.

When the train starts, and the passengers are settled
To fruit, periodicals and business letters
(And those who saw them off have left the platform)
Their faces relax from grief into relief,
To the sleepy rhythm of a hundred hours.
Fare forward, travellers! not escaping from the past
Into different lives, or into any future;
You are not the same people who left that station
Or who will arrive at any terminus,   140
While the narrowing rails slide together behind you;
And on the deck of the drumming liner
Watching the furrow that widens behind you,
You shall not think "the past is finished"
Or "the future is before us." •
At nightfall, in the rigging and the aerial,
Is a voice descanting (though not to the ear,
The murmuring shell of time, and not in any language)
"Fare forward, you who think that you are voyaging;
You are not those who saw the harbour   150
Receding, or those who will disembark.
Here between the hither and the farther shore
While time is withdrawn, consider the future
And the past with an equal mind.
At the moment which is not of action or inaction
You can receive this: 'on whatever sphere of being
The mind of a man may be intent
At the time of death'—that is the one action
(And the time of death is every moment)
Which shall fructify in the lives of others: 160
And do not think of the fruit of action.
Fare forward.
                    O voyagers, O seamen,
You who come to port, and you whose bodies
Will suffer the trial and judgement of the sea,
Or whatever event, this is your real destination."

So Krishna, as when he admonished Arjuna
On the field of battle.
              Not fare well,
But fare forward, voyagers.

IV

Lady, whose shrine stands on the promontory,
Pray for all those who are in ships, those   170
Whose business has to do with fish, and
Those concerned with every lawful traffic
And those who conduct them.

Repeat a prayer also on behalf of
Women who have seen their sons or husbands
Setting forth, and not returning:
Figlia del tuo figlio,
Queen of Heaven.

Also pray for those who were in ships, and
Ended their voyage on the sand, in the sea's lips   180
Or in the dark throat which will not reject them
Or wherever cannot reach them the sound of the sea bell's
Perpetual angelus.

V

To communicate with Mars, converse with spirits,
To report the behaviour of the sea monster,
Describe the horoscope, haruspicate or scry,
Observe disease in signatures, evoke
Biography from the wrinkles of the palm
And tragedy from fingers; release omens
By sortilege, or tea leaves, riddle the inevitable   190
With playing cards, fiddle with pentagrams
Or barbituric acids, or dissect
The recurrent image into pre-conscious terrors—

To explore the womb, or tomb, or dreams; all these are usual
Pastimes and drugs, and features of the press:
And always will be, some of them especially
When there is distress of nations and perplexity
Whether on the shores of Asia, or in the Edgware Road.
Men's curiosity searches past and future
And clings to that dimension. But to apprehend   200
The point of intersection of the timeless
With time, is an occupation for the saint—
No occupation either, but something given
And taken, in a lifetime's death in love,
Ardour and selflessness and self-surrender.
For most of us, there is only the unattended
Moment, the moment in and out of time,
The distraction fit, lost in a shaft of sunlight,
The wild thyme unseen, or the winter lightning
Or the waterfall, or music heard so deeply   210
That it is not heard at all, but you are the music
While the music lasts. These are only hints and guesses,
Hints followed by guesses; and the rest
Is prayer, observance, discipline, thought and action.
The hint half guessed, the gift half understood, is Incarnation.
Here the impossible union
Of spheres of existence is actual,
Here the past and future
Are conquered, and reconciled,
Where action were otherwise movement   220
Of that which is only moved
And has in it no source of movement—
Driven by daemonic, chthonic
Powers. And right action is freedom
From past and future also.
For most of us, this is the aim
Never here to be realised;
Who are only undefeated
Because we have gone on trying;

We, content at the last   230
If our temporal reversion nourish
(Not too far from the yew-tree)
The life of significant soil.

ROBERT FROST

Home Burial

He saw her from the bottom of the stairs
Before she saw him. She was starting down,
Looking back over her shoulder at some fear.
She took a doubtful step and then undid it
To raise herself and look again. He spoke
Advancing toward her: 'What is it you see
From up there always—for I want to know.'
She turned and sank upon her skirts at that,
And her face changed from terrified to dull.
He said to gain time: 'What is it you see,'   10
Mounting until she cowered under him.
'I will find out now—you must tell me, dear.'
She, in her place, refused him any help
With the least stiffening of her neck and silence.
She let him look, sure that he wouldn't see,
Blind creature; and a while he didn't see.
But at last he murmured, 'Oh,' and again, 'Oh.'

'What is it—what?' she said.

                              'Just that I see.'

'You don't,' she challenged. 'Tell me what it is.'   20

ROBERT FROST

'The wonder is I didn't see at once.
I never noticed it from here before.
I must be wonted to it—that's the reason.
The little graveyard where my people are!
So small the window frames the whole of it.
Not so much larger than a bedroom, is it?
There are three stones of slate and one of marble,
Broad-shouldered little slabs there in the sunlight
On the sidehill. We haven't to mind *those*.
But I understand: it is not the stones,
But the child's mound—'

                              'Don't, don't, don't, don't,' she cried.

She withdrew shrinking from beneath his arm
That rested on the banister, and slid downstairs;
And turned on him with such a daunting look,
He said twce over before he knew himself:
'Can't a man speak of his own child he's lost?'

'Not you! Oh, where's my hat? Oh, I don't need it!
I must get out of here. I must get air.
I don't know rightly whether any man can.'

'Amy! Don't go to someone else this time.
Listen to me. I won't come down the stairs.'
He sat and fixed his chin between his fists.
'There's something I should like to ask you, dear.'

'You don't know how to ask it.'

                              'Help me, then.'

Her fingers moved the latch for all reply.

'My words are nearly always an offence.
I don't know how to speak of anything

So as to please you. But I might be taught   50
I should suppose. I can't say I see how.
A man must partly give up being a man
With women-folk. We could have some arrangement
By which I'd bind myself to keep hands off
Anything special you're a-mind to name.
Though I don't like such things 'twixt those that love.
Two that don't love can't live together without them.
But two that do can't live together with them.'
She moved the latch a little. 'Don't—don't go.
Don't carry it to someone else this time.   60
Tell me about it if it's something human.
Let me into your grief. I'm not so much
Unlike other folks as your standing there
Apart would make me out. Give me my chance.
I do think, though, you overdo it a little.
What was it brought you up to think it the thing
To take your mother-loss of a first child
So inconsolably—in the face of love.
You'd think his memory might be satisfied—'

'There you go sneering now!'   70

                      'I'm not, I'm not!
You make me angry. I'll come down to you.
God, what a woman! And it's come to this,
A man can't speak of his own child that's dead.'

'You can't because you don't know how to speak.
If you had any feelings, you that dug
With your own hand—how could you?—his little grave;
I saw you from that very window there,
Making the gravel leap and leap in air,
Leap up, like that, like that, and land so lightly   80
And roll back down the mound beside the hole.
I thought, Who is that man? I didn't know you.

And I crept down the stairs and up the stairs
To look again, and still your spade kept lifting.
Then you came in. I heard your rumbling voice
Out in the kitchen, and I don't know why,
But I went near to see with my own eyes.
You could sit there with the stains on your shoes
Of the fresh earth from your own baby's grave
And talk about your everyday concerns.   90
You had stood the spade up against the wall
Outside there in the entry, for I saw it.'

'I shall laugh the worst laugh I ever laughed.
I'm cursed. God, if I don't believe I'm cursed.'

'I can repeat the very words you were saying.
"Three foggy mornings and one rainy day
Will rot the best birch fence a man can build."
Think of it, talk like that at such a time!
What had how long it takes a birch to rot
To do with what was in the darkened parlour.   100
You *couldn't* care! The nearest friends can go
With anyone to death, comes so far short
They might as well not try to go at all.
No, from the time when one is sick to death,
One is alone, and he dies more alone.
Friends make pretence of following to the grave,
But before one is in it, their minds are turned
And making the best of their way back to life
And living people, and things they understand.
But the world's evil. I won't have grief so   110
If I can change it. Oh, I won't, I won't!'

'There, you have said it all and you feel better.
You won't go now. You're crying. Close the door.
The heart's gone out of it: why keep it up.
Amy! There's someone coming down the road!'

'*You*—oh, you think the talk is all. I must go—
Somewhere out of this house. How can I make you—'

'If—you—do!' She was opening the door wider.
'Where do you mean to go? First tell me that.
I'll follow and bring you back by force. I *will!*—'   120

After Apple-Picking

My long two-pointed ladder's sticking through a tree
Toward heaven still,
And there's a barrel that I didn't fill
Beside it, and there may be two or three
Apples I didn't pick upon some bough.
But I am done with apple-picking now.
Essence of winter sleep is on the night,
The scent of apples: I am drowsing off.
I cannot rub the strangeness from my sight
I got from looking through a pane of glass   10
I skimmed this morning from the drinking trough
And held against the world of hoary grass.
It melted, and I let it fall and break.
But I was well
Upon my way to sleep before it fell,
And I could tell
What form my dreaming was about to take.
Magnified apples appear and disappear
Stem end and blossom end,
And every fleck of russet showing clear.   20
My instep arch not only keeps the ache,
It keeps the pressure of a ladder-round.
I feel the ladder sway as the boughs bend.
And I keep hearing from the cellar bin
The rumbling sound

Of load on load of apples coming in.
For I have had too much
Of apple-picking: I am overtired
Of the great harvest I myself desired.
There were ten thousand thousand fruit to touch,   30
Cherish in hand, lift down, and not let fall.
For all
That struck the earth,
No matter if not bruised or spiked with stubble,
Went surely to the cider-apple heap
As of no worth.
One can see what will trouble
This sleep of mine, whatever sleep it is.
Were he not gone,
The woodchuck could say whether it's like his   40
Long sleep, as I describe its coming on,
Or just some human sleep.

Two Witches

I

THE WITCH OF COÖS

I staid the night for shelter at a farm
Behind the mountain, with a mother and son,
Two old-believers. They did all the talking.

MOTHER. Folks think a witch who has familiar spirits
She could call up to pass a winter evening,
But won't, should be burned at the stake or something.
Summoning spirits isn't 'Button, button,
Who's got the button,' I would have them know.

SON. Mother can make a common table rear
And kick with two legs like an army mule.   10

MOTHER. And when I've done it, what good have I done?
Rather than tip a table for you, let me
Tell you what Ralle the Sioux Control once told me.
He said the dead had souls, but when I asked him
How could that be—I thought the dead were souls,
He broke my trance. Don't that make you suspicious
That there's something the dead are keeping back?
Yes, there's something the dead are keeping back.

SON. You wouldn't want to tell him what we have
Up attic, mother?   20

MOTHER. Bones—a skeleton.

SON. But the headboard of mother's bed is pushed
Against the attic door: the door is nailed.
It's harmless. Mother hears it in the night
Halting perplexed behind the barrier
Of door and headboard. Where it wants to get
Is back into the cellar where it came from.

MOTHER. We'll never let them, will we, son! We'll never!

SON. It left the cellar forty years ago
And carried itself like a pile of dishes   30
Up one flight from the cellar to the kitchen,
Another from the kitchen to the bedroom,
Another from the bedroom to the attic,
Right past both father and mother, and neither stopped it.
Father had gone upstairs; mother was downstairs.
I was a baby: I don't know where I was.

MOTHER. The only fault my husband found with me—
I went to sleep before I went to bed,
Especially in winter when the bed
Might just as well be ice and the clothes snow.   40

The night the bones came up the cellar-stairs
Toffile had gone to bed alone and left me,
But left an open door to cool the room off
So as to sort of turn me out of it.
I was just coming to myself enough
To wonder where the cold was coming from,
When I heard Toffile upstairs in the bedroom
And thought I heard him downstairs in the cellar.
The board we had laid down to walk dry-shod on
When there was water in the cellar in spring   50
Struck the hard cellar bottom. And then someone
Began the stairs, two footsteps for each step,
The way a man with one leg and a crutch,
Or a little child, comes up. It wasn't Toffile:
It wasn't anyone who could be there.
The bulkhead double-doors were double-locked
And swollen tight and buried under snow.
The cellar windows were banked up with sawdust
And swollen tight and buried under snow.
It was the bones. I knew them—and good reason.   60
My first impulse was to get to the knob
And hold the door. But the bones didn't try
The door; they halted helpless on the landing,
Waiting for things to happen in their favor.
The faintest restless rustling ran all through them.
I never could have done the thing I did
If the wish hadn't been too strong in me
To see how they were mounted for this walk.
I had a vision of them put together
Not like a man, but like a chandelier.   70
So suddenly I flung the door wide on him.
A moment he stood balancing with emotion,
And all but lost himself. (A tongue of fire
Flashed out and licked along his upper teeth.
Smoke rolled inside the sockets of his eyes.)
Then he came at me with one hand outstretched,

The way he did in life once; but this time
I struck the hand off brittle on the floor,
And fell back from him on the floor myself.
The finger-pieces slid in all directions.   80
(Where did I see one of those pieces lately?
Hand me my button-box—it must be there.)
I sat up on the floor and shouted, 'Toffile,
It's coming up to you.' It had its choice
Of the door to the cellar or the hall.
It took the hall door for the novelty,
And set off briskly for so slow a thing,
Still going every which way in the joints, though,
So that it looked like lightning or a scribble,
From the slap I had just now given its hand.   90
I listened till it almost climbed the stairs
From the hall to the only finished bedroom,
Before I got up to do anything;
Then ran and shouted, 'Shut the bedroom door,
Toffile, for my sake!' 'Company?' he said,
'Don't make me get up; I'm too warm in bed.'
So lying forward weakly on the handrail
I pushed myself upstairs, and in the light
(The kitchen had been dark) I had to own
I could see nothing. 'Toffile, I don't see it.   100
It's with us in the room though. It's the bones.'
'What bones?' 'The cellar bones—out of the grave.'
That made him throw his bare legs out of bed
And sit up by me and take hold of me.
I wanted to put out the light and see
If I could see it, or else mow the room,
With our arms at the level of our knees,
And bring the chalk-pile down. 'I'll tell you what—
It's looking for another door to try.
The uncommonly deep snow has made him think   110
Of his old song, *The Wild Colonial Boy*,
He always used to sing along the tote-road.

He's after an open door to get out-doors.
Let's trap him with an open door up attic.'
Toffile agreed to that, and sure enough,
Almost the moment he was given an opening,
The steps began to climb the attic stairs.
I heard them. Toffile didn't seem to hear them.
'Quick!' I slammed to the door and held the knob.
'Toffile, get nails.' I made him nail the door shut,   120
And push the headboard of the bed against it.
Then we asked was there anything
Up attic that we'd ever want again.
The attic was less to us than the cellar.
If the bones liked the attic, let them have it.
Let them stay in the attic. When they sometimes
Come down the stairs at night and stand perplexed
Behind the door and headboard of the bed,
Brushing their chalky skull with chalky fingers,
With sounds like the dry rattling of a shutter,   130
That's what I sit up in the dark to say—
To no one any more since Toffile died.
Let them stay in the attic since they went there.
I promised Toffile to be cruel to them
For helping them be cruel once to him.

son. We think they had a grave down in the cellar.

mother. We know they had a grave down in the cellar.

son. We never could find out whose bones they were.

mother. Yes, we could too, son. Tell the truth for once
They were a man's his father killed for me.   140
I mean a man he killed instead of me.
The least I could do was to help dig their grave.
We were about it one night in the cellar.
Son knows the story: but 'twas not for him

To tell the truth, suppose the time had come.
Son looks surprised to see me end a lie
We'd kept all these years between ourselves
So as to have it ready for outsiders.
But tonight I don't care enough to lie—
I don't remember why I ever cared.   150
Toffile, if he were here, I don't believe
Could tell you why he ever cared himself . . .

She hadn't found the finger-bone she wanted
Among the buttons poured out in her lap.
I verified the name next morning: Toffile.
The rural letter-box said Toffile Lajway.

Stopping by Woods on a Snowy Evening

Whose woods these are I think I know
His house is in the village though;
He will not see me stopping here
To watch his woods fill up with snow.

My little horse must think it queer
To stop without a farmhouse near
Between the woods and frozen lake
The darkest evening of the year.

He gives his harness bells a shake
To ask if there is some mistake.
The only other sound's the sweep
Of easy wind and downy flake.

The woods are lovely, dark and deep,
But I have promises to keep,

And miles to go before I sleep,
And miles to go before I sleep.

Fire and Ice

Some say the world will end in fire,
Some say in ice.
From what I've tasted of desire
I hold with those who favor fire.
But if it had to perish twice,
I think I know enough of hate
To say that for destruction ice
Is also great
And would suffice.

The Oven Bird

There is a singer everyone has heard,
Loud, a mid-summer and a mid-wood bird,
Who makes the solid tree trunks sound again.
He says that leaves are old and that for flowers
Mid-summer is to spring as one to ten.
He says the early petal-fall is past
When pear and cherry bloom went down in showers
On sunny days a moment overcast;
And comes that other fall we name the fall.
He says the highway dust is over all.
The bird would cease and be as other birds
But that he knows in singing not to sing.
The question that he frames in all but words
Is what to make of a diminished thing.

WALLACE STEVENS

Esthétique du Mal

I

He was at Naples writing letters home
And, between his letters, reading paragraphs
On the sublime. Vesuvius had groaned
For a month. It was pleasant to be sitting there,
While the sultriest fulgurations, flickering,
Cast corners in the glass. He could describe
The terror of the sound because the sound
Was ancient. He tried to remember the phrases: pain
Audible at noon, pain torturing itself,
Pain killing pain on the very point of pain.   10
The volcano trembled in another ether,
As the body trembles at the end of life.

It was almost time for lunch. Pain is human.
There were roses in the cool café. His book
Made sure of the most correct catastrophe.
Except for us, Vesuvius might consume
In solid fire the utmost earth and know
No pain (ignoring the cocks that crow us up
To die). This is a part of the sublime
From which we shrink. And yet, except for us,   20
The total past felt nothing when destroyed.

II

At a town in which acacias grew, he lay
On his balcony at night. Warblings became

Too dark, too far, too much the accents of
Afflicted sleep, too much the syllables
That would form themselves, in time, and communicate
The intelligence of his despair, express
What meditation never quite achieved.

The moon rose up as if it had escaped
His meditation. It evaded his mind.   30
It was part of a supremacy always
Above him. The moon was always free from him,
As night was free from him. The shadow touched
Or merely seemed to touch him as he spoke
A kind of elegy he found in space:

It is pain that is indifferent to the sky
In spite of the yellow of the acacias, the scent
Of them in the air still hanging heavily
In the hoary-hanging night. It does not regard
This freedom, this supremacy, and in   40
Its own hallucination never sees
How that which rejects it saves it in the end.

III

His firm stanzas hang like hives in hell
Or what hell was, since now both heaven and hell
Are one, and here, O terra infidel.

The fault lies with an over-human god,
Who by sympathy has made himself a man
And is not to be distinguished, when we cry

Because we suffer, our oldest parent, peer
Of the populace of the heart, the reddest lord,   50
Who has gone before us in experience.

If only he would not pity us so much,
Weaken our fate, relieve us of woe both great
And small, a constant fellow of destiny,

A too, too human god, self-pity's kin
And uncourageous genesis . . . It seems
As if the health of the world might be enough.

It seems as if the honey of common summer
Might be enough, as if the golden combs
Were part of a sustenance itself enough,   60

As if hell, so modified, had disappeared,
As if pain, no longer satanic mimicry,
Could be borne, as if we were sure to find our way.

IV

Livre de Toutes Sortes de Fleurs D'Après Nature.
All sorts of flowers. That's the sentimentalist.
When B. sat down at the piano and made
A transparence in which we heard music, made music,
In which we heard transparent sounds, did he play
All sorts of notes? Or did he play only one
In an ecstasy of its associates,   70
Variations in the tones of a single sound,
The last, or sounds so single they seemed one?

And then that Spaniard of the rose, itself
Hot-hooded and dark-blooded, rescued the rose
From nature, each time he saw it, making it,
As he saw it, exist in his own especial eye.
Can we conceive of him as rescuing less,
As muffing the mistress for her several maids,
As foregoing the nakedest passion for barefoot
Philandering? . . . The genius of misfortune   80

Is not a sentimentalist. He is
That evil, that evil in the self, from which
In desperate hallow, rugged gesture, fault
Falls out on everything: the genius of
The mind, which is our being, wrong and wrong,
The genius of the body, which is our world,
Spent in the false engagements of the mind.

v

Softly let all true sympathizers come,
Without the inventions of sorrow or the sob
Beyond invention. Within what we permit,   90
Within the actual, the warm, the near,
So great a unity, that it is bliss,
Ties us to those we love. For this familiar,
This brother even in the father's eye,
This brother half-spoken in the mother's throat
And these regalia, these things disclosed,
These nebulous brilliancies in the smallest look
Of the being's deepest darling, we forego
Lament, willingly forfeit the ai-ai

Of parades in the obscurer selvages.   100
Be near me, come closer, touch my hand, phrases
Compounded of dear relation, spoken twice,
Once by the lips, once by the services
Of central sense, these minutiae mean more
Than clouds, benevolences, distant heads.
These are within what we permit, in-bar
Exquisite in poverty against the suns
Of ex-bar, in-bar retaining attributes
With which we vested, once, the golden forms
And the damasked memory of the golden forms   110
And ex-bar's flower and fire of the festivals
Of the damasked memory of the golden forms,
Before we were wholly human and knew ourselves.

VI

The sun, in clownish yellow, but not a clown,
Brings the day to perfection and then fails. He dwells
In a consummate prime, yet still desires
A further consummation. For the lunar month
He makes the tenderest research, intent
On a transmutation which, when seen, appears
To be askew. And space is filled with his   120
Rejected years. A big bird pecks at him
For food. The big bird's boney appetite
Is as insatiable as the sun's. The bird
Rose from an imperfection of its own
To feed on the yellow bloom of the yellow fruit
Dropped down from turquoise leaves. In the landscape of
The sun, its grossest appetite becomes less gross,
Yet, when corrected, has its curious lapses,
Its glitters, its divinations of serene
Indulgence out of all celestial sight.   130

The sun is the country wherever he is. The bird
In the brightest landscape downwardly revolves
Disdaining each astringent ripening,
Evading the point of redness, not content
To repose in an hour or season or long era
Of the country colors crowding against it, since
The yellow grassman's mind is still immense,
Still promises perfections cast away.

VII

How red the rose that is the soldier's wound,
The wounds of many soldiers, the wounds of all   140
The soldiers that have fallen, red in blood,
The soldier of time grown deathless in great size.

A mountain in which no ease is ever found,
Unless indifference to deeper death

Is ease, stands in the dark, a shadows' hill,
And there the soldier of time has deathless rest.

Concentric circles of shadows, motionless
Of their own part, yet moving on the wind,
Form mystical convolutions in the sleep
Of time's red soldier deathless on his bed.   150

The shadows of his fellows ring him round
In the high night, the summer breathes for them
Its fragrance, a heavy somnolence, and for him,
For the soldier of time, it breathes a summer sleep,

In which his wound is good because life was.
No part of him was ever part of death.
A woman smoothes her forehead with her hand
And the soldier of time lies calm beneath that stroke.

VIII

The death of Satan was a tragedy
For the imagination. A capital   160
Negation destroyed him in his tenement
And, with him, many blue phenomena.
It was not the end he had foreseen. He knew
That his revenge created filial
Revenges. And negation was eccentric.
It had nothing of the Julian thunder-cloud:
The assassin flash and rumble . . . He was denied.
Phantoms, what have you left? What underground?
What place in which to be is not enough
To be? You go, poor phantoms, without place   170
Like silver in the sheathing of the sight,
As the eye closes . . . How cold the vacancy
When the phantoms are gone and the shaken realist
First sees reality. The mortal no
Has its emptiness and tragic expirations.

The tragedy, however, may have begun,
Again, in the imagination's new beginning,
In the yes of the realist spoken because he must
Say yes, spoken because under every no
Lay a passion for yes that had never been broken.   180

IX

Panic in the face of the moon—round effendi
Or the phosphored sleep in which he walks abroad
Or the majolica dish heaped up with phosphored fruit
That he sends ahead, out of the goodness of his heart,
To anyone that comes—panic, because
The moon is no longer these nor anything
And nothing is left but comic ugliness
Or a lustred nothingness. Effendi, he
That has lost the folly of the moon becomes
The prince of the proverbs of pure poverty.   190
To lose sensibility, to see what one sees,
As if sight had not its own miraculous thrift,
To hear only what one hears, one meaning alone,
As if the paradise of meaning ceased
To be paradise, it is this to be destitute.
This is the sky divested of its fountains.
Here in the west indifferent crickets chant
Through our indifferent crises. Yet we require
Another chant, an incantation, as in
Another and later genesis, music   200
That buffets the shapes of its possible halcyon
Against the haggardie . . . A loud, large water
Bubbles up in the night and drowns the cricket's sound.
It is a declaration, a primitive ecstasy,
Truth's favors sonorously exhibited.

X

He had studied the nostalgias. In these
He sought the most grossly maternal, the creature

Who most fecundly assuaged him, the softest
Woman with a vague moustache and not the mauve
Maman. His anima liked its animal   210
And liked it unsubjugated, so that home
Was a return to birth, a being born
Again in the savagest severity,
Desiring fiercely, the child of a mother fierce
In his body, fiercer in his mind, merciless
To accomplish the truth in his intelligence.
It is true there were other mothers, singular
In form, lovers of heaven and earth, she-wolves
And forest tigresses and women mixed
With the sea. These were fantastic. There were homes   220
Like things submerged with their englutted sounds,
That were never wholly still. The softest woman,
Because she is as she was, reality,
The gross, the fecund, proved him against the touch
Of impersonal pain. Reality explained.
It was the last nostalgia: that he
Should understand. That he might suffer or that
He might die was the innocence of living, if life
Itself was innocent. To say that it was
Disentangled him from sleek ensolacings.   230

XI

Life is a bitter aspic. We are not
At the centre of a diamond. At dawn,
The paratroopers fall and as they fall
They mow the lawn. A vessel sinks in waves
Of people, as big bell-billows from its bell
Bell-bellow in the village steeple. Violets,
Great tufts, spring up from buried houses
Of poor, dishonest people, for whom the steeple,
Long since, rang out farewell, farewell, farewell.

Natives of poverty, children of malheur,   240
The gaiety of language is our seigneur.

A man of bitter appetite despises
A well-made scene in which paratroopers
Select adieux; and he despises this:
A ship that rolls on a confected ocean,
The weather pink, the wind in motion; and this:
A steeple that tip-tops the classic sun's
Arrangements; and the violets' exhumo.

The tongue caresses these exacerbations.
They press it as epicure, distinguishing   250
Themselves from its essential savor,
Like hunger that feeds on its own hungriness.

                          XII

He disposes the world in categories, thus:
The peopled and the unpeopled. In both, he is
Alone. But in the peopled world, there is,
Besides the people, his knowledge of them. In
The unpeopled, there is his knowledge of himself.
Which is more desperate in the moments when
The will demands that what he thinks be true?

Is it himself in them that he knows or they   260
In him? If it is himself in them, they have
No secret from him. If it is they in him,
He has no secret from them. This knowledge
Of them and of himself destroys both worlds,
Except when he escapes from it. To be
Alone is not to know them or himself.

This creates a third world without knowledge,
In which no one peers, in which the will makes no
Demands. It accepts whatever is as true,
Including pain, which, otherwise, is false.   270
In the third world, then, there is no pain. Yes, but
What lover has one in such rocks, what woman,
However known, at the centre of the heart?

XIII

It may be that one life is a punishment
For another, as the son's life for the father's.
But that concerns the secondary characters.
It is a fragmentary tragedy
Within the universal whole. The son
And the father alike and equally are spent,
Each one, by the necessity of being   280
Himself, the unalterable necessity
Of being this unalterable animal.
This force of nature in action is the major
Tragedy. This is destiny unperplexed,
The happiest enemy. And it may be
That in his Mediterranean cloister a man,
Reclining, eased of desire, establishes
The visible, a zone of blue and orange
Versicolorings, establishes a time
To watch the fire-feinting sea and calls it good,   290
The ultimate good, sure of a reality
Of the longest meditation, the maximum,
The assassin's scene. Evil in evil is
Comparative. The assassin discloses himself,
The force that destroys us is disclosed, within
This maximum, an adventure to be endured
With the politest helplessness. Ay-mi!
One feels its action moving in the blood.

XIV

Victor Serge said, "I followed his argument
With the blank uneasiness which one might feel   300
In the presence of a logical lunatic."
He said it of Konstantinov. Revolution
Is the affair of logical lunatics.
The politics of emotion must appear
To be an intellectual structure. The cause

Creates a logic not to be distinguished
From lunacy . . . One wants to be able to walk
By the lake at Geneva and consider logic:
To think of the logicians in their graves
And of the worlds of logic in their great tombs.   310
Lakes are more reasonable than oceans. Hence,
A promenade amid the grandeurs of the mind,
By a lake, with clouds like lights among great tombs,
Gives one a blank uneasiness, as if
One might meet Konstantinov, who would interrupt
With his lunacy. He would not be aware of the lake.
He would be the lunatic of one idea
In a world of ideas, who would have all the people
Live, work, suffer and die in that idea
In a world of ideas. He would not be aware of the clouds,   320
Lighting the martyrs of logic with white fire,
His extreme of logic would be illogical.

XV

The greatest poverty is not to live
In a physical world, to feel that one's desire
Is too difficult to tell from despair. Perhaps,
After death, the non-physical people, in paradise,
Itself non-physical, may, by chance, observe
The green corn gleaming and experience
The minor of what we feel. The adventurer
In humanity has not conceived of a race   330
Completely physical in a physical world.
The green corn gleams and the metaphysicals
Lie sprawling in majors of the August heat,
The rotund emotions, paradise unknown.

This is the thesis scrivened in delight,
The reverberating psalm, the right chorale.

One might have thought of sight, but who could think

Of what it sees, for all the ill it sees?
Speech found the ear, for all the evil sound,
But the dark italics it could not propound.   340
And out of what one sees and hears and out
Of what one feels, who could have thought to make
So many selves, so many sensuous worlds,
As if the air, the mid-day air, was swarming
With the metaphysical changes that occur,
Merely in living as and where we live.

ROBINSON JEFFERS

Margrave

On the small marble-paved platform
On the turret on the head of the tower,
Watching the night deepen.
I feel the rock-edge of the continent
Reel eastward with me below the broad stars.
I lean on the broad worn stones of the parapet top
And the stones and my hands that touch them reel eastward.
The inland mountains go down and new lights
Glow over the sinking east rim of the earth.
The dark ocean comes up,   10
And reddens the western stars with its fog-breath
And hides them with its mounded darkness.

The earth was the world and man was its measure, but our
      minds have looked
Through the little mock-dome of heaven the telescope-slotted
      observatory eyeball, there space and multitude came in
And the earth is a particle of dust by a sand-grain sun, lost in a
      nameless cove of the shores of a continent.

Galaxy on galaxy, innumerable swirls of innumerable stars, en-
    dured as it were forever and humanity
Came into being, its two or three million years are a moment, in
    a moment it will certainly cease out from being
And galaxy on galaxy endure after that as it were forever . . .
    But man is conscious,
He brings the world to focus in a feeling brain,
In a net of nerves catches the splendor of things,   20
Breaks the somnambulism of nature . . . His distinction per-
    haps,
Hardly his advantage. To slaver for contemptible pleasures
And scream with pain, are hardly an advantage.
Consciousness? The learned astronomer
Analyzing the light of most remote star-swirls
Has found them—or a trick of distance deludes his prism—
All at incredible speeds fleeing outward from ours.
I thought, no doubt they are fleeing the contagion
Of consciousness that infects this corner of space.

For often I have heard the hard rocks I handled   30
Groan, because lichen and time and water dissolve them,
And they have to travel down the strange falling scale
Of soil and plants and the flesh of beasts to become
The bodies of men; they murmur at their fate
In the hollows of windless nights, they'd rather be anything
Than human flesh played on by pain and joy,
They pray for annihilation sooner, but annihilation's
Not in the book yet.

            So, I thought, the rumor
Of human consciousness has gone abroad in the world,   40
The sane uninfected far-outer universes
Flee it in a panic of escape, as men flee the plague
Taking a city: for look at the fruits of consciousness:
As in young Walter Margrave when he'd been sentenced for
    murder: he was thinking when they brought him back

To the cell in jail, "I've only a moment to arrange my thoughts,
    I must think quickly, I must think clearly,
And settle the world in my mind before I kick off," but to feel
    the curious eyes of his fellow-prisoners
And the wry-mouthed guard's and so forth torment him
    through the steel bars put his mind in a stupor, he could
    only
Sit frowning, ostentatiously unafraid. "But I can control my
    mind, their eyes can't touch my will.
One against all. What use is will at this end of everything? A
    kind of nausea is the chief feeling . . .
In my stomach and throat . . . but in my head pride: I fought
    a good fight and they can't break me; along, unbroken,   50
Against a hundred and twenty-three million people. They are
    going to kill the best brain perhaps in the world,
That might have made such discoveries in science
As would set the world centuries ahead, for I had the mind and
    the power. Boo, it's their loss. Blind fools,
Killing their best." When his mind forgot the eyes it made rapid
    capricious pictures instead of words,
But not of the medical school and the laboratories, its late in-
    tense interest; not at all of his crime; glimpses
Of the coast-range at home; the V of a westward canyon with
    the vibrating
Blue line of the ocean strung sharp across it; that domed hill up
    the valley, two cows like specks on the summit
And a beautiful-colored jungle of poison-oak at the foot; his
    sister half naked washing her hair,
"My dirty sister," whose example and her lovers had kept him
    chaste by revulsion; the reed-grown mouth of the river
And the sand-bar against the stinging splendor of the sea . . .
    and anguish behind all the pictures   60
(He began to consider his own mind again) "like a wall they
    hang on." Hang. The anguish came forward, an actual
Knife between two heartbeats, the organ stopped and then
    raced. He experimented awhile with his heart,

Making in his mind a picture of a man hanged, pretending to
    himself it was to happen next moment,
Trying to observe whether the beat suspended—"suspended,"
    he thought—in systole or in diastole.
The effect soon failed; the anguish remained. "Ah my slack
    lawyer, damn him, let slip chance after chance.
Scared traitor." Then broken pictures of the scenes in court, the
    jury, the judge, the idlers, and not one face
But bleak with hatred. "But I met their eyes, one against all,"
    Suddenly his mind became incapable
Of making pictures or words, but still wildly active, striking in
    all directions like a snake in a fire,
Finding nothing but the fiery element of its own anguish. He
    got up and felt the guard's eyes and sat down,
Turned side-face, resting his chin on his fist, frowning and
    trembling. He saw clearly in his mind the little   70
Adrenal glands perched on the red-brown kidneys, as if all his
    doomed tissues became transparent,
Pouring in these passions their violent secretion
Into his blood-stream, raising the tension unbearably. And the
    thyroids; tension, tension. A long course of that
Should work grave changes. "If they tortured a man like a
    laboratory dog for discovery: there'd be value gained: but
    by process
Of law for vengeance, because his glands and his brain have
    made him act in another than common manner:
You incredible breed of asses!" He smiled self-consciously in
    open scorn of the people, the guard at the door
To observe that smile—"my God, do I care about the turnkey's
    opinion?"—suddenly his mind again
Was lashing like a burnt snake. Then it was torpid for a while.
    This continued for months.

His father had come to visit him, he saw the ruinous white-
    haired head
Through two steel wickets under the bluish electric light that
    seemed to peel the skin from the face.   80

Walter said cheerfully too loudly, "Hullo. You look like a skull."
  The shaven sunk jaws in answer chewed
Inaudible words. Walter with an edge of pleasure thought
  "Once he was stronger than I! I used to admire
This poor old man's strength when I was a child," and said
  "Buck up, old fellow, it will soon be over. Here's nothing
To cry for. Do you think I'm afraid to die? It's good people that
  fear death, people with the soft streak
Of goodness in them fear death: but I, you know, am a monster,
  don't you read the papers? Caught at last:
I fought a hundred and twenty-three million people. How's
  Hazel? How's the farm? I could get out of this scrape
By playing dementia, but I refuse to, there's not an alienist liv-
  ing
Could catch me out. I'm the king of Spain dying for the world.
  I've been persecuted since I was born
By a secret sect, they stuck pins into me
And fed me regular doses of poison for a certain reason. Why
  do you pretend that you're my father?   90
God is. . . . Believe me, I could get by with it.
But I refuse."
                Old Margrave looked timidly at the two guards
  listening, and drew his brown tremulous hand
Across his eyes below the white hair. "I thought of going to try
  to see the governor, Walter."
"That's it!" "Don't hope for anything, Walter, they tell me that
  there's no hope. They say that I shan't even
Be allowed to see him." "By God," the young man said trem-
  bling, "you can if you want to. Never believe that lawyer.
If I'd had Dorking? but you couldn't afford him. Poor men
  have no right to breed sons. I'd not be here
If you'd had money to put me through college. Tell the governor
I know he won't pardon, but he can commute the sentence to
  life imprisonment. Then I can read and study,

I can help the penitentiary doctor, I can do something to help
    humanity. Tell him it's madness   100
To throw such a brain as mine into the garbage. Don't deny my
    guilt but tell him my reasons.
I kidnapped the little girl to get money to finish my medical
    education. What's one child's life
Against a career like mine that might have saved
Thousands of children? Say I'd isolated the organism of infantile
    paralysis: I'd have done more:
But that alone would save thousands of children. I was merci-
    ful; she died quietly; tell him that.
It was only pithing a little white frog.
Don't you think you can make him understand? I'm not a crimi-
    nal: I judge differently from others. I wasn't
Afraid to think for myself. All I did
Was for money for my education, to help humanity. And tell
    him if I've done wrong—what's wrong?—I've paid for it
With frightful suffering: the more developed the brain the
    greater the agony. He won't admit that. Oh God,   110
These brains the size of a pea! To be juried
And strangled by a hundred and twenty-three million peas. Go
    down on your knees to him. You owe me that: you'd no
    right
To breed, you're poor.
But you itched for a woman, you had to fetch me out of the
    happy hill of not-being. Pfah, to hug a woman
And make this I. That's the evil in the world, that letter. I—I—
    Tell the governor
That I'm not afraid of dying, that I laugh at death. No, no, we'll
    laugh in private. Tell him I'm crazy.
I've come to that: after being the only sane mind among a hun-
    dred and twenty-three million peas.
Anything, anything . . ."

                  He had let his nerves go wild on pur-
pose, to edge on the old man to action, now at last

Escaping utterly out of control they stumbled into a bog of
    thick sobs. The guards pulled him up   120
And walked him away as if he were half insensible. He was not
    insensible, but more acutely aware
Than ever in his life before of all that touched him, and of
    shame and anguish.

                You would be wise, you far stars,
To flee with the speed of light this infection.
For here the good sane invulnerable material
And nature of things more and more grows alive and cries.
The rock and water grow human, the bitter weed
Of consciousness catches the sun, it clings to the near stars,
Even the nearer portion of the universal God
Seems to become conscious, yearns and rejoices   130
And suffers: I believe this hurt will be healed
Some age of time after mankind has died,
Then the sun will say "What ailed me a moment?" and resume
The old soulless triumph, and the iron and stone earth
With confident inorganic glory obliterate
Her ruins and fossils, like that incredible unfading red rose
Of desert in Arizona glowing life to scorn,
And grind the chalky emptied seed-shells of consciousness
The bare skulls of the dead to powder; after some million
Courses around the sun her sadness may pass: 140
But why should you worlds of the virgin distance
Endure to survive what it were better to escape?

I also am not innocent
Of contagion, but have spread my spirit on the deep world.
I have gotten sons and sent the fire wider.
I have planted trees, they also feel while they live.
I have humanized the ancient sea-sculptured cliff
And the ocean's wreckage of rock
Into a house and a tower,
Hastening the sure decay of granite with my hammer,   150

Its hard dust will make soft flesh;
And have widened in my idleness
The disastrous personality of life with poems,
That are pleasant enough in the breeding but go bitterly at last
To envy oblivion and the early deaths of nobler
Verse, and much nobler flesh;
And I have projected my spirit
Behind the superb sufficient forehead of nature
To gift the inhuman God with this rankling consciousness.

But who is our judge? It is likely the enormous   160
Beauty of the world requires for completion our ghostly incre-
        ment,
It has to dream, and dream badly, a moment of its night.

On the little stone-belted platform
On the turret on the head of the tower,
Between the stars and the earth,
And the ocean and the continent.
One ship's light shines and eclipses
Very far out, behind the high waves on the hill of water.
In the east under the Hyades and rising Orion
Are many cities and multitudes of people,   170
But westward a long way they are few enough.
It is fortunate to look westward as to look upward.
In the south the dark river-mouth pool mirrors a star
That stands over Margrave's farmhouse. The old man has lost it,
        he isn't there any more. He went down to the river-mouth
Last December, when recent rains had opened the stream and
        the salmon were running. Fishermen very solemnly
Stood all along the low sand like herons, and sea-lions offshore
        in the rolling waves with deep wet voices
Coughed at each other; the sea air is hoarse with their voices
        that time of year. Margrave had rambled since noon
Among the little folds of the seaward field that he had forgotten
        to plow and was trying to sell

Though he used to love it, but everything was lost now. He lay
    awhile on his face in the rotting stubble and random

Unsown green blades, then he got up and drifted over the ridge
    to the river-mouth sands, unaimed,   180

Pale and gap-eyed, as the day moon a clear morning, opposite
    the sun. He noticed with surprise the many

Fishermen like herons in the shallows and along the sands; and
    then that his girl Hazel was with him: who'd feared

What he might do to himself and had come to watch him when
    he lay face down in the field. "I know what they're doing,"

He said slyly, "Hazel, they're fishing! I guess they don't know,"

He whispered, "about our trouble. Oh no, don't tell them." She
    said, "Don't go down, father, your face would tell them.

Sit here on the edge of grass, watch the brown river meet the
    blue sea. Do look: that boy's caught something.

How the line cuts the water and the small wheel sings." "If I'd
    been rich,"

Old Margrave answered, "they'd have fixed the hook for . . .
    Walter . . . with some other bait. It sticks in my mind
    that . . . Walter

Blames me too much." "Look," Hazel said, "he's landing it now.
    Oh, it's a big one." "I dreamed about fishing,

Some time ago," he answered, "but we were the fish. I saw the
    people all running reaching for prizes   190

That dangled on long lines from the sky. A lovely girl or a sack
    of money or a case of whiskey,

Or fake things like reputation, hackle-feathers and a hook. A
    man would reach up and grab and the line

Jerked, then you knew by his face that the hook was in him,
    wherever he went. Often they're played for half

A lifetime before they're landed: others, like . . . my son . . .
    pulled up short. Oh, Oh,

It's not a dream." He said gently, "He wanted money for his
    education, but you poor girl

Wanted boy friends, now you've got a round belly. That's the
    hook. I wanted children and got

Walter and you. Hm? Hooked twice is too much. Let's walk."
"Not that way: let's go up home, daddy.
It makes you unhappy to see them fishing." "No," he answered,
    "nothing can. I have it in my pocket." She walked behind
    him,
Hiding herself, ashamed of her visible pregnancy and her broth-
    er's fate; but when the old man stumbled   200
And wavered on the slope she went beside him to support him,
    her right hand under his elbow, and wreathed his body
With the other arm.

                  The clear brown river ran eagerly through
    the sand-hill, undercutting its banks,
That slid in masses; tall waves walked very slowly up stream
    from the sea, and stood
Stationary in the throat of the channel before they dissolved.
    The rock the children call Red-cap stood
High and naked among the fishermen, the orange lichen on its
    head. At the sea-end of the sand
Two boys and a man had rifles instead of rods, they meant to
    punish the salmon-devouring sea-lions
Because the fish were fewer than last year; whenever a sleek
    brown head with the big questioning eyes
Broke sea they fired. Margrave had heard the shots but taken
    no notice, but when he walked by the stream
He saw a swimmer look up from the water and its round dark
    eye   210
Suddenly burst red blood before it went down. He cried out
    and twisted himself from Hazel's hand
And ran like a squirrel along the stream-bank. "I'll not allow
    it!" He snatched at a rifle. "Why should my lad
Be hanged for killing and all you others go free?" He wrestled
    feebly to gain the rifle, the sand-bank
Slid under his feet, he slipped and lay face down in the running
    stream and was hauled astrand. Then Hazel
Came running heavily, and when he was able to walk she led
    him away. The sea-beast, blinded but a painful

Vain gleam, starved long before it could die; old Margrave still
    lives. Death's like a little gay child that runs
The world around with the keys of salvation in his foolish fin-
    gers, lends them at random where they're not wanted,
But often withholds them where most required.

                                                    Margrave's son
        at this time
Had only four days to wait, but death now appeared so dread-
    ful to him that to speak of his thoughts and the abject   220
Horror, would be to insult humanity more than it deserves. At
    last the jerked hemp snapped the neck sideways
And bruised the cable of nerves that threads the bone rings; the
    intolerably strained consciousness in a moment changed.
It was strangely cut in two parts at the noose, the head's
Consciousness from the body's; both were set free and flamed;
    the head's with flashing paradisal light
Like the wild birth of a star, but crying in bewilderment and
    suddenly extinguished; the body's with a sharp emotion
Of satisfied love, a wave of hard warmth and joy, that ebbed
    cold on darkness. After a time of darkness
The dreams that follow upon death came and subsided, like
    fibrillar twitchings
Of the nerves unorganizing themselves; and some of the small
    dreams were delightful and some, slight miseries,
But nothing intense; then consciousness wandered home from
    the cell to the molecule, was utterly dissolved and changed;
Peace was the end of the play, so far as concerns humanity. Oh
    beautiful capricious little savior,   230
Death, the gay child with the gipsy eyes, to avoid you for a time
    I think is virtuous, to fear you is insane.
On the little stone-girdled platform
Over the earth and the ocean
I seem to have stood a long time and watched the stars pass.
They also shall perish I believe.
Here to-day, gone to-morrow, desperate wee galaxies

Scattering themselves and shining their substance away
Like a passionate thought. It is very well ordered.

E. E. CUMMINGS

Somewhere I Have Never Travelled

somewhere i have never travelled, gladly beyond
any experience, your eyes have their silence:
in your most frail gesture are things which enclose me,
or which i cannot touch because they are too near

your slightest look easily will unclose me
though i have closed myself as fingers,
you open always petal by petal myself as Spring opens
(touching skilfully, mysteriously) her first rose

or if your wish be to close me, i and
my life will shut very beautifully, suddenly,
as when the heart of this flower imagines
the snow carefully everywhere descending;

nothing which we are to perceive in this world equals
the power of your intense fragility: whose texture
compels me with the color of its countries,
rendering death and forever with each breathing

(i do not know what it is about you that closes
and opens; only something in me understands

the voice of your eyes is deeper than all roses)
nobody, not even the rain, has such small hands

Anyone Lived in a Pretty How Town

anyone lived in a pretty how town
(and up so floating many bells down)
spring summer autumn winter
he sang his didn't he danced his did.

Women and men (both little and small)
cared for anyone not at all
they sowed their isn't they reaped their same
sun moon stars rain

children guessed (but only a few
and down they forgot as up they grew   10
autumn winter spring summer)
that noone loved him more by more

when by now and tree by leaf
she laughed his joy she cried his grief
bird by snow and stir by still
anyone's any was all to her

someones married their everyones
laughed their cryings and did their dance
(sleep wake hope and then) they
said their nevers they slept their dream   20

From *50 Poems*, published by Duell, Sloan & Pearce, Inc. Copyright, 1939, 1940, by E. E. Cummings.

stars rain/sun moon
(and only the snow can begin to explain
how children are apt to forget to remember
with up so floating many bells down)

one day anyone died i guess
(and noone stooped to kiss his face)
busy folk buried them side by side
little by little and was by was

all by all and deep by deep
and more by more they dream their sleep   30
noone and anyone earth by april
wish by spirit and if by yes.

Women and men (both dong and ding)
summer autumn winter spring
reaped their sowing and went their came
sun moon stars rain

Nobody Loses All the Time

nobody loses all the time

i had an uncle named
Sol who was a born failure and
nearly everybody said he should have gone
into vaudeville perhaps because my Uncle Sol could
sing McCann He Was A Diver on Xmas Eve like Hell Itself
    which
may or may not account for the fact that my Uncle

Sol indulged in that possibly most inexcusable
of all to use a highfalootin phrase

From *Collected Poems of E. E. Cummings,* published by Harcourt, Brace and Company, Inc. Copyright, 1926, by Horace Liveright.

luxuries that is or to   10
wit farming and be
it needlessly
added

my Uncle Sol's farm
failed because the chickens
ate the vegetables
so my Uncle Sol had a
chicken farm till the
skunks ate the chickens when

my Uncle Sol   20
had a skunk farm but
the skunks caught cold and
died and so
my Uncle Sol imitated the
skunks in a subtle manner
or by drowning himself in the watertank
but somebody who'd given my Uncle Sol a Victor
Victrola and records while he lived presented to
him upon the auspicious occasion of his decease a
scrumptious not to mention splendiferous funeral with   30
tall boys in black gloves and flowers and everything and

i remember we all cried like the Missouri
when my Uncle Sol's coffin lurched because
somebody pressed a button
(and down went
my Uncle
Sol

and started a worm farm)

HART CRANE

For the Marriage of Faustus and Helen

> "And so we may arrive by Talmud skill
> And profane Greek to raise the building up
> Of Helen's house against the Ismaelite,
> King of Thogarma, and his habergeons
> Brimstony, blue and fiery; and the force
> Of King Abaddon, and the beast of Cittim;
> Which Rabbi David Kimchi, Onkelos,
> And Aben Ezra do interpret Rome."
>
> —THE ALCHEMIST

I

The mind has shown itself at times
Too much the baked and labeled dough
Divided by accepted multitudes.
Across the stacked partitions of the day—
Across the memoranda, baseball scores,
The stenographic smiles and stock quotations
Smutty wings flash out equivocations.

The mind is brushed by sparrow wings;
Numbers, rebuffed by asphalt, crowd
The margins of the day, accent the curbs,   10
Convoying divers dawns on every corner
To druggist, barber and tobacconist,
Until the graduate opacities of evening
Take them away as suddenly to somewhere
Virginal perhaps, less fragmentary, cool.

> *There is the world dimensional for*
> *those untwisted by the love of things*
> *irreconcilable . . .*

And yet, suppose some evening I forgot
The fare and transfer, yet got by that way
Without recall,—lost yet poised in traffic.
Then I might find your eyes across an aisle,
Still flickering with those prefigurations—   20
Prodigal, yet uncontested now,
Half-riant before the jerky window frame.

There is some way, I think, to touch
Those hands of yours that count the nights
Stippled with pink and green advertisements.
And now, before its arteries turn dark,
I would have you meet this bartered blood.
Imminent in his dream, none better knows
The white wafer cheek of love, or offers words
Lightly as moonlight on the eaves meets snow.   30

Reflective conversion of all things
At your deep blush, when ecstasies thread
The limbs and belly, when rainbows spread
Impinging on the throat and sides . . .
Inevitable, the body of the world
Weeps in inventive dust for the hiatus
That winks above it, bluet in your breasts.

The earth may glide diaphanous to death;
But if I lift my arms it is to bend
To you who turned away once, Helen, knowing   40
The press of troubled hands, too alternate
With steel and soil to hold you endlessly.
I meet you, therefore, in that eventual flame
You found in final chains, no captive then—

Beyond their million brittle, bloodshot eyes;
White, through white cities passed on to assume
That world which comes to each of us alone.

Accept a lone eye riveted to your plane,
Bent axle of devotion along companion ways
That beat, continuous, to hourless days—   50
One inconspicuous, glowing orb of praise.

II

Brazen hypnotics glitter here;
Glee shifts from foot to foot,
Magnetic to their tremolo.
This crashing opéra bouffe,
Blest excursion! this ricochet
From roof to roof—
Know, Olympians, we are breathless
While nigger cupids scour the stars!

A thousand light shrugs balance us   60
Through snarling hails of melody.
White shadows slip across the floor
Splayed like cards from a loose hand;
Rhythmic ellipses lead into canters
Until somewhere a rooster banters.

Greet naïvely—yet intrepidly
New soothings, new amazements
That cornets introduce at every turn—
And you may fall downstairs with me
With perfect grace and equanimity.   70
Or, plaintively scud past shores
Where, by strange harmonic laws
All relatives, serene and cool,
Sit rocked in patent armchairs.

O, I have known metallic paradises
Where cuckoos clucked to finches
Above the deft catastrophes of drums.
While titters hailed the groans of death
Beneath gyrating awnings I have seen
The incunabula of the divine grotesque.   80
This music has a reassuring way.

The siren of the springs of guilty song—
Let us take her on the incandescent wax
Striated with nuances, nervosities
That we are heir to: she is still so young,
We cannot frown upon her as she smiles,
Dipping here in this cultivated storm
Among slim skaters of the gardened skies.

III

Capped arbiter of beauty in this street
That narrows darkly into motor dawn,—   90
You, here beside me, delicate ambassador
Of intricate slain numbers that arise
In whispers, naked of steel;
                          religious gunman!
Who faithfully, yourself, will fall too soon,
And in other ways than as the wind settles
On the sixteen thrifty bridges of the city:
Let us unbind our throats of fear and pity.

                                    We even,
Who drove speediest destruction
In corymbulous formations of mechanics,—
Who hurried the hill breezes, spouting malice   100
Plangent over meadows, and looked down
On rifts of torn and empty houses
Like old women with teeth unjubilant
That waited faintly, briefly and in vain:

We know, eternal gunman, our flesh remembers
The tensile boughs, the nimble blue plateaus,
The mounted, yielding cities of the air!
That saddled sky that shook down vertical
Repeated play of fire—no hypogeum
Of wave or rock was good against one hour.   110

We did not ask for that, but have survived,
And will persist to speak again before
All stubble streets that have not curved
To memory, or known the ominous lifted arm
That lowers down the arc of Helen's brow
To saturate with blessing and dismay.

A goose, tobacco and cologne—
Three-winged and gold-shod prophecies of heaven,
The lavish heart shall always have to leaven
And spread with bells and voices, and atone   120
The abating shadows of our conscript dust.

Anchises' navel, dripping of the sea,—
The hands Erasmus dipped in gleaming tides,
Gathered the voltage of blown blood and vine;
Delve upward for the new and scattered wine,
O brother-thief of time, that we recall.
Laugh out the meager penance of their days
Who dare not share with us the breath released,
The substance drilled and spent beyond repair
For golden, or the shadow of gold hair.   130

Distinctly praise the years, whose volatile
Blamed bleeding hands extend and thresh the height
The imagination spans beyond despair,
Outpacing bargain, vocable and prayer.

KARL SHAPIRO

The Progress of Faust

He was born in Deutschland, as you would suspect,
And graduated in magic from Cracow
In Fifteen Five. His portraits show a brow
Heightened by science. The eye is indirect,
As of bent light upon a crooked soul,
And that he bargained with the Prince of Shame
For pleasures intellectually foul
Is known by every court that lists his name.

His frequent disappearances are put down
To visits in the regions of the damned   10
And to the periodic deaths he shammed,
But, unregenerate and in Doctor's gown,
He would turn up to lecture at the fair
And do a minor miracle for a fee.
Many a life he whispered up the stair
To teach the black art of anatomy.

He was as deaf to angels as an oak
When, in the fall of Fifteen Ninety-four,
He went to London and crashed through the floor
In mock damnation of the playgoing folk.   20
Weekending with the scientific crowd,
He met Sir Francis Bacon and helped draft
"Colours of Good and Evil" and read aloud
An obscene sermon at which no one laughed.

He toured the Continent for a hundred years
And subsidized among the peasantry
The puppet play, his tragic history;
With a white glove he boxed the devil's ears
And with a black his own. Tired of this,
He published penny poems about his sins,   30
In which he placed the heavy emphasis
On the white glove which, for a penny, wins.

Some time before the hemorrhage of the Kings
Of France, he turned respectable and taught;
Quite suddenly everything that he had thought
Seemed to grow scholars' beards and angels' wings.
It was the Overthrow. On Reason's throne
He sat with the fair Phrygian on his knees
And called all universities his own,
As plausible a figure as you please.   40

Then back to Germany as the sages' sage
To preach comparative science to the young
Who came from every land in a great throng
And knew they heard the master of the age.
When for a secret formula he paid
The Devil another fragment of his soul,
His scholars wept, and several even prayed
That Satan would restore him to them whole.

Backwardly tolerant, Faustus was expelled
From the Third Reich in Nineteen Thirty-nine.   50
His exit caused the breaching of the Rhine,
Except for which the frontier might have held.
Five years unknown to enemy and friend
He hid, appearing on the sixth to pose
In an American desert at war's end
Where, at his back, a dome of atoms rose.

Homecoming

Lost in the vastness of the void Pacific
My thousand days of exile, pain,
Bid me farewell. Gone is the Southern Cross
To her own sky, fallen a continent
Under the wave, dissolved the bitterest isles
In their salt element,
And here upon the deck the mist encloses
My smile that would light up all darkness
And ask forgiveness of the things that thrust
Shame and all death on millions and on me.   10

We bring no raw materials from the East
But green-skinned men in blue-lit holds
And lunatics impounded between-decks;
The mighty ghoul-ship that we ride exhales
The sickly-sweet stench of humiliation,
And even the majority, untouched by steel
Or psychoneurosis, stare with eyes in rut,
Their hands a rabble to snatch the riches
Of glittering shops and girls.

Because I am angry at this kindness which   20
Is both habitual and contradictory
To the life of armies, now I stand alone
And hate the swarms of khaki men that crawl
Like lice upon the wrinkled hide of earth,
Infesting ships as well. Not otherwise
Could I lean outward piercing fog to find
Our sacred bridge of exile and return.
My tears are psychological, not poems
To the United States; my smile is prayer.

Gnawing the thin slops of anxiety,   30
Escorted by the ground swell and by gulls,
In silence and with mystery we enter
The territorial waters. Not till then
Does that convulsive terrible joy, more sudden
And brilliant than the explosion of a ship,
Shatter the tensions of the heaven and sea
To crush a hundred thousand skulls
And liberate in that high burst of love
The imprisoned souls of soldiers and of me.

The Convert

Deep in the shadowy bethel of the tired mind,
Where spooks and death lights ride, and Marys, too,
Materialize like senseless ectoplasm
Smiling in blue, out of the blue,
Quite gradually, on a common afternoon,
With no more inner fanfare than a sigh,
With no cross in the air, drizzle of blood,
Beauty of blinding voices from up high,
The man surrenders reason to the ghost
And enters church, via the vestry room.   10

The groan of positive science, hiss of friends,
Substantiate what doctors call
His rather shameful and benign disease,
But ecumenical heaven clearly sees
His love, his possibilities.
O victory of the Unintelligence,
What mystic rose developing from rock
Is more a miracle than this overthrow?
What Constitution ever promised more
Than his declared insanity?   20

Yet he shall be less perfect than before,
Being no longer neutral to the Book
But answerable. What formerly were poems,
Precepts, and commonplaces now are laws,
Dantean atlases, and official news.
The dust of ages settles on his mind
And in his ears he hears the click of beads
Adding, adding, adding like a prayer machine
His heartfelt sums. Upon his new-found knees
He treasures up the gold of never-ending day.   30

All arguments are vain—that Notre Dame
Has plumbing, Baptists shoot their fellowmen,
Hindus are pious, nuns have Cadillacs;
Apologetics anger him who is
The living proof of what he newly knows;
And proudly sorrowing for those who fail
To read his simple summa theologica,
He prays that in the burning they be spared,
And prays for mercy as the south wind blows,
And for all final sins that tip the scale.   40

Peace on a hundred thousand temples falls
With gently even light, revealing some
With wounded walls and missing faces, some
Spared by the bombardier, and some by God.
In mournful happiness the clerics move
To put the altars back, and the new man,
Heartbroken, walks among the broken saints,
Thinking how heavy is the hand that hates,
How light and secret is the sign of love
In the time of many significant conversions.   50

The Grammar of Science

(1903)

HENRY ADAMS

Of all the travels made by man since the voyages of Dante, this new exploration along the shores of Multiplicity and Complexity promised to be the longest, though as yet it had barely touched two familiar regions—race and sex. Even within these narrow seas the navigator lost his bearings and followed the winds as they blew. By chance it happened that Raphael Pumpelly helped the winds; for, being in Washington on his way to Central Asia he fell to talking with Adams about these matters, and said that Willard Gibbs thought he got most help from a book called the "Grammar of Science," by Karl Pearson. To Adams's vision, Willard Gibbs stood on the same plane with the three or four greatest minds of his century, and the idea that a man so incomparably superior should find help anywhere filled him with wonder. He sent for the volume and read it. From the time he sailed for Europe and reached his den on the Avenue du Bois until he took his return steamer at Cherbourg on December 26, he did little but try to find out what Karl Pearson could have taught Willard Gibbs.

Here came in, more than ever, the fatal handicap of ignorance in mathematics. Not so much the actual tool was needed, as the right to judge the product of the tool. Ignorant as one was

of the finer values of French or German, and often deceived by
the intricacies of thought hidden in the muddiness of the medium, one could sometimes catch a tendency to intelligible
meaning even in Kant or Hegel; but one had not the right to a
suspicion of error where the tool of thought was algebra. Adams
could see in such parts of the "Grammar" as he could understand, little more than an enlargement of Stallo's book already
twenty years old. He never found out what it could have taught
a master like Willard Gibbs. Yet the book had a historical value
out of all proportion to its science. No such stride had any Englishman before taken in the lines of English thought. The progress of science was measured by the success of the "Grammar,"
when, for twenty years past, Stallo had been deliberately ignored
under the usual conspiracy of silence inevitable to all thought
which demands new thought-machinery. Science needs time to
reconstruct its instruments, to follow a revolution in space; a
certain lag is inevitable; the most active mind cannot instantly
swerve from its path; but such revolutions are portentous, and
the fall or rise of half-a-dozen empires interested a student of
history less than the rise of the "Grammar of Science," the more
pressingly because, under the silent influence of Langley, he was
prepared to expect it.

For a number of years Langley had published in his Smith-
sonian Reports the revolutionary papers that foretold the over-
flow of nineteenth-century dogma, and among the first was the
famous address of Sir William Crookes on psychical research,
followed by a series of papers on Roentgen and Curie, which
had steadily driven the scientific lawgivers of Unity into the
open; but Karl Pearson was the first to pen them up for slaughter
in the schools. The phrase is not stronger than that with which
the "Grammar of Science" challenged the fight: "Anything more
hopelessly illogical than the statements with regard to Force and
Matter current in elementary textbooks of science, it is difficult
to imagine," opened Mr. Pearson, and the responsible author of
the "elementary textbook," as he went on to explain, was Lord
Kelvin himself. Pearson shut out of science everything which

the nineteenth century had brought into it. He told his scholars that they must put up with a fraction of the universe, and a very small fraction at that—the circle reached by the senses, where sequence could be taken for granted—much as the deep-sea fish takes for granted the circle of light which he generates. "Order and reason, beauty and benevolence, are characteristics and conceptions which we find solely associated with the mind of man." The assertion, as a broad truth, left one's mind in some doubt of its bearing, for order and beauty seemed to be associated also in the mind of a crystal, if one's senses were to be admitted as judge; but the historian had no interest in the universal truth of Pearson's or Kelvin's or Newton's laws; he sought only their relative drift or direction, and Pearson went on to say that these conceptions must stop: "Into the chaos beyond sense-impressions we cannot scientifically project them." We cannot even infer them: "In the chaos behind sensations, in the 'beyond' of sense-impressions, we cannot infer necessity, order or routine, for these are concepts formed by the mind of man on this side of sense-impressions"; but we must infer chaos: "Briefly chaos is all that science can logically assert of the supersensuous." The kinetic theory of gas is an assertion of ultimate chaos. In plain words, Chaos was the law of nature; Order was the dream of man.

No one means all he says, and yet very few say all they mean, for words are slippery and thought is viscous; but since Bacon and Newton, English thought had gone on impatiently protesting that no one must try to know the unknowable at the same time that every one went on thinking about it. The result was as chaotic as kinetic gas; but with the thought a historian had nothing to do. He sought only its direction. For himself he knew, that, in spite of all the Englishmen that ever lived, he would be forced to enter supersensual chaos if he meant to find out what became of British science—or indeed of any other science. From Pythagoras to Herbert Spencer, every one had done it, although commonly science had explored an ocean which it preferred to regard as Unity or a Universe, and called Order. Even Hegel, who taught that every notion included its own negation, used the negation only to reach a "larger synthesis," till he reached the universal which thinks itself, contradiction and all. The Church alone had constantly protested that anarchy was not order, that Satan was not God, that pantheism was worse than atheism, and that Unity could not be proved as a contradiction. Karl Pearson seemed to agree with the Church, but every one else, including Newton, Darwin and Clerk Maxwell, had sailed gaily into the supersensual, calling it:—

> "One God, one Law, one Element,
>   And one far-off, divine event,
>   To which the whole creation moves."

Suddenly, in 1900, science raised its head and denied.

Yet, perhaps, after all, the change had not been so sudden as it seemed. Real and actual, it certainly was, and every newspaper betrayed it, but sequence could scarcely be denied by one who had watched its steady approach, thinking the change far more interesting to history than the thought. When he reflected about it, he recalled that the flow of tide had shown itself at least twenty years before; that it had become marked as early as 1893; and that the man of science must have been sleepy indeed who did not jump from his chair like a scared dog when, in 1898, Mme. Curie threw on his desk the metaphysical bomb she called radium. There remained no hole to hide in. Even metaphysics swept back over science with the green water of the deep-sea ocean and no one could longer hope to bar out the unknowable, for the unknowable was known.

The fact was admitted that the uniformitarians of one's youth had wound about their universe a tangle of contradictions meant only for temporary support to be merged in "larger synthesis," and had waited for the larger synthesis in silence and in vain. They had refused to hear Stallo. They had betrayed little interest in Crookes. At last their universe had been wrecked by rays, and Karl Pearson undertook to cut the wreck loose with an axe, leaving science adrift on a sensual raft in the midst of a supersensual chaos. The confusion seemed, to a mere passenger, worse than that of 1600 when the astronomers upset the world; it resembled rather the convulsion of 310 when the *Civitas Dei* cut itself loose from the *Civitas Romae,* and the Cross took the place of the legions; but the historian accepted it all alike; he knew that his opinion was worthless; only, in this case, he found himself on the raft, personally and economically concerned in its drift.

English thought had always been chaos and multiplicity itself, in which the new step of Karl Pearson marked only a consistent progress; but German thought had affected system, unity, and abstract truth, to a point that fretted the most patient foreigner, and to Germany the voyager in strange seas of thought alone might resort with confident hope of renewing his youth. Turning his back on Karl Pearson and England, he plunged into Germany, and had scarcely crossed the Rhine when he fell into libraries of new works bearing the names of Ostwald, Ernst Mach, Ernst Haeckel, and others less familiar, among whom Haeckel was easiest to approach, not only because of being the oldest and clearest and steadiest spokesman of nineteenth-century mechanical convictions, but also because in 1902 he had published a vehement renewal of his faith. The volume contained only one paragraph that concerned a historian; it was that in which Haeckel sank his voice almost to a religious whisper in avowing with evident effort, that the "proper essence of substance appeared to him more and more marvellous and enigmatic as he penetrated further into the knowledge of its attributes—matter and energy—and as he learned to know their innumerable phenomena and their evolution." Since Haeckel seemed to have begun the voyage into multiplicity that Pearson had forbidden to Englishmen, he should have been a safe pilot to the point, at least, of a "proper essence of substance" in its attributes of matter and energy; but Ernst Mach seemed to go yet one step further, for he rejected matter altogether, and admitted but two processes in nature—change of place and inter-conversion of forms. Matter was Motion—Motion was Matter—the thing moved.

A student of history had no need to understand these scientific ideas of very great men; he sought only the relation with the ideas of their grandfathers, and their common direction towards the ideas of their grandsons. He had long ago reached, with Hegel, the limits of contradiction; and Ernst Mach scarcely added a shade of variety to the identity of opposites; but both of them seemed to be in agreement with Karl Pearson on the facts of the supersensual universe which could be known only as unknowable.

With a deep sigh of relief, the traveller turned back to France. There he felt safe. No Frenchman except Rabelais and Montaigne had ever taught anarchy other than as path to order. Chaos would be unity in Paris even if child of the guillotine. To make this assurance mathematically sure, the highest scientific authority in France was a great mathematician, M. Poincaré of the Institut, who published in 1902 a small volume called "La Science et l'Hypothèse," which purported to be relatively readable. Trusting to its external appearance, the traveller timidly bought it, and greedily devoured it, without understanding a single consecutive page, but catching here and there a period that startled him to the depths of his ignorance, for they seemed to show that M. Poincaré was troubled by the same historical landmarks which guided or deluded Adams himself: "[In science] we are led," said M. Poincaré, "to act as though a simple law, when other things were equal, must be more probable than a complicated law. Half a century ago one frankly confessed it, and proclaimed that nature loves simplicity. She has since given us too often the lie. To-day this tendency is no longer avowed, and only as much of it is preserved as is indispensable so that science shall not become impossible."

Here at last was a fixed point beyond the chance of confusion with self-suggestion. History and mathematics agreed. Had M. Poincaré shown anarchistic tastes, his evidence would have weighted less heavily; but he seemed to be the only authority in science who felt what a historian felt so strongly—the need of unity in a universe. "Considering everything we have made some approach towards unity. We have not gone as fast as we hoped fifty years ago; we have not always taken the intended road; but definitely we have gained much ground." This was the most clear and convincing evidence of progress yet offered to the navigator of ignorance; but suddenly he fell on another view which seemed to him quite irreconcilable with the first: "Doubtless if our means of investigation should become more and more penetrating, we should discover the simple under the complex; then the complex under the simple; then anew the simple under the complex; and so on without ever being able to foresee the last term."

A mathematical paradise of endless displacement promised eternal bliss to the mathematician, but turned the historian green with horror. Made miserable by the thought that he knew no mathematics, he burned to ask whether M. Poincaré knew any history, since he began by begging the historical question altogether, and assuming that the past showed alternating phases of simple and complex—the precise point that Adams, after fifty years of effort, found himself forced to surrender; and then going on to assume alternating phases for the future which, for the weary Titan of Unity, differed in nothing essential from the kinetic theory of a perfect gas.

Since monkeys first began to chatter in trees, neither man nor beast had ever denied or doubted Multiplicity, Diversity, Complexity, Anarchy, Chaos. Always and everywhere the Complex had been true and the Contradiction had been certain. Thought started by it. Mathematics itself began by counting one—two —three; then imagining their continuity, which M. Poincaré was still exhausting his wits to explain or defend; and this was his explanation: "In short, the mind has the faculty of creating symbols, and it is thus that it has constructed mathematical continuity which is only a particular system of symbols." With the same light touch, more destructive in its artistic measure than the heaviest-handed brutality of Englishmen or Germans, he went on to upset relative truth itself: "How should I answer the question whether Euclidian Geometry is true? It has no sense! . . . Euclidian Geometry is, and will remain, the most convenient."

Chaos was a primary fact even in Paris—especially in Paris—as it was in the Book of Genesis; but every thinking being in Paris or out of it had exhausted thought in the effort to prove Unity, Continuity, Purpose, Order, Law, Truth, the Universe, God, after having begun by taking it for granted, and discovering, to their profound dismay, that some minds denied it. The direction of mind, as a single force of nature, had been constant since history began. Its own unity had created a universe the essence of which was abstract Truth; the Absolute; God! To Thomas Aquinas, the universe was still a person; to Spinoza, a substance; to Kant, Truth was the essence of the "I"; an innate conviction; a categorical imperative; to Poincaré, it was a convenience; and to Karl Pearson, a medium of exchange.

The historian never stopped repeating to himself that he knew nothing about it; that he was a mere instrument of measure, a barometer, pedometer, radiometer; and that his whole share in the matter was restricted to the measurement of thought-motion as marked by the accepted thinkers. He took their facts for granted. He knew no more than a firefly about rays—or about race—or sex—or ennui—or a bar of music—or a pang of love—or a grain of musk—or of phosphorus—or conscience—or duty—or the force of Euclidian Geometry—or non-Euclidian—or heat—or light—or osmosis—or electrolysis—or the magnet—or ether—or *vis inertiae*—or gravitation—or cohesion—or elasticity—or surface tension—or capillary attraction—or Brownian motion—or of some scores, or thousands, or millions of chemical attractions, repulsions or indifferences which were busy within and without him; or, in brief, of Force itself, which, he was credibly informed, bore some dozen definitions in the textbooks, mostly contadictory, and all, as he was assured, beyond his intelligence; but summed up in the dictum of the last and highest science, that Motion seems to be Matter and Matter seems to be Motion, yet "we are probably incapable of discovering" what either is. History had no need to ask what either might be; all it needed to know was the admission of ignorance; the mere fact of multiplicity baffling science. Even as to the fact, science disputed, but radium happened to radiate something that seemed to explode the scientific magazine, bringing thought, for the time, to a standstill; though, in the line of thought-movement in history, radium was merely the next position, familiar and inexplicable since Zeno and his arrow: continuous from the beginning of time, and discontinuous at each successive point. History set it down on the record—pricked its position on the chart—and waited to be led, or misled, once more.

The historian must not try to know what is truth, if he values his honesty; for, if he cares for his truths, he is certain to falsify his facts. The laws of history only repeat the lines of force or thought. Yet though his will be iron, he cannot help now and then resuming his humanity or simianity in face of a fear. The motion of thought had the same value as the motion of a cannon-ball seen approaching the observer on a direct line through the air. One could watch its curve for five thousand years. Its first violent acceleration in historical times had ended in the catastrophe of 310. The next swerve of direction occurred towards 1500. Galileo and Bacon gave a still newer curve to it, which altered its values; but all these changes had never altered the continuity. Only in 1900, the continuity snapped.

Vaguely conscious of the cataclysm, the world sometimes dated it from 1893, by the Roentgen rays, or from 1898, by the Curies' radium; but in 1904, Arthur Balfour announced on the part of British science that the human race without exception had lived and died in a world of illusion until the last year of the century. The date was convenient, and convenience was truth.

The child born in 1900 would, then, be born into a new world which would not be a unity but a multiple. Adams tried to imagine it, and an education that would fit it. He found himself in a land where no one had ever penetrated before; where order was an accidental relation obnoxious to nature; artificial compulsion imposed on motion: against which every free energy of the universe revolted; and which, being merely occasional, resolved it-self back into anarchy at last. He could not deny that the law of the new multiverse explained much that had been most obscure, especially the persistently fiendish treatment of man by man, the perpetual effort of society to establish law, and the perpetual revolt of society against the law it had established; the perpetual building up of authority by force, and the perpetual appeal to force to overthrow it; the perpetual symbolism of a higher law, and the perpetual relapse to a lower one; the perpetual victory of the principles of freedom, and their perpetual conversion into principles of power; but the staggering problem was the outlook ahead into the despotism of artificial order which nature abhorred. The physicists had a phrase for it, unintelligible to the vulgar: "All that we win is a battle—lost in advance—with the irreversible phenomena in the background of nature."

All that a historian won was a vehement wish to escape. He saw his education complete, and was sorry he ever began it. As a matter of taste, he greatly preferred his eighteenth-century education when God was a father and nature a mother, and all was for the best in a scientific universe. He repudiated all share in the world as it was to be, and yet he could not detect the point where his responsibility began or ended.

As history unveiled itself in the new order, man's mind had behaved like a young pearl oyster, secreting its universe to suit its conditions until it had built up a shell of *nacre* that embodied all its notions of the perfect. Man knew it was true because he made it, and he loved it for the same reason. He sacrificed millions of lives to acquire his unity, but he achieved it, and justly thought it a work of art. The woman especially did great things, creating her deities on a higher level than the male, and, in the end, compelling the man to accept the Virgin as guardian of the man's God. The man's part in his Universe was secondary, but the woman was at home there, and sacrificed herself without limit to make it habitable, when man permitted it, as sometimes happened for brief intervals of war and famine; but she could

THE GRAMMAR OF SCIENCE

not provide protection against forces of nature. She did not
think of her universe as a raft to which the limpets stuck for life
in the surge of a supersensual chaos; she conceived herself and
her family as the centre and flower of an ordered universe which
she knew to be unity because she had made it after the image of
her own fecundity; and this creation of hers was surrounded by
beauties and perfections which she knew to be real because she
herself had imagined them.

Even the masculine philosopher admired and loved and celebrated her triumph, and the greatest of them sang it in the
noblest of his verses:—

> "Alma Venus, coeli subter labentia signa
> Quae mare navigerum, quae terras frugiferenteis
> Concelebras . . . .
> Quae quoniam rerum naturam sola gubernas,
> Nec sine te quidquam dias in luminis oras
> Exoritur, neque fit laetum neque amabile quidquam;
> Te sociam studeo!"

Neither man nor woman ever wanted to quit this Eden of their
own invention, and could no more have done it of their own ac-
cord than the pearl oyster could quit its shell; but although the
oyster might perhaps assimilate or embalm a grain of sand
forced into its aperture, it could only perish in face of the
cyclonic hurricane or the volcanic upheaval of its bed. Her
supersensual chaos killed her.

Such seemed the theory of history to be imposed by science
on the generation born after 1900. For this theory, Adams
felt himself in no way responsible. Even as historian he had
made it his duty always to speak with respect of everything that
had ever been thought respectable—except an occasional states-
man; but he had submitted to force all his life, and he meant to
accept it for the future as for the past. All his efforts had been
turned only to the search for its channel. He never invented his
facts; they were furnished him by the only authorities he could
find. As for himself, according to Helmholz, Ernst Mach, and
Arthur Balfour, he was henceforth to be a conscious ball of vi-
brating motions, traversed in every direction by infinite lines of

rotation or vibration, rolling at the feet of the Virgin at Chartres
or of M. Poincaré in an attic at Paris, a centre of supersensual
chaos. The discovery did not distress him. A solitary man of
sixty-five years or more, alone in a Gothic cathedral or a Paris
apartment, need fret himself little about a few illusions more or
less. He should have learned his lesson fifty years earlier; the
times had long passed when a student could stop before chaos
or order; he had no choice but to march with his world.

Nevertheless, he could not pretend that his mind felt flattered
by this scientific outlook. Every fabulist has told how the human
mind has always struggled like a frightened bird to escape the
chaos which caged it; how—appearing suddenly and inex-
plicably out of some unknown and unimaginable void; passing
half its known life in the mental chaos of sleep; victim even
when awake, to its own ill-adjustment, to disease, to age, to
external suggestion, to nature's compulsion; doubting its sensations, and, in the last resort, trusting only to instruments and
averages—after sixty or seventy years of growing astonishment,
the mind wakes to find itself looking blankly into the void of
death. That it should profess itself pleased by this performance
was all that the highest rules of good breeding could ask; but
that it should actually be satisfied would prove that it existed
only as idiocy.

Satisfied, the future generation could scarcely think itself, for
even when the mind existed in a universe of its own creation, it
had never been quite at ease. As far as one ventured to inter-
pret actual science, the mind had thus far adjusted itself by an
infinite series of infinitely delicate adjustments forced on it by
the infinite motion of an infinite chaos of motion; dragged at one
moment into the unknowable and unthinkable, then trying to
scramble back within its senses and to bar the chaos out, but
always assimilating bits of it, until at last, in 1900, a new avalanche of unknown forces had fallen on it, which required new
mental powers to control. If this view was correct, the mind
could gain nothing by flight or by fight; it must merge in its
supersensual multiverse, or succumb to it.

On Being Original

IRVING BABBITT

There has been a radical change during the last hundred years in the world's attitude toward originality. An age of conformity has given way to an age of self-assertion; so that nowadays a man makes a bid for fame by launching a paradox, much as he might have done in the time of Pope by polishing a commonplace. Then, even a person of genuine originality was in danger of being accounted freakish. Now, many a man passes for original who is in reality only freakish. Boileau, speaking for the old criticism, says that Perrault was "bizarre;" Sainte-Beuve, speaking for the new, says that Perrault had genius. From the outset, the neo-classic critics stifled free initiative in the name of the "rules," and opposed to every attempt at innovation the authority of Aristotle and the ancients. The relation of the literary aspirant to the "models" during this period is not unfairly summed up in the words of the comic opera,—

> "Of course you can never be like us,
> But be as like us as you're able to be."

Later, under French influence, the tyranny of etiquette was added to the tyranny of classical imitation. Aristotle was reinforced by the dancing master. Social convention so entwined itself about the whole nature of a Frenchman of the Old Régime that it finally became almost as hard for him as we may suppose it is for a Chinaman to disengage his originality from the coils of custom. The very word original was often used as a

Reprinted from *Literature and the American College* by Irving Babbitt, 1908. Reprinted by permission of the publishers, Houghton Mifflin Company.

term of ridicule and disparagement. Brossette writes of the Oriental traveler Tavernier that he is "brutal and even a bit original." "When it is desired to turn any one to ridicule," writes Boursault about the same time, "he is said to be an *original sans copie.*" Anything in literature or art that departed from the conventional type was pronounced "monstrous." La Harpe applies this epithet to the "Divine Comedy," and points out how inferior the occasional felicities of this "absurd and shapeless rhapsody" are to the correct beauties of a true epic like Voltaire's "Henriade."

And so we might go on, as Mr. Saintsbury, for example, does for scores of pages in his "History of Criticism," exposing the neo-classic narrowness, and setting forth in contrast the glories of our modern emancipation. But this is to give one's self the pleasure, as the French would say, of smashing in open doors. Instead of engaging in this exhilarating pastime, we might, perhaps, find more profit in inquiring, first, into the definite historical reasons that led to the triumph of the so-called school of good sense over the school of genius and originality; and second, in seeking for the element of truth that lurked beneath even the most arid and unpromising of the neo-classic conventions. For if, like Mr. Saintsbury and many other romanticists, we reject the truth along with the convention, we shall simply fall from one extreme into another.

The whole subject of originality is closely bound up with what is rather vaguely known as individualism. We must recollect that before the disciplinary classicism of the later Renaissance there was an earlier Renaissance which was in a high degree favorable to originality. At the very beginning of this earlier period, Petrarch made his famous plea for originality, in a letter to Boccaccio, and established his claim, in this as in other respects, to be considered the first modern man. "Every one," says Petrarch, "has not only in his countenance and gestures, but also in his voice and language, something peculiarly his own (*quiddam suum ac proprium*), which it is both easier and wiser to cultivate and correct than it is to alter." And so many of the Italians who followed Petrarch set out to cultivate the *quiddam suum ac proprium,* often showing real ardor for self-expression, and still oftener, perhaps, using the new liberty merely as a cloak for license. Society finally took alarm, not only at the license, but at the clash of rival originalities, each man indulging in his own individual sense without much reference to the general or common sense of mankind. We need not, however, repeat what we have already said in our first essay about the reaction of the later Renaissance against an excessive individualism. This reaction, especially in France and Italy, soon ran into excesses of its own. Yet we must not forget that, at the moment when the neo-classic disciplinarian appeared on the scene, the great creative impulse of the early Renaissance was already dying out or degenerating into affectation. The various forms of bad taste that spread like an epidemic over Europe at the end of the sixteenth century and beginning of the seventeenth (cultism, Marinism, euphuism, préciosité, etc.), have their common source in a straining to be original in defiance of sound reason. We may say of the writers of these different schools as a class that, in spite of occasional lyrical felicities, they have "all the nodosities of the oak without its strength and all the contortions of the Sibyl without the inspiration."

The school of good sense was the natural and legitimate protest against this pseudo-originality. But this school can be justified on higher grounds than simply as a reaction from a previous excess. It tried to apply, however imperfectly, the profound doctrine of Aristotle that the final test of art is not its originality, but its truth to the universal. The question is one of special interest because we are living in an age that comes at the end of a great era of expansion, comparable in some ways to that of the Renaissance. Now, as then, there is a riot of so-called originality. In the name of this originality art is becoming more and more centrifugal and eccentric. As the result of our loss of standards, the classicist would complain, we are inbreeding personal and national peculiarities and getting farther and farther away from what is universally human.

In other words, the chief ambition of our modern art, which resembles in this respect some of the art of the later Renaissance, is to be original. The first aim of both classic and neo-classic art, on the other hand, was to be representative. Aristotle had said that it is not enough to render a thing as it is in this or that particular case, but as it is in general; and he goes on to say that the superiority of poetry over history lies in the fact that it has more of this universality, that it is more concerned with the essentials and less with the accidents of human nature. The weakness of neo-classic art was that it substituted the rule of thumb and servile imitation for direct observation in deciding what were accidents and what were essentials. It was ready to proscribe a thing as "monstrous,"—that is, as outside of nature, —when in reality it was simply outside the bounds set by certain commentators on Aristotle. The artist had to conform to the conventional types established in this way, even if he sacrificed to them poignancy and directness of emotion. He was limited by the type not only in dealing with any particular literary form,—tragedy, epic, and so forth,—but even in his creating of individual characters. For example, he must be careful not to paint a particular soldier, but the typical soldier, and of course he was not to depart too far from the classical models in deciding what the traits of the typical soldier are. Thus Rymer condemns Iago because he is not true to the "character constantly worn by soldiers for some thousands of years in the world." According to Rymer, again, the queen in one of Beaumont and Fletcher's plays oversteps the bounds of decorum. Some particular queen, Rymer admits, may have acted in this way; but she must be rid of all her "accidental historical impudence" before she can become an orthodox, typical queen, entitled to "stalk in tragedy on her high shoes."

The attempt of the neo-classicists to tyrannize over originality and restrict the creative impulse in the name of the type was bound in the long run to provoke a reaction. To carry through the difficult and delicate task of breaking with convention some man of more than Socratic wisdom was needed; instead, this task was undertaken by the "self-torturing sophist, wild Rousseau." In almost the opening sentence of his "Confessions" Rousseau strikes the note that is heard throughout the nineteenth century, from the early romanticists to Ibsen and Sudermann: "If I am not better than other men, at least I am different." By this gloating sense of his own departure from the type Rousseau became the father of eccentric individualists. By his insistence on the rights and legitimacy of unrestrained emotion he inaugurated the age of storm and stress, not only in Germany, but throughout Europe. Our modern impressionists, who would make of their own sensibility the measure of all things, are only his late-born disciples.

Emotion, insists the classicist, must be disciplined and subdued to what is typical; else it will be eccentric and not true to the human heart. "The human heart of whom?" cries Alfred de Musset, like a true disciple of Jean-Jacques. "The human heart of what? Even though the devil be in it, I have my human heart of my own—*j'ai mon coeur humain, moi.*" The whole of French romanticism is in that *moi.* Away with stale authority, usage, and tradition, that would come between a man and his own spontaneity, and keep him from immediate contact with "nature." Let him once more see the world bathed in the fresh wonder of the dawn. To this end let him discard books ("a dull and endless strife") and live as if "none had lived before him."

Every man, in short, is to be an original genius. It was the assumption of this attitude by Rousseau's followers in Germany that gave its name to a whole literary period (*Geniezeit*). Germany sought its emancipation from convention, not, as Lessing would have wished, through the discipline of reason, but through "genius" and "originality," which meant in practice the opening of the floodgates of sentiment. We can imagine the disgust with which Lessing looked on the Rousseauism of the youthful Goethe. In "Werther," critics are accused of being in a conspiracy against originality. Their rules are compared to a system of dams and trenches with which the critics protect their own little cabbage-patches against genius, whose impetuous waves would otherwise burst forth and overwhelm them, and at the same time astound the world. One thinks of Lessing's admirable defense of criticism, of the passage in which he confesses that he owes all he has, not to genius and originality, but to a patient assimilation of the wisdom of the past. "Without criticism I should be poor, cold, short-sighted. I am, therefore, always ashamed or annoyed when I hear or read anything in disparagement of criticism. It is said to suppress genius, and I flattered myself that I had gained from it something very nearly approaching genius. I am a lame man who cannot possibly be edified by abuse of his crutch."

We are still inclined to side with original genius against what Lessing calls criticism. Criticism itself has come to mean nowadays mere appreciativeness, instead of meaning, as it did for Lessing, the application of standards of judgment. It may, however, appear some day how much the great romantic leaders, Shelley for example, suffered from the absence of just what Lessing called criticism. Men may then grow weary of a genius and originality that are at bottom only an outpouring of undisciplined emotion. One whole side of our American transcendental school is only a belated echo of German romanticism, which itself continues the age of original genius. There is special danger even in Emerson's conception of originality, and the unbounded deference with which it fills him for the untrained individual. Every man, to become great, merely needs, it would appear, to plant himself indomitably on his instincts; but it is not safe for the average person to trust so blindly to what Rymer would have called his own "maggot." Hawthorne, the best observer of the group, has left an account of some of the nightmare originalities that were developed under the Concord influence.

We read of a certain character in one of Marivaux's plays: "He is a man whose first impulse is to ask, not, 'Do you esteem me?' but, 'Are you surprised at me?' His purpose is not to convince us that he is better than other people, but that he resembles himself alone." The comedy in which this eighteenth-century Bernard Shaw figures was written a number of years before Rousseau assumed the Armenian costume and began to agitate Europe with his paradoxes. Since Rousseau the world has become increasingly familiar with the man who poses and attitudinizes before it and is not satisfied until he can draw its attention to the traits that establish his own uniqueness. The eccentric individualist not only rejoices in his own singularity, but is usually eager to thrust it on other people. His aim is to startle, or, as the French would say, to *épater le bourgeois*, to make the plain citizen "stare and gasp." Dr. Johnson said of Lord Monboddo that if he had had a tail he would have been as proud of it as a squirrel. Perhaps Rousseau was never more deeply hurt than by the lady who said, on breaking with him, "You're just like other men." This, as a French critic remarks, was a home thrust that one of Molière's soubrettes could not have improved upon. The claim of Rousseau and his earlier followers was to be not simply unique, but unique in feeling. This sentiment of uniqueness in feeling speedily became that of uniqueness in suffering—on the familiar principle, no doubt, that life, which is a comedy for those who think, is a tragedy for those who feel. Hence arose in the romantic school a somewhat theatrical affectation of grief. Byron was far from being the first who paraded before the public "the pageant of his bleeding heart." Chateaubriand especially nourished in himself the sense of fated and preëminent sorrow, and was ready to exclaim at the most ordinary mischance: "Such things happen only to me!" Sainte-Beuve makes an interesting comparison between Chateaubriand and another native of Brittany, the author of "Gil Blas." "A book like 'René,'" says Sainte-Beuve, "encourages a subtle spiritual pride. A man seeks in his imagination some unique misfortune to which he may abandon himself and which he may fold about him in solitude. He says to himself that a great soul must contain more sorrow than a little one; and adds in a whisper that he himself may be this great soul. 'Gil Blas,' on the other hand, is a book that brings you into full contact with life and the throng of your fellow creatures. When you are very gloomy and believe in fatality and imagine that certain extraordinary things happen to you alone, read 'Gil Blas,' and you will find that he had that very misfortune or one just like it, and that he took it as a simple mishap and got over it."

The same contrast might be brought out by comparing Montaigne and Rousseau, the two writers who, in a broad sense, are the masters respectively of Lesage and Chateaubriand. This contrast is easily missed, because at first glance Montaigne seems an arch-egotist like Rousseau, and is almost equally ready to bestow his own idiosyncrasies on the reader. Yet in the final analysis Montaigne is interested in Montaigne because he is a human being; Rousseau is interested in Rousseau because he is Jean-Jacques. Montaigne observes himself impartially as a normal specimen of the genus homo. Rousseau, as we have seen, positively gloats over his own otherwiseness. Montaigne aims to be the average, or, it would be less misleading to say, the representative man; Rousseau's aim is to be the extraordinary man, or original genius. Rousseau is an eccentric, Montaigne a concentric individualist. The sentence of Montaigne that sums him up is, "Every man bears within him the entire image of the human lot." Rousseau is rather summed up in his phrase, "There are souls that are too privileged to follow the common path," with its corollary that he is himself one of these privileged souls.

The nineteenth century saw the rise of a race of eccentric individualists, especially in art and literature, who, like Rousseau, scorned the common path and strove to distinguish themselves from the bourgeois and philistine in everything, from the details of their dress to the refinements of their sensations. In this quest of the rare and the original they attained to a departure from the norm that was not only eccentric, but pathological. Every man was to have the right to express not only his own particular vision of life, but his own particular nightmare. We finally come to a writer like Baudelaire, who builds himself a "little strangely scented and strangely colored kiosk on the extreme tip of the romantic Kamchatka" and "cultivates his hysteria with delight and terror;" who, instead of being true to the human heart, as the old-fashioned classicist would say, makes it his ambition to create a "new shudder." All the modern writer cares for, says M. Anatole France, is to be thought original. In his fear of becoming commonplace he prides himself, like Victor Hugo, on reading only those books that other men do not read, or else he does not read at all, and so comes to resemble that eighteenth-century Frenchwoman who was said to have "respected in her ignorance the active principle of her originality." The danger of the man who is too assimilative, who possesses too perfectly the riches of tradition, is to feel that originality is henceforth impossible. It is related of a French critic that he used to turn away wearily from every new volume of poetry that was submitted to him, with the remark: "All the verses are written."

Genuine originality, however, is a hardy growth, and usually gains more than it loses by striking deep root into the literature of the past. La Bruyère begins his "Characters" by observing that "Everything has been said," and then goes on to write one of the most original books in French. Montaigne wrote a still more original book which often impresses the reader as a mere cento of quotations. An excessive respect for the past is less harmful than the excess from which we are now suffering. For example, one of our younger writers is praised in a review for his "stark freedom from tradition . . . as though he came into the world of letters without ever a predecessor. He is the expression in literary art of certain enormous repudiations." It is precisely this notion of originality that explains the immense insignificance of so much of our contemporary writing. The man who breaks with the past in this way will think that he is original when he is in reality merely ignorant and presumptuous. He is apt to imagine himself about a century ahead of his age when he is at least four or five centuries behind it. "He comes to you," as Bagehot puts it, "with a notion that Noah discarded in the ark, and attracts attention to it as if it were a stupendous novelty of his own."

We may be sure that the more enlightened of the Cave Dwellers had already made deeper discoveries in human nature than many of our modern radicals. Goethe said that if as a young man he had known of the masterpieces that already existed in Greek he would never have written a line. Goethe carries his modesty too far; but how grateful just a touch of it would be in the average author of to-day! With even a small part of Goethe's knowledge and insight, he would no longer go on serving up to us the dregs and last muddy lees of the romantic and naturalistic movements as originality and genius. He would see that his very paradoxes were stale. Instead of being a half-baked author, he would become a modest and at the same time judicious reader; or, if he continued to write, he would be less anxious to create and more anxious to humanize his creations. Sooner or later every author, as well as the characters he conceives, will have to answer the question that was the first addressed to anyone who designed to enter the Buddhist church: "Are you a human being?" The world's suffrage will go in the long run to the writer or artist who dwells habitually in the centre and not on the remote periphery of human nature. Gautier paid a doubtful compliment to Victor Hugo when he said that Hugo's works seemed to proceed not from a man, but an element, that they were Cyclopean, "as it were, the works of Polyphemus." Hugo remained the original genius to the end, in contrast with Goethe, who attained humane restraint after having begun as a Rousseauist.

Romanticism from the very beginning tended to become eccentric through over-anxiety to be original; and romanticism is now running to seed. Many of our contemporary writers are as plainly in an extreme as the most extreme of the neo-classicists. They think that to be original they need merely to arrive at self-expression without any effort to be representative. The neo-classicist, on the other hand, strove so hard to be representative that he often lost the personal flavor entirely and fell into colorless abstraction. Both extremes fail equally of being humane. For, to revert to our fundamental principle, the humanist must combine opposite extremes and occupy all the space between them. Genuine originality is so immensely difficult because it imposes the task of achieving work that is of general human truth and at the same time intensely individual. Perhaps the best examples of this union of qualities are found in Greek. The original man for the Greek was the one who could create in the very act of imitating the past. Greek literature at its best is to a remarkable degree a creative imitation of Homer.

The modern does not, like the Greek, hope to become original by assimilating tradition, but rather by ignoring it, or, if he is a scholar, by trying to prove that it is mistaken. We have been discussing thus far almost entirely the originality of the Rousseauist or sentimental naturalist; but we should not fail to note the curious points of contact here as elsewhere between sentimental and scientific naturalism. The Baconian aims less at the assimilation of past wisdom than at the advancement of learning. With him too the prime stress is on the new and the original. Formerly there was a pedantry of authority and prescription. As a result of the working together of Rousseauist and Baconian there has arisen a veritable pedantry of originality. The scientific pedant who is entirely absorbed in his own bit of research is first cousin to the artistic and literary pedant who is entirely absorbed in his own sensation. The hero of modern scholarship is not the humanist, but the investigator. The man who digs up an unpublished document from some musty archive outranks the man who can deal judiciously with the documents already in print. His glory will be all the greater if he can make the new document a pretext for writing a book, for attempting a rehabilitation. The love of truth shades imperceptibly into the love of paradox; and Rousseauist and Baconian often coexist in the same person.

A royal road to a reputation for originality is to impugn the verdicts of the past,—to whitewash what is traditionally black or to blackwash what is traditionally white. Only the other day one of the English reviews published the "Blackwashing of Dante." A still better example is Renan's blackwashing of King David, which concludes as follows: "Pious souls, when they take delight in the sentiments filled with resignation and tender melancholy contained in the most beautiful of the liturgical books, will imagine that they are in communion with this bandit. Humanity will believe in final justice on the testimony of David, who never gave it a thought, and of the Sibyl, who never existed," etc. The whitewashings have been still more numerous. Rehabilitations have appeared of Tiberius, the Borgias, and Robespierre. A book has also been written to prove that the first Napoleon was a man of an eminently peace-loving disposition. Mr. Stephen Phillips undertakes to throw a poetical glamour over the character of Nero, that amiable youth, who, as the versifier in "Punch" observes,—

> "would have doubtless made his mark,
> Had he not, in a mad, mad, boyish lark,
> Murdered his mother!"

If this whitewashing and blackwashing goes on, the time will soon come when the only way left to be original will be to make a modest plea for the traditional good sense of the world. This traditional good sense was never treated with an easier contempt than at present. A writer named Bax, who recently published a volume rehabilitating the revolutionary monster Marat, says in his preface: "It is in fact a fairly safe rule to ascertain for oneself what most people think on such questions" (*i.e.* as the character of Marat), "and then assume the exact opposite to be true." Of most books of this kind we may say what Fitzgerald said when Henry Irving made himself up in the rôle of Shylock to look like the Saviour: "It is an attempt to strike out an original idea in the teeth of common sense and tradition." Of course there are in every age and individual, as we have said elsewhere, elements that run counter to the main tendency. One of the regular recipes for writing German doctors' theses is to seize on one of these elements, exaggerate it, and take it as a point of departure for refuting the traditional view. Thus Rousseau says in one place that he has always detested political agitators. We may be sure in advance that some German will start from this to prove that Rousseau has been cruelly maligned in being looked on as a revolutionist.

Even our more serious scholars are finding it hard to resist that something in the spirit of the age which demands that their results be not only just, but novel. Even our older universities are becoming familiar with the professor who combines in about equal measure his love of research and his love of the limelight. In public opinion, the perfection of the type is the Chicago professor whose originality has become the jest of the cheap newspapers. Here are a few Chicago "discoveries," selected almost at random from the many that have been announced from time to time in the daily press:—

Kissing causes lockjaw.

The Pennsylvanians are turning into Indians.

A man does not need to take exercise after the age of thirty-five.

Music is antiseptic.

A dog will not follow an uneducated man.

Marriage is a form of insanity.

Americans are incapable of friendship.

Boccaccio was a Swede.

John D. Rockefeller is as great a man as Shakespeare.

Some day a wounded or even worn-out heart of a human being may be replaced by a healthy heart from a living monkey, etc.

The Chicago professors would say, and no doubt rightly, that they are misrepresented by these newspaper statements.[1] But we are only giving the general impression. Even the utterance of Dr. Osler that at once gave him such a start over all his academic rivals in the race for notoriety becomes comparatively unsensational when read in its context. The professor with an

---

[1] Chicago instructors have told me that the University is the victim of a sort of conspiracy on the part of certain newspapers.

itch for the limelight has only to pattern himself on Rousseau, the great master of paradox. Rousseau's method has been compared to that of a man who fires off a pistol in the street to attract a crowd. When Rousseau has once drawn his crowd, he may proceed to attenuate his paradox, until sometimes it is in danger of dwindling into a commonplace.

Most good observers would probably agree that contemporary scholarship and literature are becoming too eccentric and centrifugal; they would agree that some unifying principle is needed to counteract this excessive striving after originality. For example, Professor Gummere, who is one of the most distinguished representatives of the scholarly tradition that ultimately goes back to Herder and the Grimm brothers, diagnoses our present malady with great clearness in a recent article on "Originality and Convention in Literature." [1] The higher forms of poetry and creative art, he says, are being made impossible by the disintegrating influences at work in modern life, and by an excess of analysis. He suggests as remedy that we jettison this intellectual and analytical element, and seek to restore once more the bond of communal sympathy. This remedy betrays at once its romantic origin. It is only one form of Rousseau's assumption that an unaided sympathy will do more to draw men together than the naked forces of egoism and self-assertion will do to drive them asunder. Even in his studies of the beginnings of poetry Professor Gummere should, perhaps, have insisted more on communal discipline as a needful preliminary to communal sympathy. However that may be, our present hope does not seem to lie in the romanticist's attempt to revert to the unity of instinct and feeling that he supposes to have existed in primitive life. We need to commune and unite in what is above rather than in what is below our ordinary selves, and the pathway to this higher unity is not through sympathy, communal or otherwise, but through restraint. If we have got so far apart, it is because of the lack, not of sympathy, but of humane standards.

[1] *Quarterly Review*, January, 1906.

Without trying to enter fully into so large a topic as the impressionism of our modern society, its loss of traditional standards, and its failure as yet to find new, we may at least point out that education should be less infected than it is with a pedantic straining after originality. In general, education should represent the conservative and unifying element in our national life. The college especially must maintain humane standards, if it is to have any reason at all for existing as something distinct from university and preparatory school. Its function is not, as is so often assumed, merely to help its students to self-expression, but even more to help them to become humane. In the words of Cardinal Newman, the college is "the great ordinary means to a great but ordinary end;" this end is to supply principles of taste and judgment and train in sanity and centrality of view; to give background and perspective, and inspire, if not the spirit of conformity, at least a proper respect for the past experience of the world. Most of us have heard of Mrs. Shelley's reply when advised to send her boy to a school where he would be taught to think for himself: "My God! teach him rather to think like other people." Mrs. Shelley had lived with a man who was not only a real genius, but also an original genius in the German sense, and knew whereof she spoke. Now the college should not necessarily teach its students to think like other people, but it should teach them to distinguish between what is original and what is merely odd and eccentric, both in themselves and others. According to Lowell, this is a distinction that Wordsworth could never make, and Wordsworth is not alone in this respect among the romantic leaders. We must insist, at the risk of causing scandal, that the college is not primarily intended to encourage originality and independence of thought as these terms are often understood. The story is told of a professor in one of our Eastern colleges that he invariably gave a high mark to the undergraduates who contradicted the received opinions in his subject; but the highest mark he reserved for the undergraduate who in addition to contradicting the traditional view set up a new view of his own. As this fact became known, the professor was gratified by a rapid growth among his students of independent and original thinking.

The college should guard against an undue stress on self-expression and an insufficient stress on humane assimilation. This danger is especially plain in the teaching of English composition. A father once said to me of a "daily theme" course that it had at least set his son's wits to working. But what if it set them to working in the void? The most that can be expected of youths who are put to writing with little or no background of humane assimilation is a clever impressionism. They will be fitted, not to render serious service to literature, but at most to shine in the more superficial kinds of journalism. It is still an open question whether any direct method of teaching English really takes the place of the drill in the niceties of style that can be derived from translation, especially the translation of Latin; whether a student, for example, who rendered Cicero with due regard for the delicate shades of meaning would not gain more mastery of English (to say nothing of Latin) than a student who devoted the same amount of time to daily themes and original composition. We must, however, be fair to our departments of English. They have to cope with conditions not entirely of their own making, of which the most serious is something approaching illiteracy in many of the students that are forced upon them from the preparatory schools. In practice they have to devote most of their time to imparting, not the elegancies, but the simplest decencies of the English language. Ultimately a great deal of what goes on in the more elementary college courses in English may well be relegated to the lower schools,—and the home, —and the work that is done in the advanced courses in composition will probably either be omitted entirely, or else done, as it is in France, in connection with the reading and detailed study of great writers. Assimilation will then keep pace as it should with expression.

Spinoza says that a man should constantly keep before his eyes a sort of exemplar of human nature (*idea hominis, tamquam naturae humanae exemplar*). He should, in other words, have a humane standard to which he may defer, and which will not proscribe originality, but will help him to discriminate between what is original and what is merely freakish and abnormal in himself and others. Now this humane standard may be gained by a few through philosophic insight, but in most cases it will be attained, if at all, by a knowledge of good literature—by a familiarity with that golden chain of masterpieces which links together into a single tradition the more permanent experience of the race; books which so agree in essentials that they seem, as Emerson puts it, to be the work of one all-seeing, all-hearing gentleman. In short, the most practical way of promoting humanism is to work for a revival of the almost lost art of reading. As a general rule, the humane man will be the one who has a memory richly stored with what is best in literature, with the sound sense perfectly expressed that is found only in the masters. Conversely, the decline of humanism and the growth of Rousseauism has been marked by a steady decay in the higher uses of the memory. For the Greeks the Muses were not the daughters of Inspiration or of Genius, as they would be for a modern, but the daughters of Memory. Sainte-Beuve says that "from time to time we should raise our eyes to the hill-tops, to the group of revered mortals, and ask ourselves: What would they say of us?" No one whose memory is not enriched in the way we have described can profit by this advice. Sainte-Beuve himself in giving it was probably only remembering Longinus.[1]

[1] See *On the Sublime,* section xiv.

Human Nature and Conduct: Introduction

JOHN DEWEY

"Give a dog a bad name and hang him." Human nature has
been the dog of professional moralists, and consequences ac-
cord with the proverb. Man's nature has been regarded with
suspicion, with fear, with sour looks, sometimes with enthusiasm for its possibilities but only when these were placed in contrast with its actualities. It has appeared to be so evilly disposed
that the business of morality was to prune and curb it; it would
be thought better of if it could be replaced by something else.
It has been supposed that morality would be quite superfluous
were it not for the inherent weakness, bordering on depravity,
of human nature. Some writers with a more genial conception
have attributed the current blackening to theologians who have
thought to honor the divine by disparaging the human. Theologians have doubtless taken a gloomier view of man than have
pagans and secularists. But this explanation doesn't take us far.
For after all these theologians are themselves human, and they
would have been without influence if the human audience had
not somehow responded to them.

Morality is largely concerned with controlling human nature.
When we are attempting to control anything we are acutely
aware of what resists us. So moralists were led, perhaps, to think
of human nature as evil because of its reluctance to yield to control, its rebelliousness under the yoke. But this explanation
only raises another question. Why did morality set up rules so

---

From *Human Nature and Conduct*, by John Dewey. By permission of
Henry Holt and Company, Inc., 1922, 1950.

foreign to human nature? The ends it insisted upon, the regulations it imposed, were after all outgrowths of human nature. Why then was human nature so averse to them? Moreover rules can be obeyed and ideals realized only as they appeal to something in human nature and awaken in it an active response. Moral principles that exalt themselves by degrading human nature are in effect committing suicide. Or else they involve human nature in unending civil war, and treat it as a hopeless mess of contradictory forces.

We are forced therefore to consider the nature and origin of that control of human nature with which morals has been occupied. And the fact which is forced upon us when we raise this question is the existence of classes. Control has been vested in an oligarchy. Indifference to regulation has grown in the gap which separates the ruled from the rulers. Parents, priests, chiefs, social censors have supplied aims, aims which were foreign to those upon whom they were imposed, to the young, laymen, ordinary folk; a few have given and administered rule, and the mass have in a passable fashion and with reluctance obeyed. Everybody knows that good children are those who make as little trouble as possible for their elders, and since most of them cause a good deal of annoyance they must be naughty by nature. Generally speaking, good people have been those who did what they were told to do, and lack of eager compliance is a sign of something wrong in their nature.

But no matter how much men in authority have turned moral rules into an agency of class supremacy, any theory which attributes the origin of rule to deliberate design is false. To take advantage of conditions after they have come into existence is one thing; to create them for the sake of an advantage to accrue is quite another thing. We must go back of the bare fact of social division into superior and inferior. To say that accident produced social conditions is to perceive they were not produced by intelligence. Lack of understanding of human nature is the primary cause of disregard for it. Lack of insight always ends in despising or else unreasoned admiration. When men

had no scientific knowledge of physical nature they either pas-
sively submitted to it or sought to control it magically. What
cannot be understood cannot be managed intelligently. It has
to be forced into subjection from without. The opagueness of
human nature to reason is equivalent to a belief in its intrinsic
irregularity. Hence a decline in the authority of social oligarchy
was accompanied by a rise of scientific interest in human nature.
This means that the make-up and working of human forces
afford a basis for moral ideas and ideals. Our science of human
nature in comparison with physical sciences is rudimentary,
and morals which are concerned with the health, efficiency and
happiness of a development of human nature are correspond-
ingly elementary. These pages are a discussion of some phases
of the ethical change involved in positive respect for human
nature when the latter is associated with scientific knowledge.
We may anticipate the general nature of this change through
considering the evils which have resulted from severing morals
from the actualities of human physiology and psychology. There
is a pathology of goodness as well as of evil; that is, of that sort
of goodness which is nurtured by this separation. The badness
of good people, for the most part recorded only in fiction, is the
revenge taken by human nature for the injuries heaped upon it
in the name of morality. In the first place, morals cut off from
positive roots in man's nature is bound to be mainly negative.
Practical emphasis falls upon avoidance, escape of evil, upon
not doing things, observing prohibitions. Negative morals assume as many forms as there are types of temperament subject
to it. Its commonest form is the protective coloration of a neutral respectability, an insipidity of character. For one man who
thanks God that he is not as other men there are a thousand to
offer thanks that they are as other men, sufficiently as others are
to escape attention. Absence of social blame is the usual mark
of goodness for it shows that evil has been avoided. Blame is
most readily averted by being so much like everybody else that
one passes unnoticed. Conventional morality is a drab morality,
in which the only fatal thing is to be conspicuous. If there be

flavor left in it, then some natural traits have somehow escaped being subdued. To be so good as to attract notice is to be priggish, too good for this world. The same psychology that brands the convicted criminal as forever a social outcast makes it the part of a gentleman not to obtrude virtues noticeably upon others.

The Puritan is never popular, not even in a society of Puritans. In case of a pinch, the mass prefer to be good fellows rather than to be good men. Polite vice is preferable to eccentricity and ceases to be vice. Morals that professedly neglect human nature end by emphasizing those qualities of human nature that are most commonplace and average; they exaggerate the herd instinct to conformity. Professional guardians of morality who have been exacting with respect to themselves have accepted avoidance of conspicuous evil as enough for the masses. One of the most instructive things in all human history is the system of concessions, tolerances, mitigations and reprieves which the Catholic Church with its official supernatural morality has devised for the multitude. Elevation of the spirit above everything natural is tempered by organized leniency for the frailties of flesh. To uphold an aloof realm of strictly ideal realities is admitted to be possible only for a few. Protestantism, except in its most zealous forms, has accomplished the same result by a sharp separation between religion and morality in which a higher justification by faith disposes at one stroke of daily lapses into the gregarious morals of average conduct.

There are always ruder forceful natures who cannot tame themselves to the required level of colorless conformity. To them conventional morality appears as an organized futility; though they are usually unconscious of their own attitude since they are heartily in favor of morality for the mass as making it easier to manage them. Their only standard is success, putting things over, getting things done. Being good is to them practically synonymous with ineffectuality; and accomplishment, achievement is its own justification. They know by experience that much is forgiven to those who succeed, and they leave goodness to the stupid, to those whom they qualify as boobs. Their gregarious nature finds sufficient outlet in the conspicuous tribute they pay to all established institutions as guardians of ideal interests, and in their denunciations of all who openly defy conventionalized ideals. Or they discover that they are the chosen agents of a higher morality and walk subject to specially ordained laws. Hypocrisy in the sense of a deliberate covering up of a will to evil by loud-voiced protestations of virtue is one of the rarest of occurrences. But the combination in the same person of an intensely executive nature with a love of popular approval is bound, in the face of conventional morality, to produce what the critical term hypocrisy.

Another reaction to the separation of morals from human nature is a romantic glorification of natural impulse as something superior to all moral claims. There are those who lack the persistent force of the executive will to break through conventions and to use them for their own purposes, but who unite sensitiveness with intensity of desire. Fastening upon the conventional element in morality, they hold that all morality is a conventionality hampering to the development of individuality. Although appetites are the commonest things in human nature, the least distinctive or individualized, they identify unrestraint in satisfaction of appetite with free realization of individuality. They treat subjection to passion as a manifestation of freedom in the degree in which it shocks the bourgeois. The urgent need for a transvaluation of morals is caricatured by the notion that an avoidance of the avoidances of conventional morals constitutes positive achievement. While the executive type keeps its eyes on actual conditions so as to manipulate them, this school abrogates objective intelligence in behalf of sentiment, and withdraws into little coteries of emancipated souls.

There are others who take seriously the idea of morals separated from the ordinary actualities of humanity and who attempt to live up to it. Some become engrossed in spiritual egotism. They are preoccupied with the state of their character, concerned for the purity of their motives and the goodness of their souls. The exaltation of conceit which sometimes accompanies this absorption can produce a corrosive inhumanity which exceeds the possibilities of any other known form of selfishness. In other cases, persistent preoccupation with the thought of an ideal realm breeds morbid discontent with surroundings, or induces a futile withdrawal into an inner world where all facts are fair to the eye. The needs of actual conditions are neglected, or dealt with in a half-hearted way, because in the light of the ideal they are so mean and sordid. To speak of evils, to strive seriously for change, shows a low mind. Or, again, the ideal becomes a refuge, an asylum, a way of escape from tiresome responsibilities. In varied ways men come to live in two worlds, one the actual, the other the ideal. Some are tortured by the sense of their irreconcilability. Others alternate between the two, compensating for the strains of renunciation involved in membership in the ideal realm by pleasureable excursions into the delights of the actual.

If we turn from concrete effects upon character to theoretical issues, we single out the discussion regarding freedom of will as typical of the consequences that come from separating morals from human nature. Men are wearied with bootless discussion, and anxious to dismiss it as a metaphysical subtlety. But nevertheless it contains within itself the most practical of all moral questions, the nature of freedom and the means of its achieving. The separation of morals from human nature leads to a separation of human nature in its moral aspects from the rest of nature, and from ordinary social habits and endeavors which are found in business, civic life, the run of companionships and recreations. These things are thought of at most as places where moral notions need to be applied, not as places where moral ideas are to be studied and moral energies generated. In short, the severance of morals from human nature ends by driving morals inwards from the public open out-of-doors air and light of day into the obscurities and privacies of an inner life. The

significance of the traditional discussion of free will is that it
reflects precisely a separation of moral activity from nature and
the public life of men.

One has to turn from moral theories to the general human
struggle for political, economic and religious liberty, for freedom
of thought, speech, assemblage and creed, to find significant
reality in the conception of freedom of will. Then one finds himself out of the stiflingly close atmosphere of an inner consciousness and in the open-air world. The cost of confining moral
freedom to an inner region is the almost complete severance of
ethics from polities and economics. The former is regarded as
summed up in edifying exhortations, and the latter as connected with arts of expediency separated from larger issues of
good.

In short, there are two schools of social reform. One bases itself upon the notion of a morality which springs from an inner
freedom, something mysteriously cooped up within personality.
It asserts that the only way to change institutions is for men to
purify their own hearts, and that when this has been accomplished, change of institutions will follow of itself. The other
school denies the existence of any such inner power, and in
so doing conceives that it has denied all moral freedom. It says
that men are made what they are by the forces of the environment, that human nature is purely malleable, and that till institutions are changed, nothing can be done. Clearly this leaves
the outcome as hopeless as does an appeal to an inner rectitude
and benevolence. For it provides no leverage for change of environment. It throws us back upon accident, usually disguised
as a necessary law of history or evolution, and trusts to some
violent change, symbolized by civil war, to usher in an abrupt
millennium. There is an alternative to being penned in between
these two theories. We can recognize that all conduct is *interaction* between elements of human nature and the environment,
natural and social. Then we shall see that progress proceeds in
two ways, and that freedom is found in that kind of interaction

which maintains an environment in which human desire and choice count for something. There are in truth forces in man as well as without him. While they are infinitely frail in comparison with exterior forces, yet they may have the support of a foreseeing and contriving intelligence. When we look at the problem as one of an adjustment to be intelligently attained, the issue shifts from within personality to an engineering issue, the establishment of arts of education and social guidance.

The idea persists that there is something materialistic about natural science and that morals are degraded by having anything seriously to do with material things. If a sect should arise proclaiming that men ought to purify their lungs completely before they ever drew a breath it ought to win many adherents from professed moralists. For the neglect of sciences that deal specifically with facts of the natural and social environment leads to a side-tracking of moral forces into an unreal privacy of an unreal self. It is impossible to say how much of the remediable suffering of the world is due to the fact that physical science is looked upon as merely physical. It is impossible to say how much of the unnecessary slavery of the world is due to the conception that moral issues can be settled within conscience or human sentiment apart from consistent study of facts and application of specific knowledge in industry, law and politics. Outside of manufacturing and transportation, science gets its chance in war. These facts perpetuate war and the hardest, most brutal side of modern industry. Each sign of disregard for the moral potentialities of physical science drafts the conscience of mankind away from concern with the interactions of man and nature which must be mastered if freedom is to be a reality. It diverts intelligence to anxious preoccupation with the unrealities of a purely inner life, or strengthens reliance upon outbursts of sentimental affection. The masses swarm to the occult for assistance. The cultivated smile contemptuously. They might smile, as the saying goes, out of the other side of their mouths if they realized how recourse to the occult exhibits the practical logic of their own beliefs. For both rest upon a separation of moral ideas and feelings from knowable facts of life, man and the world.

It is not pretended that a moral theory based upon realities of human nature and a study of the specific connections of these realities with those of physical science would do away with moral struggle and defeat. It would not make the moral life as simple a matter as wending one's way along a well-lighted boulevard. All action is an invasion of the future, of the unknown. Conflict and uncertainty are ultimate traits. But morals based upon concern with facts and deriving guidance from knowledge of them would at least locate the points of effective endeavor and would focus available resources upon them. It would put an end to the impossible attempt to live in two unrelated worlds. It would destroy fixed distinction between the human and the physical, as well as that between the moral and the industrial and political. A morals based on study of human nature instead of upon disregard for it would find the facts of man continuous with those of the rest of nature and would thereby ally ethics with physics and biology. It would find the nature and activities of one person coterminous with those of other human beings, and therefore link ethics with the study of history, sociology, law and economics.

Such a morals would not automatically solve moral problems, nor resolve perplexities. But it would enable us to state problems in such forms that action could be courageously and intelligently directed to their solution. It would not assure us against failure, but it would render failure a source of instruction. It would not protect us against the future emergence of equally serious moral difficulties, but it would enable us to approach the always recurring troubles with a fund of growing knowledge which would add significant values to our conduct even when we overtly failed—as we should continue to do. Until the integrity of morals with human nature and of both with the environment is recognized, we shall be deprived of the aid of past experience to cope with the most acute and deep prob-

lems of life. Accurate and extensive knowledge will continue
to operate only in dealing with purely technical problems. The
intelligent acknowledgment of the continuity of nature, man
and society will alone secure a growth of morals which will be
serious without being fanatical, aspiring without sentimentality,
adapted to reality without conventionality, sensible without
taking the form of calculation of profits, idealistic without being
romantic.

"Highbrow" and "Lowbrow"

VAN WYCK BROOKS

———————

I

At the time when he was trying to release humanity from the
cross of gold on which, as he said, it was crucified, the Apostle
of Free Silver—in this matter, at least, representing the old
American frame of mind—announced that the opinion of all
the professors in the United States would not affect his opinions in the least. Now this, plainly, was a very formidable di-
lemma. For on the one hand stood a body of supposed experts
in economic theory, on the other a man whose profession it
was to change and reform economic practice,—the one knowing, the other doing; and not only was there no compatibility
between them but an openly avowed and cynical contempt of
theory on the part of practice was a principal element in the
popularity of a popular hero. Was Mr. Bryan, however, to blame
for it? To know anything of the economic theory which is
taught in American universities—in many cases compulsorily

From a chapter in "America's Coming of Age," from *Three Essays on
America*, by Van Wyck Brooks. Copyright, 1915, 1934, by E. P. Dutton &
Co., Inc.

taught—is to confess that blame is not the right word. For this economic theory is at the least equally cynical. It revolves round and round in its tree-top dream of the economic man; and no matter how much the wind blows political economy never comes down. Incompatibility, mutual contempt between theory and practice, is in the very nature of things.

One might extend the illustration to literature, merely substituting one professor for another and putting any typical best-selling novelist in the place of Mr. Bryan. It is a peculiar twist in the academic mind to suppose that a writer belongs to literature only when he is dead; living he is, vaguely, something else; and an habitual remoteness from the creative mood has made American professors quite peculiarly academic. "Literature," as distinguished from excellent writing, is, in the American universities, a thing felt to have been done, and while for all one knows it may continue to be done the quality in it which makes it literature only comes out, like the quality in wines, with age.

Now I suppose that most of the American novelists in our day are university men; they have learned to regard literature as an august compound of Browning, Ben Jonson, and Hesiod; and consequently when they themselves begin to write it is in a spirit of real humility that they set themselves to the composition of richly rewarded trash. I am sure of this: it is modesty that lies behind the "best-seller"; and there is an aspect in which the spectacle of writers regarding themselves as humble tradesfolk has a certain charm. But the conception of literature as something, so to speak, high and dry, gives to the craft of authorship in America a latitude like that of morality in Catholic countries: so long as the heavenly virtues are upheld mundane virtues may shift as they will. In a word, writers are relieved of responsibility, and while their ethical conscience remains quite sound they absolve themselves from any artistic conscience whatsoever. And the worst of it is that precisely these writers of immitigable trash are often the bright, vigorous, intuitive souls who *could* make literature out of American life. Has it ever been considered how great a knowledge of men, what psycho-

logical gifts of the first order their incomparable achievement
of popularity implies?

These two attitudes of mind have been phrased once for all
in our vernacular as "Highbrow" and "Lowbrow." I have proposed these terms to a Russian, an Englishman, and a German,
asking each in turn whether in his country there was anything
to correspond with the conceptions implied in them. In each
case they have been returned to me as quite American, authen-
tically our very own, and, I should add, highly suggestive.

What side of American life is not touched by this antithesis?
What explanation of American life is more central or more illuminating? In everything one finds this frank acceptance of
twin values which are not expected to have anything in common: on the one hand a quite unclouded, quite unhypocritical
assumption of transcendent theory ("high ideals"); on the other
a simultaneous acceptance of catchpenny realities. Between
university ethics and business ethics, between American culture
and American humor, between Good Government and Tammany, between academic pedantry and pavement slang, there
is no community, no genial middle ground.

The very accent of the words "Highbrow" and "Lowbrow"
implies an instinctive perception that this is a very unsatisfactory state of affairs. For both are used in a derogatory sense. The
"Highbrow" is the superior person whose virtue is admitted but
felt to be an inept unpalatable virtue; while the "Lowbrow" is a
good fellow one readily takes to, but with a certain scorn for
him and all his works. And what is true of them as personal
types is true of what they stand for. They are equally undesir-
able, and they are incompatible; but they divide American life
between them.

II

They always have divided American life between them; and
to understand them one has to go back to the beginning of
things,—for without doubt the Puritan Theocracy is the all-in-
fluential fact in the history of the American mind. It was the

Puritan conception of the Deity as not alone all-determining but precisely responsible for the practical affairs of the race, as constituting, in fact, the State itself, which precluded in advance any central bond, any responsibility, any common feeling in American affairs and which justified the unlimited centrifugal expediency which has always marked American life. And the same instinct that made against centrality in government made against centrality in thought, against common standards of any kind. The imminent eternal issues the Puritans felt so keenly, the equally imminent practical issues they experienced so monotonously threw almost no light on one another; there was no middle ground between to mitigate, combine, or harmonize them.

So it is that from the beginning we find two main currents in the American mind running side by side but rarely mingling— a current of overtones and a current of undertones—and both equally unsocial: on the one hand, the current of Transcendentalism, originating in the piety of the Puritans, becoming a philosophy in Jonathan Edwards, passing through Emerson, producing the fastidious refinement and aloofness of the chief American writers, and, as the coherent ideals and beliefs of Transcendentalism gradually faded out, resulting in the final unreality of most contemporary American culture; and on the other hand the current of catchpenny opportunism, originating in the practical shifts of Puritan life, becoming a philosophy in Franklin, passing through the American humorists, and resulting in the atmosphere of contemporary business life.

Thus the literature of the seventeenth century in America is composed in equal parts, one may fairly say, of piety and advertisement; and the revered chronicles of New England had the double effect of proving how many pilgrim souls had been elected to salvation and of populating with hopeful immigrants a land where heaven had proved so indulgent.

For three generations the prevailing American character was compact in one type, the man of action who was also the man of God. Not until the eighteenth century did the rift appear and with it the essential distinction between "Highbrow" and "Low-brow." It appeared in the two philosophers, Jonathan Edwards and Benjamin Franklin, who share the eighteenth century between them. In their amazing purity of type and in the apparent incompatibility of their aims they determined the American character as a racial fact, and after them the Revolution became inevitable. Channing, Lincoln, Emerson, Whitman, Grant, Webster, Garrison, Edison, Mr. Rockefeller, Mrs. Eddy are all, in one way or another, permutations and combinations of these two grand progenitors of the American character.

Strange that at the very outset two men should have arisen so aptly side by side and fixed the poles of our national life! For no one has ever more fully and typically than Jonathan Edwards displayed the infinite inflexibility of the upper levels of the American mind, nor any one more typically than Franklin the infinite flexibility of its lower levels.

The intellect of Jonathan Edwards was like the Matterhorn, steep, icy, and pinnacled. At its base were green slopes and singing valleys filled with all sorts of little tender wild-flowers—for he was the most lovable of men; but as soon as the ground began to rise in good earnest all this verdurous life came to an abrupt end: not one green or living thing could subsist in that frozen soil, on those pale heights. It was the solitude of logic that led him to see in destiny only a wrathful tyrant and a viper's trail in the mischievous ways of little boys and girls.

I confess to an old-time and so to speak aboriginal affection for this man, so gently solicitous to make up in his daily walk and conversation for the ferocious impulsions of that brain of his. He was even the most romantic of men, as I thought once, and I well remember that immense old musty book of his theology, covered with mildew, with its desert of tiny print, which I carried out with me into the fields and read, in the intervals of birdnesting, under the hedgerows and along the borders of the wood: the sun fell for the first time on those clammy old pages and the pallid thoughts that lay in them, and the field-sparrows all about were twittering in a language which, to tell the truth, was no more unintelligible to me. But everything that springs from solitude shines by a light of its own, and Manfred among the Alps was not more lonely than this rapt scholar in his parsonage among the Indians.

There are, however, solitudes and solitudes. Great poets and fruitful thinkers live apart themselves, perhaps, but they have society and the ways of men in their blood. They recollect in tranquillity, as it were, gestate, live again, and reveal the last significance of active generations rich in human stuff, in experience, in emotion, in common reason. Nothing like this existed in the background of Jonathan Edwards, no profound and complex race-life. Intellect in him, isolated and not responsible to the other faculties, went on its way unchecked; and he was able to spin those inept sublimities of his by subtracting from his mind every trace of experience, every touch of human nature as it really was among his innocent country-folk.

Notoriously, of course, our great Dr. Franklin simplified existence in precisely the opposite way; for the opposite of unmitigated theory is unmitigated practice. Who can deny that in *Poor Richard* the "Lowbrow" point of view for the first time took definite shape, stayed itself with axioms, and found a sanction in the idea of "policy"? It emerges there full-fledged, in its classical form, a two-dimensional wisdom, a wisdom shorn of overtones, the most accommodating wisdom in the world.

Were ever two views of life more incompatible than these? What indeed could Poor Richard have in common with an Angry God?

And what can Mr. Bryan have in common with political economy?

III

"Our people," said Emerson, "have their intellectual culture from one country and their duties from another." In how many spheres that phrase can be applied! Desiccated culture at one end and stark utility at the other have created a deadlock in the

American mind, and all our life drifts chaotically between the two extremes. Consider, for example, our use of the English language. Literary English in England is naturally a living speech, which occupies the middle of the field and expresses the flesh and blood of an evolving race. Literary English with us is a tradition, just as Anglo-Saxon law with us is a tradition. They persist not as the normal expressions of a race, the essential fibre of which is permanently Anglo-Saxon, but through prestige and precedent and the will and habit of a dominating class largely out of touch with a national fabric unconsciously taking form "out of school." No wonder that our literary style is "pure," that our literary tradition, our tradition especially in oratory and political prose, retains the spirit of the eighteenth century. But at what a cost! At the cost of expressing a popular life which bubbles with energy and spreads and grows and slips away ever more and more from the control of tested ideas, a popular life "with the lid off," which demands an intellectual outlet and finds one in slang, journalism, and unmannerly fiction.

After seventy years Carlyle's well-known appeal to Emerson still applies to the spirit of American culture: "For the rest, I have to object still (what you will call objecting against the Law of Nature) that we find you a speaker indeed, but as it were a *Soliloquizer* on the eternal mountain-tops only, in vast solitudes where men and their affairs lie all hushed in a very dim remoteness; and only *the man* and the stars and the earth are visible—whom, so fine a fellow seems he, we could perpetually punch into, and say, 'Why won't you come and help us then? We have terrible need of one man like you down among us! It is cold and vacant up there; nothing paintable but rainbows and emotions; come down and you shall do life-pictures, passions, facts. . . .'"

And what a comment on the same utterance that at this very moment an amiable New Englander should have been painting in Parson Wilbur and Hosea Biglow, respectively, unconscious of any tragic symbolism of things to come, the unbridgeable chasm between literate and illiterate America! Morally, no doubt, in Jaalam, they understood one another and got along very well, as Yankees will. But in Chicago?

IV

To pass now from the social to the personal question, since the question is at bottom a personal one, let us figure to ourselves how this divergence comes about and how it is that our educational system, instead of creating what President Eliot calls a "serviceable fellowship" between theory and practice, tends to set them apart and to confirm us all either in the one extreme or in the other.

Let us figure to ourselves a typical American who has grown up, as an American typically does grow up, in a sort of orgy of lofty examples, moralized poems, national anthems, and baccalaureate sermons; until he is charged with all manner of ideal purities, ideal honorabilities, ideal femininities, flag-wavings and skyscrapings of every sort;—until he comes to feel in himself the hovering presence of all manner of fine potentialities, remote, vaporous, and evanescent as a rainbow. All this time, it can fairly be said, he has not been taught to associate himself personally with ends even much lower than these, he has not been taught that life is a legitimate progress toward spiritual or intellectual ends at all, his instincts of acquisition, pleasure, enterprise, and desire have in no way been linked and connected with disinterested ends; he has had it very firmly embedded in his mind. . . .

Let us imagine that, having grown up in this way, he is sent to college. And here, in order to keep the case a typical one, we shall have to exercise a little discrimination in the choice of a university.

It will not be Harvard, because the ideal of Harvard, as I shall point out, is not a typically modern American ideal. Nor will it be one of the modern utilitarian universities, which have no ideal at all. It will be any one of the others; and when I say this I mean that each of the others is in one way or another a development of the old American country college; its ideal, its experience, its tradition spring out of and lead one back to that. Now among these old colleges Harvard might have been figured as an ever-developing, ever-liberalizing catholicism, of which they were all sectarian offshoots, established on a principle of progressive theological fragmentation, each one defending an orthodoxy its predecessors had outworn or violently setting up in defense of some private orthodoxy of its own. They founded themselves each on a remote dogma or system of dogma as their central and sufficient basis, and all their wheels turned in relation to the central theological dynamo. In a sense of course this was true also of Harvard, but with a marked difference. For the theologians who founded Harvard were men of action as well; in the seventeenth century a New England minister was also a politician, and the education of ministers for which Harvard was mainly established implied an education for public affairs as well, an education for society, so far as the word society can be used in connection with the early Puritans at all. Thus at the outset the founders of Harvard drove in the wedge of secularism: Harvard had from the beginning a sort of national basis, at least among New Englanders, and its dogmatic structure consequently reflected and shifted with and accommodated itself to the currents of national thought. Remaining in touch with society, it educated to a certain extent, relatively to an extraordinary extent, the social function of its students; and it is thus no accident that so large a proportion of the political, the literary, and the scientific life of America has sprung from it. But in the eighteenth century the conditions under which Harvard was established had ceased to be true. The minister was no longer a man of affairs,—he was a stark theologian, and usually of a type which the majority of his flock had outgrown. Yale, Princeton, and virtually all the other typically American colleges were founded by men of this type. Jonathan Edwards may figure for them all; the motive which led him to become the president of Princeton being precisely that his flock in Connecticut could no longer see the anger of God eye to eye with him. Already in his time the fathers and mothers of young America had submitted to the charms of *Poor Richard's Almanac*—they had themselves for the most part become inveterately "Lowbrow"; but they seem to have believed that an Angry God might still be a good influence over young America himself.

To return now to the typical case with whom we began, let us imagine that he makes a typical choice and goes to a typical university. Having arrived there will he be confronted with an Angry God, or any sort of direct theological dogma? By no means. But there will have remained in the air a certain fragrance and vibration, as if an ideal had passed that way and not stayed, there will be intangible whispers and seductions, there will be a certain faint, rarified, remote, but curiously pervasive and insistent influence—like the sound of an Aeolian harp or the recollection of Plato in some uncouth slum; there will be memories and portraits of many an old metaphysician, white, unearthly, fragile. It will all seem very much as if, the significance of these remote dogmas having evaporated, only the remoteness, in a way, had remained.

One would have to be very insensitive not to feel the quite unbalancing charm of this quality—so different from its comparatively robust Oxford parallel—in the old New England colleges, as in Princeton, Yale, and the other universities which have developed out of them; but one cannot help feeling also, I think, something vaguely Circean in it. And in fact, given the preliminary method of bringing up which I have sketched, what will be its effect in the case we are considering? Suddenly confronted during four years with just this remote influence of ideals, out of which the intellectual structure has evaporated and which never possessed a social structure, will he not find them too vague, too intangible, too unprepared for to be incorporated into his nature? . . .

Indeed there is nothing so tragic and so ominous as the familiar saying that college is the happiest time of one's life. Yet perhaps a majority of college men think of their college life in this way. They deliberately put their Golden Age behind them—

and, as things are, they know it is behind them. But consider what a comment this is on the American university itself,—a place, one can fairly say, where ideals are cherished precisely because they are ineffectual, because they are ineptly and mournfully beautiful, because they make one cynical, because they make life progressively uninteresting, because, practically and in effect, they are illusions and frauds and infinitely charming lies. There surely is the last and the most impenetrable stronghold of Puritanism, refined to the last degree of intangibility, which persists in making the world a world inevitably sordid, basely practical, and whose very definition of the ideal consequently is, that which has no connection with the world!

Thus far then for our typical university graduate. He has been consistently educated in twin values which are incompatible. . . .

Now supposing he has already become interested in the study, let us say, of economics, three paths are open to him: either he can give himself once for all to economics, or he can go the way of all flesh, i.e., into business, or he can hesitate between the two, becoming an economist for the time being and eventually going into business.

It is just here, at the moment of choice, that the want of ballast in his education becomes manifest. There is nothing for him but to lurch violently to the one extreme or the other; and this, according as there is in his nature a crude preponderance either of intellect or of the sense of action, he does. If he is preponderantly intellectual he adopts the first course; that is to say, he dedicates himself to the service of a type of economic theory that bears no relation to this wicked world at all, leaving all the good people who are managing the economic practice of society (and, for the want of him, chiefly muddling it)—leaving all these good people to talk nonsense in the wilderness. If he is preponderantly a man of action, he adopts the second course; that is to say, he dedicates himself to the service of a private end which knows nothing of theory, which is most cynically contemptuous of ideals, flatulent or other, and which is precisely as indifferent to the economic life of society as the professor of economics himself.

Well, good riddance to both of them, one might be inclined to say, except that on second thought the professor and the business man between them hold in their hands so great a part of human destiny. It is the third case that is really interesting and really tragic. For just so far as our typical student is a normal man, just so far as he shares the twin elements of intellect and action in equal parts, just so far will he be on the fence. The probability is that in this case he will become a professor for as long as he can stand it and then burst into business and become a first-rate millionaire as quickly as possible. The sense of action in him will rebel against the sense of theory and finding in theory no basis for action, no relation to action, will press him into a fresh life where the theoretical side of his nature will at least be of some slight use in furthering his own aggrandizement, and that alone.

v

Naturally the question of economics is only typical. Any branch of human activity which is represented by professors at all—and which is not?—would serve as well. Human nature itself in America exists on two irreconcilable planes, the plane of stark theory and the plane of stark business; and in the back of its mind is heaven knows what world of poetry, hidden away, too inaccessible, too intangible, too unreal in fact ever to be brought into the open, or to serve, as the poetry of life rightly should serve, in harnessing thought and action together, turning life into a disinterested adventure.

Argue which way you will, from the individual to society or from society to the individual, it is the same. Just as the American attitude toward the State has been the attitude of an oratorical and vague patriotism which has not based itself on a concrete interest in public affairs; just as, in consequence of this, the "invisible government" of business has swept in and taken possession of the field and become the actual government under which we live, overgrowing and supplanting the government we recognize: so also in the case of the individual; the cherishing of ideals that are simply unmapped regions to which nobody has the least intention of building roads, the baccalaureate sermons that are no just, organic comment on the educational system that precedes them—precisely these themselves strengthen the forces from below; the invisible government of self-interest, built up carefully from the beginning by maxim and example, fills the vacuum a disinterested purpose ought to have occupied.

Twenty, even ten years, ago, it would have been universally assumed that the only hope for American society lay in somehow lifting the "Lowbrow" elements in it to the level of the "Highbrow" elements. But that quickening realism which belongs to contemporary thought makes it plain on the one hand that the mere idealism of university ethics, the mere loftiness of what is called culture, the mere purity of so-called Good Government, left to themselves, not only produce a glassy inflexible priggishness on the upper levels which paralyzes life; but that the lower levels have a certain humanity, flexibility, tangibility which are indispensable in any programme: that Tammany has quite as much to teach Good Government as Good Government has to teach Tammany, that slang has quite as much in store for so-called culture as culture has for slang—that the universities, while emphatically not becoming more "practical," must base their disinterestedness on human, moral, social, artistic, and personal needs, impulses, and experience.

But society cannot become humane of itself; and it is for this reason that the movements of Reform are so external and so superficial. The will to reform springs from a conviction *ex post facto*, and is strictly analogous to the frame of mind of business men who retire at sixty and collect pictures. Nothing so exemplifies it as the spectacle of Mr. Carnegie, spending three quarters of his life in providing steel for battleships and the last quarter of it in trying to abolish war. He himself surely has not been conscious of any inward revolution; plainly with him as with others the will to create disorder and the will to reform it spring from the same inner condition of mind. The impetus of Reform is evidently derived from the hope that a sufficient number of reformers can be trained and brought into the field to match the forces of business—the one group cancelling the other group. The ideal of Reform, in short, is the attainment of zero.

Nothing is more absurd than to attack business as such. But the motives and circumstances of business vary from age to age, and there is a world of difference between industry conceived as a social process and trade conceived as a private end. A familiar distinction between the nineteenth century and the twentieth is that the problem of civilization is no longer the problem of want but the problem of surplus. Roughly speaking, the hereditary American class—the prevailing class, I mean—is faced with the problem not of making money but of spending it; the prevailing American class is in a position of relative, but relatively great, economic freedom, and under these conditions it is plain that in them economic self-assertion ("enterprise") has become to a large extent a vicious anachronism. . . .

Because it was for so long the law of the tribe economic self-assertion still remains to most Americans a sort of moral obligation; while self-fulfillment still looks like a pretty word for selfishness. Yet self-fulfillment through science, or literature, or mechanics, or industry itself—the working out of one's own personality, one's own inventiveness through forms of activity that are directly social, as all these activities *are* directly social, gives a man, through his very sociality, through the feeling he has that as a good workman he is coöperating with all other good workmen, a life-interest apart from his rewards. And just as this principle becomes generally diffused and understood the incentive is withdrawn from economic self-assertion, a relative competence being notoriously satisfying to the man whose prime end is the fulfilling of his own creative instincts; and the wealth of the world is already socialized. . . .

The only serious approach to society is the personal approach, and what I have called the quickening realism of contemporary social thought is at bottom simply a restatement for the mass of commercialized men, and in relation to issues which directly concern the mass of men as a whole, of those personal instincts that have been the essence of art, religion, literature—the essence of personality itself—since the beginning of things. It will remain of the least importance to patch up politics, to become infected with social consciousness, or to do any of the other easy popular contemporary things unless, in some way, personality can be made to release itself on a middle plane between vaporous idealism and self-interested practicality; unless, in short, self-fulfillment as an ideal can be substituted for self-assertion as an ideal. On the economic plane that implies socialism; on every other plane it implies something which a majority of Americans in our day certainly do not possess. . . .

VI

It is perhaps just as well that Cervantes lived and died in Spain three hundred years ago. Had he been born an American of the twentieth century he might have found the task of satire an all too overwhelming one. Yet his fable, which has its personal bearing in all men always, has in America a social bearing that is perhaps unique. Don Quixote is the eternal "Highbrow" under a polite name, just as Sancho Panza is the eternal "Lowbrow"; and if the adorable Dulcinea is not a vision of the night and a daily goal in the mind of our professors, then there is no money in Wall Street. One admits the charm of both extremes, the one so fantastically above, the other so fantastically below the level of right reason; to have any kind of relish for muddled humanity is necessarily to feel the charm of both extremes. But where is all that is real, where is personality and all its works, if it is not essentially somewhere, somehow, in some not very vague way, between?

Advice to Young Men

H. L. MENCKEN

I

TO HIM THAT HATH

The most valuable of all human possessions, next to a superior and disdainful air, is the reputation of being well to do. Nothing else so neatly eases one's way through life, especially in democratic countries. There is in ninety-nine per cent of all democrats an irresistible impulse to crook the knee to wealth, to defer humbly to the power that goes with it, to see all sorts of high merits in the man who has it, or is said to have it. True enough, envy goes with the pliant neck, but it is envy somehow purged of all menace: the inferior man is afraid to do evil to the man with money in eight banks; he is even afraid to *think* evil of him—that is, in any patent and offensive way. Against capital as an abstraction he rants incessantly, and all of the laws that he favors treat it as if it were criminal. But in the presence of the concrete capitalist he is singularly fawning. What makes him so is easy to discern. He yearns with a great yearning for a chance to tap the capitalist's purse, and he knows very well, deep down in his heart, that he is too craven and stupid to do it by force of arms. So he turns to politeness, and tries to cajole. Give out the news that one has just made a killing in the stock market, or robbed some confiding widow of her dower, or swindled the government in some patriotic enterprise, and at once one will discover that one's shabbiness is a charming eccentric-

ity, and one's judgment of wines worth hearing, and one's politics worthy of attention and respect. The man who is thought
to be poor never gets a fair chance. No one wants to listen to
him. No one gives a damn what he thinks or knows or feels. No
one has any active desire for his good opinion.

I discovered this principle early in life, and have put it to use
ever since. I have got a great deal more out of men (and
women) by having the name of being a well-heeled fellow than
I have ever got by being decent to them, or by dazzling them
with my sagacity, or by hard industry, or by a personal beauty
that is singular and ineffable.

II

THE VENERABLE EXAMINED

The older I grow the more I distrust the familiar doctrine that
age brings wisdom. It is my honest belief that I am no wiser to-
day than I was five or ten years ago; in fact, I often suspect that
I am appreciably *less* wise. Women can prevail over me to-day
by devices that would have made me hoof them out of my studio when I was thirty-five. I am also an easier mark for male
swindlers than I used to be; at fifty I'll probably be joining
clubs and buying Mexican mine stock. The truth is that every
man goes up-hill in sagacity to a certain point, and then begins
sliding down again. Nearly all the old fellows that I know are
more or less balmy. Theoretically, they should be much wiser
than younger men, if only because of their greater experience,
but actually they seem to take on folly faster than they take on
wisdom. A man of thirty-five or thirty-eight is almost woman-
proof. For a woman to marry him is a herculean feat. But by the
time he is fifty he is quite as easy as a Yale sophomore. On other
planes the same decay of the intelligence is visible. Certainly it
would be difficult to imagine any committee of relatively young
men, of thirty or thirty-five, showing the unbroken childishness,
ignorance and lack of humor of the Supreme Court of the
United States. The average age of the learned justices must be

well beyond sixty, and all of them are supposed to be of finished and mellowed sagacity. Yet their knowledge of the most ordinary principles of justice often turns out to be extremely meager, and when they spread themselves grandly upon a great case their reasoning powers are usually found to be precisely equal to those of a respectable Pullman conductor.

III

DUTY

Some of the loosest thinking in ethics has duty for its theme. Practically all writers on the subject agree that the individual owes certain unescapable duties to the race—for example, the duty of engaging in productive labor, and that of marrying and begetting offspring. In support of this position it is almost always argued that if *all* men neglected such duties the race would perish. The logic is hollow enough to be worthy of the college professors who are guilty of it. It simply confuses the conventionality, the pusillanimity, the lack of imagination of the majority of men with the duty of *all* men. There is not the slightest ground for assuming, even as a matter of mere argumentation, that *all* men will ever neglect these alleged duties. There will always remain a safe majority that is willing to do whatever is ordained—that accepts docilely the government it is born under, obeys its laws, and supports its theory. But that majority does not comprise the men who render the highest and most intelligent services to the race; it comprises those who render nothing save their obedience.

For the man who differs from this inert and well-regimented mass, however slightly, there are no duties *per se*. What he is spontaneously inclined to do is of vastly more value to all of us than what the majority is willing to do. There is, indeed, no such thing as duty-in-itself; it is a mere chimera of ethical theorists. Human progress is furthered, not by conformity, but by aberration. The very concept of duty is thus a function of inferiority; it belongs naturally only to timorous and incompetent men. Even on such levels it remains largely a self-delusion, a soothing apparition, a euphemism for necessity. When a man succumbs to duty he merely succumbs to the habit and inclination of other men. Their collective interests invariably pull against his individual interests. Some of us can resist a pretty strong pull—the pull, perhaps, of thousands. But it is only the miraculous man who can withstand the pull of a whole nation.

IV

MARTYRS

"History," says Henry Ford, "is bunk." I inscribe myself among those who dissent from this doctrine; nevertheless, I am often hauled up, in reading history, by a feeling that I am among unrealities. In particular, that feeling comes over me when I read about the religious wars of the past—wars in which thousands of men, women and children were butchered on account of puerile and unintelligible disputes over transubstantiation, the atonement, and other such metaphysical banshees. It does not surprise me that the majority murdered the minority; the majority, even to-day, does it whenever it is possible. What I can't understand is that the minority went voluntarily to the slaughter. Even in the worst persecutions known to history— say, for example, those of the Jews of Spain—it was always possible for a given member of the minority to save his hide by giving public assent to the religious notions of the majority. A Jew who was willing to be baptized, in the reign of Ferdinand and Isabella, was practically unmolested; his descendants today are 100% Spaniards. Well, then, why did so many Jews refuse? Why did so many prefer to be robbed, exiled, and sometimes murdered?

The answer given by philosophical historians is that they were a noble people, and preferred death to heresy. But this merely begs the question. Is it actually noble to cling to a religious idea so tenaciously? Certainly it doesn't seem so to me. After all, no human being really *knows* anything about the exalted

matters with which all religions deal. The most he can do is
to match his private guess against the guesses of his fellowmen.
For any man to say absolutely, in such a field, that this or that
is wholly and irrefragably true and this or that is utterly false is
simply to talk nonsense. Personally, I have never encountered a
religious idea—and I do not except even the idea of the existence of God—that was instantly and unchallengeably convincing, as, say, the Copernican astronomy is instantly and unchallengeably convincing. But neither have I ever encountered
a religious idea that could be dismissed offhand as palpably
and indubitably false. In even the worst nonsense of such theological mountebanks as the Rev. Dr. Billy Sunday, Brigham
Young and Mrs. Eddy there is always enough lingering plau-
sibility, or, at all events, possibility, to give the judicious pause.
Whatever the weight of the probabilities against it, it nevertheless *may* be true that man, on his decease, turns into a gaseous
vertebrate, and that this vertebrate, if its human larva has engaged in embezzlement, bootlegging, profanity or adultery on
this earth, will be boiled for a million years in a cauldron of
pitch. My private inclination, due to my defective upbringing,
is to doubt it, and to set down any one who believes it as an ass,
but it must be plain that I have no means of disproving it.

   In view of this uncertainty it seems to me sheer vanity for
any man to hold his religious views too firmly, or to submit to
any inconvenience on account of them. It is far better, if they
happen to offend, to conceal them discreetly, or to change them
amiably as the delusions of the majority change. My own views
in this department, being wholly skeptical and tolerant, are
obnoxious to the subscribers to practically all other views; even
atheists sometimes denounce me. At the moment, by an accident of American political history, these dissenters from my
theology are forbidden to punish me for not agreeing with them.
But at any succeeding moment some group or other among
them may seize such power and proceed against me in the immemorial manner. If it ever happens, I give notice here and

now that I shall get converted to their nonsense instantly, and so retire to safety with my right thumb laid against my nose and my fingers waving like wheat in the wind. I'd do it even to-day, if there were any practical advantage in it. Offer me a case of Rauenthaler 1903, and I engage to submit to baptism by any rite ever heard of, provided it does not expose my gothic nakedness. Make it ten cases, and I'll agree to be both baptized and confirmed. In such matters I am broad-minded. What, after all, is one more lie?

v

THE DISABLED VETERAN

The science of psychological pathology is still in its infancy. In all its literature in three languages, I can't find a line about the permanent ill effects of acute emotional diseases—say, for example, love affairs. The common assumption of the world is that when a love affair is over it is over—that nothing remains behind. This is probably grossly untrue. It is my belief that every such experience leaves scars upon my psyche, and that they are quite as plain and quite as dangerous as the scars left on the neck by a carbuncle. A man who has passed through a love affair, even though he may eventually forget the lady's very name, is never quite the same thereafter. His scars may be small, but they are permanent. The sentimentalist, exposed incessantly, ends as a psychic cripple; he is as badly off as the man who has come home from the wars with shell-shock. The precise nature of the scars remains to be determined. My own notion is that they take the form of large yellow patches upon the self-esteem. Whenever a man thinks of one of his dead love affairs, and in particular whenever he allows his memory to dredge up an image of the woman he loved, he shivers like one taken in some unmanly and discreditable act. Such shivers, repeated often enough, must inevitably shake his inner integrity off its base. No man can love, and yet remain truly proud. It is a disarming and humiliating experience.

VI

PATRIOTISM

Patriotism is conceivable to a civilized man in times of stress and storm, when his country is wobbling and sore beset. His country then appeals to him as any victim of misfortune appeals to him—say, a street-walker pursued by the police. But when it is safe, happy and prosperous it can only excite his loathing. The things that make countries safe, happy and prosperous—a secure peace, an active trade, political serenity at home—are all intrinsically corrupting and disgusting. It is as impossible for a civilized man to love his country in good times as it would be for him to respect a politician.

Symbolism

EDMUND WILSON

It is my purpose in this book to try to trace the origins of certain tendencies in contemporary literature and to show their development in the work of six contemporary writers. To persons already familiar with the field, my explanations in this first chapter will seem rudimentary; but I believe that it is still true in general, for reasons which I shall suggest, that the sources and fundamental principals of many of the books which have excited most discussion during the period since the War are singularly little understood. It is not usually recognized that writers such as W. B. Yeats, James Joyce, T. S. Eliot, Gertrude Stein, Marcel Proust and Paul Valéry represent the culmination

Reprinted from *Axel's Castle* by Edmund Wilson; copyright, 1931, by Charles Scribner's Sons; used by permission of the publishers.

of a self-conscious and very important literary movement; and even when we have become aware that these writers have something in common, that they belong to a common school, we are likely to be rather vague as to what its distinguishing features are.

We do, however, to-day as a rule have a pretty clear idea of the issues which were raised by the Romantic Movement of the beginning of the nineteenth century. We still debate Classicism and Romanticism, and when we attempt to deal with contemporary literary problems, we often tend to discuss them in those terms. Yet the movement of which in our own day we are witnessing the mature development is not merely a degeneration or an elaboration of Romanticism, but rather a counterpart to it, a second flood of the same tide. And even the metaphor of a tide is misleading: what we have to-day is an entirely distinct movement, which has arisen from different conditions and must be dealt with in different terms.

Romanticism, as everyone has heard, was a revolt of the individual. The "Classicism" against which it was a reaction meant, in the domain of politics and morals, a preoccupation with society as a whole; and, in art, an ideal of objectivity. In *Le Misanthrope*, in *Bérénice*, in *The Way of the World*, in *Gulliver's Travels*, the artist is out of the picture: he would consider it artistic bad taste to identify his hero with himself and to glorify himself with his hero, or to intrude between the reader and the story and give vent to his personal emotions. But in *René*, in *Rolla*, in *Childe Harold*, in *The Prelude*, the writer is either his own hero, or unmistakably identified with his hero, and the personality and emotions of the writer are presented as the principal subject of interest. Racine, Molière, Congreve and Swift ask us to be interested in what they have made; but Chateaubriand, Musset, Byron, and Wordsworth ask us to be interested in themselves. And they ask us to be interested in themselves by virtue of the intrinsic value of the individual: they vindicate the rights of the individual against the claims of society as a whole—against government, morals, conventions, academy or church. The Romantic is nearly always a rebel.

In this connection, it is illuminating to consider the explanation of the Romantic Movement given by A. N. Whitehead in his *Science and the Modern World*. The Romantic Movement, Whitehead says, was really a reaction against scientific ideas, or rather against the mechanistic ideas to which certain scientific discoveries gave rise. The seventeenth and eighteenth centuries were in Europe the great period of the development of mathematical and physical theory; and in the literature of the so-called Classical period, Descartes and Newton were influences as important as those of the classics themselves. The poets, like the astronomers and mathematicians, had come to regard the universe as a machine, obeying logical laws and susceptible of reasonable explanation: God figured merely as the clockmaker who must have existed to make the clock. People applied this conception also to society, which, from the point of view of Louis XIV and of the American Constitution alike, had the character of a planetary system or a well-regulated machine; and they examined human nature dispassionately, in the same lucid and reasonable spirit, to find the principles on which it worked. Thus the theorems of the physicist were matched by the geometrical plays of Racine and the balanced couplets of Pope.

But this conception of a fixed mechanical order came eventually to be felt as a constraint: it excluded too much of life— or rather, the description it supplied did not correspond to actual experience. The Romantics had become acutely conscious of aspects of their experience which it was impossible to analyze or explain on the theory of a world run by clock-work. The universe was not a machine, after all, but something more mysterious and less rational.

> The atoms of Democritus,
>   And Newton's particles of light
> Are sands upon the Red Sea shore,
>   Where Israel's tents do shine so bright!

Blake had already contradicted contemptuously the physical theory of the eighteenth century. And to Wordsworth, the countryside of his boyhood meant neither agriculture nor neo-classic idylls, but a light never seen on land or sea. When the poet looked into his own soul, he beheld something which did not seem to him reducible to a set of principles of human nature such, for example, as La Rochefoucauld's *Maxims:* he saw fantasy, conflict, confusion. And he either set himself, like Wordsworth and Blake, to affirm the superior truth of this vision as compared to the mechanical universe of the physicists; or, accepting this mechanical universe, like Byron or Alfred de Vigny, as external to and indifferent to man, he pitted against it, in defiance, his own turbulent insubordinate soul.

In any case, it is always, as in Wordsworth, the individual sensibility, or, as in Byron, the individual will, with which the Romantic poet is preoccupied; and he has invented a new language for the expression of its mystery, its conflict and confusion. The arena of literature has been transferred from the universe conceived as a machine, from society conceived as an organization, to the individual soul.

What has really taken place, says Whitehead, is a philosophical revolution. The scientists of the seventeenth century who presented the universe as a mechanism had caused people to draw the conclusion that man was something apart from nature, something introduced into the universe from outside and remaining alien to all that he found. But a Romantic poet like Wordsworth has come to feel the falsity of this assumption: he has perceived that the world is an organism, that nature includes planets, mountains, vegetation and people alike, that what we are and what we see, what we hear, what we feel and what we smell, are inextricably related, that all are involved in the same great entity. Those who make fun of the Romantics are mistaken in supposing that there is no intimate connection between the landscape and the poet's emotions. There is no real dualism, says Whitehead, between external lakes and hills, on the one hand, and personal feelings, on the other: human

feelings and inanimate objects are interdependent and developing together in some fashion of which our traditional notions of
laws of cause and effect, of dualities of mind and matter or of
body and soul, can give us no true idea. The Romantic poet,
then, with his turbid or opalescent language, his sympathies
and passions which cause him to seem to merge with his surroundings, is the prophet of a new insight into nature: he is
describing things as they really are; and a revolution in the
imagery of poetry is in reality a revolution in metaphysics.

Whitehead drops the story at this point; but he has provided
the key to what follows. In the middle of the nineteenth century,
science made new advances, and mechanistic ideas were
brought back into fashion again. But they came this time from
a different quarter—not from physics and mathematics, but
from biology. It was the effect of the theory of Evolution to
reduce man from the heroic stature to which the Romantics had
tried to exalt him, to the semblance of a helpless animal, again
very small in the universe and at the mercy of the forces about
him. Humanity was the accidental product of heredity and environment, and capable of being explained in terms of these.
This doctrine in literature was called Naturalism, and it was put
into practice by novelists like Zola, who believed that compos-
ing a novel was like performing a laboratory experiment: you
had only to supply your characters with a specific environment
and heredity and then watch their automatic reactions; and by
historians and critics like Taine, who asserted that virtue and
vice were as much the products of automatic processes as alkalis
and acids, and who attempted to account for masterpieces by
studying the geographical and climatic conditions of the countries in which they had been produced.

Not, however, that the movement known as Naturalism arose
directly from *The Origin of Species*. There had already set in,
about the middle of the century, quite independent of the theory
of Evolution, a reaction against the sentimentality and the looseness of Romanticism, and in the direction of the objectivity and
the severity of Classicism again; and this reaction had already

been characterized by a kind of scientific observation which closely corresponded to that of biological science. This reaction is seen most clearly in France. The Parnassian group of poets, who made their first appearance in the fifties—Gautier, Leconte de Lisle, Hérédia—seemed to have taken it for their aim merely to picture historical incidents and natural phenomena as objectively and accurately as possible in impassive perfect verse. Leconte de Lisle's elephants crossing the desert is a celebrated example: the elephants appear and disappear with a certain classical dignity and grandeur, and the poet leaves it at that.

It is less easy, in English poetry, to give clear examples of the reaction toward Naturalism: the English did not, after the Romantic Movement, take much interest in literary methods till toward the end of the nineteenth century. But the tendency toward what we call realism had set in, none the less: Browning, though he had, of course, nothing of the classical form of the Parnassians, was addicted to historical reconstruction of a kind more pedantic and less flamboyant than that of the true Romantics, and when he dealt with contemporary life, did so at least as realistically as any of the Victorian novelists—themselves going in Zola's direction without quite being aware of the fact. And we can see very plainly in Tennyson, who was much preoccupied with the doctrines of Evolution, something of the same exactitude of description combined with something of the same severity of verse—though with less hardness and more grace—that we find in the French poets.

> Nor wilt thou snare him in the white ravine,
> Nor find him dropt upon the firths of ice,
> That huddling slant in furrow-cloven fells
> To roll the torrent out of dusky doors:
> But follow; let the torrent dance thee down
> To find him in the valley; let the wild
> Lean-headed eagles yelp alone.

And it is interesting to compare Tennyson, in this connection with Pope on the rare occasions (though not so rare as people sometimes suppose) when he is describing natural objects:

> The silver eel, in shining volumes roll'd,
> The yellow carp, in scales bedropp'd with gold.

These lines have the technical perfection and the precise observation of Tennyson, but they are heavier and more metallic. Pope is often, as a matter of fact, very close to the French Parnassians. The latter represent, in reality, a second classical-scientific movement, the counterpart to that represented by Pope.

But the highest developments of Naturalism took place, not in poetry, but in prose. The plays of Ibsen and the novels of Flaubert are the masterpieces of this second period of modern classicism, as Racine and Swift are of the first. The art of Flaubert and Ibsen is again, like the art of the seventeenth-century writers, scrupulously non-personal and objective, and it insists upon precision of language and economy of form. Compare the lucidity, the logic and the limited number of characters of such a tragedy of Ibsen's as *Rosmersholm* with the rigorous conventions of Racine; or compare *Gulliver's Travels* with *Bouvard et Pécuchet* or *L'Education Sentimentale*. Yet, though the earlier works resemble the later ones in many obvious ways, they differ from them in this: where a seventeenth-century moralist like La Rouchefoucauld would have sought to discover and set forth the universal principles of human behavior, a nineteenth-century writer like Ibsen or Flaubert has begun to study man in relation to his particular environment and time. The method of approach in both cases, however, may be described as "scientific," and it tends to lead us to mechanistic conclusions.

Now Flaubert and Ibsen both had been suckled on Romanticism. Flaubert had begun by writing a Romantic *Saint-Antoine* before he chastened it and cut it down to the more sober one which he published; and Ibsen had written in verse his Faustian *Brand* and *Peer Gynt* before he arrived at his realistic plays in prose. Each, beginning in Romanticism, had evolved for himself a new discipline and developed a new point of view. For *Madame Bovary* is not merely arranged and written differently from a novel by Victor Hugo: it also constitutes an ob-

jective criticism of a case of Romantic personality; and Ibsen
was occupied all his life with situations produced by the conflict of the essentially Romantic conception of one's duty to
one's own personality with the conception of one's duty to society.

But in the later prose plays of Ibsen, the trolls and ghosts of
his early dramatic poems have begun to creep back into the
bourgeois drawing-rooms: the Naturalist has been finally compelled to make cracks in his own mold. All that vaporous, confused and grandiose world of Romanticism had been resolutely
ordered and compressed; but now the objective point of view
of Naturalism, the machine-like technique which went with it,
begin to cramp the poet's imagination, to prove inadequate to
convey what he feels. The reader begins to chafe at the strain,
and the artist begins to betray it. Huysmans described Leconte
de Lisle as "the sonorous hardware man"; we remember Wordsworth's strictures on Pope. Literature is rebounding again from
the scientific-classical pole to the poetic-romantic one. And this
second reaction at the end of the century, this counterpart to
the Romantic reaction of the end of the century before, was
known in France as Symbolism.

Now in attempting to write literary history, one must guard
against giving the impression that these movements and coun-
ter-movements necessarily follow one another in a punctual
and well-generalled fashion—as if eighteenth-century reason
had been cleanly put to rout by nineteenth-century Romanticism, which then proceeded to hold the field till it was laid by
the heels by Naturalism, and as if Mallarmé and Rimbaud had
then blown up Naturalism with bombs. What really happens, of
course, is that one set of methods and ideas is not completely
superseded by another; but that, on the contrary, it thrives in
its teeth—so that, on the one hand, Flaubert's prose has learned
to hear, see and feel with the delicate senses of Romanticism at
the same time that Flaubert is disciplining and criticizing the
Romantic temperament; and so that, on the other hand, certain members of a school, unaffected by new influences abroad,

will continue to practise its methods and to exploit its possibilities further and further, when nearly everybody else has abandoned it.

I have here purposely been selecting writers who seemed to represent some tendency or school in its purest or most highly developed form. We must, however, now consider some Romantics who, in certain ways, carried Romanticism further than even Chateaubriand or Musset, or than Wordsworth or Byron, and who became the first precursors of Symbolism and were afterwards placed among its saints.

One of these was the French writer who called himself Gérard de Nerval. Gérard de Nerval suffered from spells of insanity; and, partly no doubt as a result of this, habitually confused his own fancies and feelings with external reality. He believed, even in his lucid periods—and no doubt Whitehead would approve his metaphysics—that the world which we see about us is involved in some more intimate fashion than is ordinarily supposed with the things that go on in our minds, that even our dreams and hallucinations are somehow bound up with reality. And in one of his sonnets he outdoes Wordsworth, with his "Presences of Nature in the sky" and his "Souls of lonely places," by imagining shuttered eyes coming to life in the very walls and "a pure spirit under the bark of stones."

But a more important prophet of Symbolism was Edgar Allan Poe. It was in general true that, by the middle of the century, the Romantic writers in the United States—Poe, Hawthorne, Melville, Whitman, and even Emerson—were, for reasons which it would be interesting to determine, developing in the direction of Symbolism; and one of the events of prime importance in the early history of the Symbolist Movement was the discovery of Poe by Baudelaire. When Baudelaire, a late Romantic, first read Poe in 1847, he "experienced a strange commotion." When he began to look up Poe's writings in the files of American magazines, he found among them stories and poems which he said that he himself had already "thought vaguely and confusedly" of writing, and his interest became a veritable passion. In 1852, Baudelaire published a volume of translations of Poe's tales; and from then on the influence of Poe played an important part in French literature. Poe's critical writings provided the first scriptures of the Symbolist Movement, for he had formulated what amounted to a new literary programme which corrected the Romantic looseness and lopped away the Romantic extravagance, at the same time that it aimed, not at Naturalistic, but at ultra-Romantic effects. There was, of course, a good deal in common between Poe's poetry and such Romantic poetry as Coleridge's *Kubla Khan,* as there was between his poems in prose and such Romantic prose as that of De Quincey. But Poe, by insisting on and specially cultivating certain aspects of Romanticism, helped to transform it into something different. "I *know*," we find Poe writing, for example, "that indefiniteness is an element of the true music [of poetry]—I mean of the true musical expression . . . a suggestive indefiniteness of vague and therefore of spiritual *effect*." And to approximate the indefiniteness of music was to become one of the principal aims of Symbolism.

This effect of indefiniteness was produced not merely by the confusion I have mentioned between the imaginary world and the real; but also by means of a further confusion between the perceptions of the different senses.

> *Comme de longs échos qui de loin se confondent . . .*
> *Les parfums, les couleurs et les sons se répondent,*

wrote Baudelaire. And we find Poe, in one of his poems, *hearing* the approach of the darkness, or writing such a description as the following of the sensations which follow death: "Night arrived; and with its shadows a heavy discomfort. It oppressed my limbs with the oppression of some dull weight, and was palpable. There was also a moaning sound, not unlike the distant reverberation of surf, but more continuous, which beginning with the first twilight, had grown in strength with the darkness. Suddenly lights were brought into the room . . . and issuing from the flame of each lamp, there flowed unbrokenly into my ears a strain of melodious monotone."

This notation of super-rational sensations was a novelty in the forties of the last century—as was the dream-like irrational musical poetry of *Annabel Lee* and *Ulalume;* and they helped to effect a revolution in France. For an English-speaking reader of to-day Poe's influence may be hard to understand; and even when such a reader comes to examine the productions of French Symbolism it may surprise him that they should have caused amazement. The medley of images; the deliberately mixed metaphors; the combination of passion and wit—of the grand and the prosaic manners; the bold amalgamation of material with spiritual—all these may seem to him quite proper and familiar. He has always known them in the English poetry of the sixteenth and seventeenth centuries—Shakespeare and the other Elizabethans did all these things without theorizing about them. Is this not the natural language of poetry? Is it not the norm against which, in English Literature, the eighteenth century was a heresy and to which the Romantics did their best to return?

But we must remember that the development of French poetry has been quite different from that of English. Michelet says that in the sixteenth century the future of French literature had hung in the balance between Rabelais and Ronsard, and he regrets that it was Ronsard who triumphed. For Rabelais in France was a sort of equivalent to our own Elizabethans, whereas Ronsard, who represented to Michelet all that was poorest, dryest and most conventional in the French genius, was one of the fathers of that classical tradition of lucidity, sobriety and purity which culminated in Molière and Racine. In comparison with the Classicism of the French, which has dominated their whole literature since the Renaissance, the English Classicism of the eighteenth century, the age of Dr. Johnson and Pope, was a brief ineffective deviation. And from the point of view of English readers, the most daring innovations of the Romantic revolution in France, in spite of all the excitement which accompanied them, must appear of an astonishingly moderate character. But the age and the rigor of the tradition were the measure of the difficulty of breaking out of it. After all, Coleridge, Shelley, and Keats—in spite of Pope and Doctor Johnson—had only to look back to Milton and Shakespeare, whose dense forests had all along been in view beyond the formal eighteenth-century gardens. But to an eighteenth-century Frenchman like Voltaire, Shakespeare was incomprehensible; and to the Frenchman of the classical tradition of the beginning of the nineteenth century, the rhetoric of Hugo was a scandal: the French were not used to such rich colors or to so free a vocabulary; moreover, the Romantics broke metrical rules far stricter than any we have had in English. Yet Victor Hugo was still very far from the variety and freedom of Shakespeare. It is enlightening to compare Shelley's lyric which begins "O World! O Life! O Time!" with the poem of Alfred de Musset's which begins, "J'ai perdu ma force et ma vie." These two lyrics are in some ways curiously similar: each is the breath of a Romantic sigh over the passing of the pride of youth. Yet the French poet, even in his wistfulness, makes epigrammatic points: his language is always logical and precise; whereas the English poet is vague and gives us images unrelated by logic. And it will not be till the advent of the Symbolists that French poetry will really become capable of the fantasy and fluidity of English.

The Symbolist Movement broke those rules of French metrics which the Romantics had left intact, and it finally succeeded in throwing overboard completely the clarity and logic of the French classical tradition, which the Romantics had still to a great extent respected. It was nourished from many alien sources —German, Flemish, modern Greek—and especially, precisely, from English. Verlaine had lived in England, and knew English well; Mallarmé was a professor of English; and Baudelaire, as I have said, had provided the movement with its first programs by translating the essays of Poe. Two of the Symbolist poets, Stuart Merrill and Francis Vielé-Griffin, were Americans who lived in Paris and wrote French; and an American, reading to-

day the latter's *Chevauchée d'Yeldis,* for example, may wonder
how, when Symbolism was new, such a poem could ever have
been regarded as one of the movement's acknowledged masterpieces: to us, it seems merely agreeable, not in the least revolutionary or novel, but like something which might not impossibly
have been written by Thomas Bailey Aldrich if he had been
influenced by Browning. We are surprised to learn that Vielé-
Griffin is still considered an important poet. But the point was
that he had performed a feat which astonished and impressed
the French and of which it is probable that no Frenchman was
capable: he had succeeded in wrecking once for all the classical
Alexandrine, hitherto the basis of French poetry—or rather, as
an English reader at once recognizes, he had dispensed with it
altogether and begun writing English metres in French. The
French called this "vers libre," but it is "free" only in the sense
of being irregular, like many poems of Matthew Arnold and
Browning.

What made Poe particularly acceptable to the French, however, was what had distinguished him from most of the other
Romantics of the English-speaking countries: his interest in
aesthetic theory. The French have always reasoned about literature far more than the English have; they always want to know
what they are doing and why they are doing it: their literary
criticism has acted as a constant interpreter and guide to the
rest of their literature. And it was in France that Poe's literary
theory, to which no one seems to have paid much attention elsewhere, was first studied and elucidated. So that, though the
effects and devices of Symbolism were of a kind that was familiar in English, and though the Symbolists were sometimes in-
debted to English literature directly—the Symbolist Movement
itself, by reason of its origin in France, had a deliberate self-
conscious aesthetic which made it different from anything in
English. One must go back to Coleridge to find in English a
figure comparable to the Symbolist leader Stéphane Mallarmé.
Paul Valéry says of Mallarmé that, as he was the greatest French
poet of his time, he could also have been one of the most popu-

lar. But Mallarmé was an unpopular poet: he taught English for a living, and wrote little and published less. Yet, ridiculed and denounced by the public, who reiterated that his poetry was nonsense and yet were irritated by his seriousness and obstinacy, he exercised, from his little Paris apartment, where he held Tuesday receptions, an influence curiously far-reaching over the young writers—English and French alike—of the end of the century. There in the sitting-room which was also the dining-room on the fourth floor in the Rue de Rome, where the whistle of locomotives came in through the windows to mingle with the literary conversation, Mallarmé, with his shining pensive gaze from under his long lashes and always smoking a cigarette "to put some smoke," as he used to say, "between the world and himself," would talk about the theory of poetry in a "mild, musical and unforgettable voice." There was an atmosphere "calm and almost religious." Mallarmé had "the pride of the inner life," said one of his friends; his nature was "patient, disdainful and imperiously gentle." He always reflected before he spoke and always put what he said in the form of a question. His wife sat beside him embroidering; his daughter answered the door. Here came Huysmans, Whistler, Degas, Moréas, Laforgue, Vielé-Griffin, Paul Valéry, Henri de Régnier, Pierre Louis, Paul Claudel, Remy de Gourmont, André Gide, Oscar Wilde, Arthur Symons, George Moore and W. B. Yeats. For Mallarmé was a true saint of literature: he had proposed to himself an almost impossible object, and he pursued it without compromise or distraction. His whole life was dedicated to the effort to do something with the language of poetry which had never been done before. "Donner un sens plus pur," he had written in a sonnet on Poe, "aux mots de la tribu." He was, as Albert Thibaudet has said, engaged in "a disinterested experiment on the confines of poetry, at a limit where other lungs would find the air unbreathable."

What, then, was this purer sense which Mallarmé believed he was following Poe in wishing to give to the words of the tribe? What, precisely, was the nature of this experiment on the con-

fines of poetry which Mallarmé found so absorbing and which
so many other writers tried to repeat? What, precisely, did the
Symbolists propose? I have called attention, in speaking of Poe,
to the confusion between the perceptions of the different senses,
and to the attempt to make the effects of poetry approximate to
those of music. And I should add, in this latter connection, that
the influence on Symbolist poetry of Wagner was as important
as that of any poet: at the time when Romantic music had come
closest to literature, literature was attracted toward music. I
have also spoken, in connection with Gérard de Nervel, of the
confusion between the imaginary and the real, between our
sensations and fancies, on the one hand, and what we actually
do and see, on the other. It was the tendency of Symbolism—
that second swing of the pendulum away from a mechanistic
view of nature and from a social conception of man—to make
poetry even more a matter of the sensations and emotions of the
individual than had been the case with Romanticism: Symbolism, indeed, sometimes had the result of making poetry so much
a private concern of the poet's that it turned out to be incom-
municable to the reader. The peculiar subtlety and difficulty of
Symbolism is indicated by the name itself. This name has often
been complained of as being inadequate for the movement to
which it was given and inappropriate to certain of its aspects;
and it may prove misleading to English readers. For the symbols of Symbolism have to be defined a little differently from
symbols in the ordinary sense—the sense in which the Cross is
the symbol of Christianity or the Stars and Stripes the symbol
of the United States. This symbolism differs even from such
symbolism as Dante's. For the familiar kind of symbolism is
conventional and fixed; the symbolism of the *Divine Comedy*
is conventional, logical and definite. But the symbols of the
Symbolist school are usually chosen arbitrarily by the poet to
stand for special ideas of his own—they are a sort of disguise for
these ideas. "The Parnassians, for their part," wrote Mallarmé,
"take the thing just as it is and put it before us—and consequently they are deficient in mystery: they deprive the mind

of the delicious joy of believing that it is creating. To name an object is to do away with the three-quarters of the enjoyment of the poem which is derived from the satisfaction of guessing little by little: to suggest it, to evoke it—that is what charms the imagination."

To intimate things rather than state them plainly was thus one of the primary aims of the Symbolists. But there was more involved in their point of view than Mallarmé here explains. The assumptions which underlay Symbolism lead us to formulate some such doctrine as the following: Every feeling or sensation we have, every moment of consciousness, is different from every other; and it is, in consequence, impossible to render our sensations as we actually experience them through the conventional and universal language of ordinary literature. Each poet has his unique personality; each of his moments has its special tone, its special combination of elements. And it is the poet's task to find, to invent, the special language which will alone be capable of expressing his personality and feelings. Such a language must make use of symbols: what is so special, so fleeting and so vague cannot be conveyed by direct statement or description, but only by a succession of words, of images, which will serve to suggest it to the reader. The Symbolists themselves, full of the idea of producing with poetry effects like those of music, tended to think of these images as possessing an abstract value like musical notes and chords. But the words of our speech are not musical notation, and what the symbols of Symbolism really were, were metaphors detached from their subjects—for one cannot, beyond a certain point, in poetry, merely enjoy color and sound for their own sake: one has to guess what the images are being applied to. And Symbolism may be defined as an attempt by carefully studied means— a complicated association of ideas represented by a medley of metaphors—to communicate unique personal feelings.

The Symbolist Movement proper was first largely confined to France and principally limited to poetry of rather an esoteric kind; but it was destined, as time went on, to spread to the whole western world and its principles to be applied on a scale which the most enthusiastic of its founders could scarcely have foreseen. Remy de Gourmont, who was eventually to become the most distinguished critical champion of the movement, tells of his excitement, one afternoon in the eighties, at discovering the new poetry in a little magazine which he had picked up at a book-stall in the Odéon: "As I looked through it, I experienced the little aesthetic thrill and that exquisite impression of novelty which has so much charm for youth. I seemed to myself to have been dreaming rather than reading. The Luxembourg was pink with early April: I crossed it toward the Rue d'Assas, thinking a great deal more about the new literature which was coinciding for me that day with the renewal of the world than about the business which had brought me to that part of Paris. All that I had written up to that time inspired me with profound disgust. . . . In less than an hour my literary orientation was radically modified." And Yeats wrote in 1897: "The reaction against the rationalism of the eighteenth century has mingled with a reaction against the materialism of the nineteenth century, and the symbolical movement, which has come to perfection in Germany in Wagner, in England in the Pre-Raphaelites, and in France in Villiers de L'Isle-Adam and Mallarmé and Maeterlinck, and has stirred the imagination of Ibsen and D'Annunzio, is certainly the only movement that is saying new things."

We do not talk about Symbolism to-day in dealing with English literature; we do not even, as Yeats did at the end of the last century, think of writers whom he mentions as all belonging to a "symbolical movement"; yet the influence of Mallarmé and his fellow poets was felt widely and deeply outside of France, and it is difficult to understand certain of the things which have been happening lately in English literature without some knowledge of the Symbolist school. I believe, in fact, that if English and American criticism have sometimes shown themselves at a loss when confronted with the work of certain recent writers, it is partly because the work of these writers is the result of a literary revolution which occurred outside English literature. The case of the Romantic Movement was different: Wordsworth's prefaces were English manifestoes; Lockhart's attack on Keats and Byron's attack on Jeffrey were blows struck in an English civil war. But in spite of the Pre-Raphaelites, who were launched by an impulse somewhat similar to that of the Symbolists, and in spite of the English "aesthetics" and "decadents," who for the most part imitated the French without very much originality, the battle of Symbolism has never properly been fought out in English. So that whereas French writers like Valéry and Proust who have grown out of the Symbolist Movement are well understood and appreciated by French literary criticism, the critics of the English-speaking countries have often seemed not to know how to deal with writers such as Eliot and Joyce. Even when these writers have brought back into English qualities which are natural to it and resources which it originally possessed, these elements have returned by way of France and have taken on the complexion of the French mind —critical, philosophical, much occupied with aesthetic theory and tending always to aim self-consciously at particular effects and to study scrupulously appropriate means.

It has perhaps been peculiarly easy for certain of the leaders of contemporary English literature—that is, of the literature since the War—to profit by the example of Paris, because they have themselves not been English. Of the writers in English I shall discuss in this book, Yeats is an Irishman who turns almost as easily toward Paris as toward London; Joyce an Irishman who has done most of his work on the Continent and who has scarcely lived in England at all; and T. S. Eliot and Gertrude Stein are Americans living abroad. The work of these writers has been largely a continuance or extension of Symbolism. Yeats, the ablest of the *fin de siécle* group who tried in London to emulate the French, managed to make Symbolism flourish triumphantly by transplanting it to the more favorable soil of Ireland. T. S. Eliot in his earliest poems seems to have been as susceptible to the influence of the Symbolists as to that of the

English Elizabethans. Joyce, a master of Naturalism as great as Flaubert, has at the same time succeeded in dramatizing Symbolism by making use of its methods for differentiating between his various characters and their varying states of mind. And Gertrude Stein has carried Mallarmé's principles so far in the direction of that limit where other lungs find the air unbreathable as perhaps finally to reduce them to absurdity. It is true, however, that under proper conditions, these principles remain valid; and both the strength and the weaknesses characteristic of much of the literature since the War derive naturally from the Symbolist poets and may already be studied in their work. The literary history of our time is to a great extent that of the development of Symbolism and of its fusion or conflict with Naturalism.

Social Themes in American Realism

JAMES T. FARRELL

———

I

Since the 1890's, American writers of the realistic tradition have been trying to tell the story of the human consequences of the advance of American civilization. As is well known, a pioneer in this tradition was Theodore Dreiser. A significant distinction can be made between his work and that of such writers as Henry James, Stephen Crane, and Harold Frederic. While these writers differ greatly from one another, they were all

Reprinted by permission of Vanguard Press Inc. from *Literature and Morality* by James T. Farrell. Copyright, 1946, 1947, by James T. Farrell.

concerned with the same theme of self-development, of awareness. This theme is even involved in the manner in which
James creates suspense. Crane's *The Red Badge of Courage* is
not merely a war novel. Using the setting of war, he tells the
story of how a boy becomes a man. Frederic's *The Damnation
of Theron Ware* also deals with the theme of awareness or
development, though negatively. Theron Ware becomes aware
of values superior to, and more sophisticated than, those embodied in his ministerial education and in his life as a minister
in a small community in upstate New York. His "damnation"
or disintegration is the result of his inability to live by these
superior values.

With Dreiser, the conditions of life and the ideals of success
in America are thematic: the motif of development or awareness, when treated by him, is secondary to these. His characters
usually take on the color of their environment. Failure and
tragedy in his novels are to be interpreted as consequences of
the pitiless force of circumstances. His heroes and heroines are
seeking to rise socially, to change their class status. If they fail,
it is because of the circumstances of their lives—a lack of education, a lack of physical magnetism, or a lack of control of the
levers of social power, most notably, money. Money provides
the means for wielding power and, if it is gained, the individual
is in a better position to satisfy desire. Human beings—for instance, Roberta Alden, in *An American Tragedy,* or Jennie
Gerhardt—are sacrificed in the interests of success and social
prestige in a society dominated by those who control because
they are rich or, at least, well off. And only those who are born
into the upper classes, or those who are particularly strong-
willed, magnetic, shrewd, or lucky, can escape the alternative
fates of tragedy and failure or apathetic mediocrity. In the
Dreiserian world, the emotional capacities of men and women
for affection and the powers of the individual will are weaker
than the forces of social circumstance. In this sense, Dreiser
wrote realistic novels about the conditions of American life.

II

In recent years the cultural climate provided by the "New Deal" has had a manifest influence on American writing. In a political speech, the late President Franklin D. Roosevelt said: "Always the heart and soul of our country will be the heart and soul of the common man—the men and women who never have ceased to believe in democracy, who never have ceased to love their families, their homes, and their country." The faith of America, he declared, is the faith of the common man. The New Deal cultural climate which evolved in America during the 1930's, and which was patently exemplified in many motion pictures, radio plays, and novels of the war period, helped to produce a pseudo-populist literature of the common man. This neo-populist art and literature emphasizes the concept of Americanism as the means of unifying all races, creeds, and classes. Instead of a literature which penetratingly describes class differences and which also reveals the consequences of the conditions of life that thwart the boy and girl of plebeian origin in the struggle for success and growth, as Dreiser did, this literature has generally stressed and sentimentalized the theme that the common man is human; it has also used the theme that the rich are Americans, too, and that they are like the common man.[1]

The cultural influence of populism, like its political influence, cannot be interpreted in the same way for the 1940's as for the nineteenth century. The agrarian populist movement, reaching its political height with the rise of William Jennings Bryan, played a profound role in the shaping of American literature and in influencing American social thinking. It is one of the social, political, economic developments which stand behind twentieth-century American literature. One of the best illustrations of the populist influence can be found in Frank Norris,

---

[1] Cf. Barbara Deming, "Exposition of a Method" (*Chimera*, Winter and Spring issues, 1945). I have dealt with some aspects of this development in "The Fate of Writing in America," included in this volume.

a major initiator of modern American literature. His books are democratic, popular, anti-snobbish. In his essay "The Responsibilities of the Novelist," he agrues that the novelist must accept the responsibility of writing truthfully for the large mass of the people. *The Octopus,* Volume I of Norris' uncompleted trilogy, *An Epic of the Wheat,* portrays economic struggle and class relationships on the level of personal experience. It recounts the conflict between independent wheat-growers of the West and the railroad "octopus." Although the former think of themselves as the "people," they are independent capitalists who are producing wheat on a capitalist basis and with the use of the most advanced machinery of the time; thus, while they think they are fighting the battles of the people against the railroad, they are also reducing smaller producers to the status of tenants or of agricultural laborers. A poet character, Pressley, speaks in these pages for the author; he formalizes and generalizes this populist theme by conceiving it in terms of the interests of the people as a whole. In this sense *The Octopus* can be called "populist." However, populism is not introduced as a vehicle for rhetorical persuasiveness; rather, it is implanted in the novel as a conviction which is integral in the narrative; it is socially rooted and empirically developed as part of the story.

In contrast to this, recent works of a "populist" character are tendentiously organized and rely for conviction on the author's editorializations. A most notable example of this is to be seen in the radio plays of Norman Corwin. This difference is important, both artistically and sociologically. Some recent works that grew out of the New Deal cultural climate present life in America on the level of newspaper editorials, oversimplifying character and situation. Oversimplification of this kind is to be found, for instance, in such books as *The Grapes of Wrath.*

III

The American realistic novel has treated the American Way of Life in terms of the human costs of American success and expansion. Dreiser's "successful" characters do not find inner harmony. This is exemplified by his financier, Cowperwood, and by Carrie Meeber of *Sister Carrie*. The most notable characters who fail, Hurstwood and Clyde Griffiths, suffer a terrible and tragic end. Sherwood Anderson, influenced by Dreiser, wrote principally of the little man of the lower middle class, the man on the level of the handicraftsman. Many of his characters have already lost their social identity before the stories commence or are in the process of losing it as the stories progress. With capitalist relationships conquering in the small town —in fact, all over the country—types such as those which Anderson describes are declassed. Anderson deals, then, with the consequences of such a development. This is even seen in his emphasis on hands—on working with one's hands. And the feeling of human need in his writings is seen in the need for contacts, for physical contacts. Through contacts, need will be satisfied, and some sense of personal and social identity will be regained. The Andersonian emphasis on sex grows out of this; sex is a way out of confusion, a form of intimate contact which might make more happy the lot of the confused child of a confused world.

Dreiser presents more formally the result of conflict between the need for sexual expression and the repressions imposed by the Puritan moral code. David Graham Phillips also does this in his novel, *Susan Lenox: Her Fall and Rise*. His heroine, Susan, is presented as a superior and attractive girl. However, she is socially ostracized because she was born out of wedlock. She is socially punished because of her mother's "sin." Both Dreiser and Phillips (the latter in a more sentimentally romantic vein) reveal social aspects of class relationships and class differences through their treatment of sex. As a result of social ostracism, Susan is driven out of her class; she is made a victim of the sexual appetites of men of a superior class. This is the essence of her "fall" in the first portions of this work. Dreiser's heroines, Carrie Meeber and Jennie Gerhardt, also have lovers who are of a social class superior to the one from which they come. Jennie is punished for her sin. Here, class injustice is involved in the punishment which society metes out to the girl who "sins." Sex in works of this kind serves as a focus which permits the author to reveal social consequences rooted in class differentiation. At the same time, we are shown the social snobbery, the social hypocrisy, and the double standard prevalent in the upper classes.

IV

In the literature of the 1920's, leisure and consumption are of growing thematic importance. Also, the commodity and commodity values become either an open or a concealed theme. Babbitt's shallowness, for instance, is related to the fact that his social life and his inner world are controlled by commodities and cash values. Even his pleasures are bought, and a cash value placed on them. His thoughts and his life are governed to a great extent by the fact that he must impress those who are impressing him with cost prices. Childish display and ostentation are dominating factors in his life. Babbitt is living on the other side of the Success Dream. In a small way, he has become a success. But his individuality has been lost. In a time of standardized commodities, he is a standardized man. This suggests the major criticism Sinclair Lewis makes of American civilization. The representative American, Babbitt, does not know how to use and enjoy his leisure, does not, with his success and greater leisure, learn how to *consume* more civilized and more sophisticated cultural values.

Other writers of this period, for instance F. Scott Fitzgerald, Hemingway, and Ring Lardner, also deal with the theme of leisure. Fitzgerald describes the social disillusionments and ballroom romanticism of the young people of the upper classes and the loneliness of Gatsby, who gives large parties and has an extensive social life; yet he is lonely, and his guests scarcely know him. Hemingway's characters live in a tourist world, and one of their major problems is that of consuming time itself. It is interesting to observe that his works are written from the standpoint of the spectator. His characters are usually people who are looking—looking at bull fights, scenery, and at one another across café tables. Ring Lardner's satire is directed against the snobbery and stupidity of people who are trying to enjoy themselves and do not know how. Most of his characters are seen in their leisure. If we see them at work, it is at some occupation concerned with the amusement or entertainment of others. Thus he shows us baseball players, prize fighters, a golf caddy, and songwriters at work. Leisure as a theme in such works is treated in terms of satire and social disillusionment.

v

After the Depression, with the entry of a new generation into literature, we can observe another thematic change in realistic American fiction. By and large, the plebeian classes, the lower class, and special groups of the American population were not centrally treated in American fiction before the end of the Twenties. But suddenly we can observe the change. It is mirrored in the racial backgrounds of writers, in the themes, in the subjects, and in the conditions of life which are treated. The orphan asylum, the streets of the city, poolrooms, lower-class homes and family life, the backward sections of America, such as parts of Georgia or the decaying sections of New England, hobo life—all this is introduced into the American novel and short story, and introduced from the inside rather than the outside. At the same time, first- and second-generation Americans of diverse racial and national backgrounds become characters in the American novel and short story.

With this, the problems of lower-class childhood are carefully and realistically introduced into the American novel. The burden placed on the child in a society which is gradually becoming more stratified is dealt with more painfully and in greater detail than was usually the case in earlier fiction. One of the first books suggesting the new trend was *Bottom Dogs*, by Edward Dahlberg, a novel dealing with the life of a boy in an orphan asylum and his subsequent migratory existence. One could use the title of this novel to suggest the new emphasis. A bottom-dog literature, in the social sense, began to develop.[2]

An important feature of this literature is that social snobbery —thematically dealt with in earlier realistic novels (like those of Dreiser and Phillips)—is revealed here as ugly racial prejudice. There should be nothing surprising in this fact. Snobbery and prejudice find different outlets on different levels of society. The snobbery of the upper classes is pressed down on the lower classes. The lower classes are undefended in the face of a class educational system which favors the sons and daughters of the upper classes. Possession of money and the sense of security it usually provides can easily give a tone, a veneer, a seeming graciousness to upper-class life. Prejudice in such circles is a matter of excluding others, of not inviting them to one's home or social functions. Toward the bottom of the social ladder there is more interracial contact. The burden of all social problems weighs down most heavily on the areas of lower-class life. The personal psychological frustrations of those in the lower classes are additionally emphasized by economic frustra-

---

[2] Here the term "bottom-dog" literature has advantages over "proletarian" literature. If we use "proletarian" in the strictly Marxist sense, many of these works cannot be said to deal with the proletariat but rather with the lower middle class, the urban lumpen proletariat, the poor farmer. For a discussion of the concept "proletarian" as a literary category, see my book, A Note On Literary Criticism (New York: Vanguard Press, 1936). Examples of such works are the following: Bottom Dog and From Flushing to Calvary, by Edward Dahlberg; Call It Sleep, by Henry Roth; Somebody in Boots and Never Come Morning, by Nelson Algren; the short stories of Erskine Caldwell, collected in a number of volumes; Summer in Williamsburg, by Daniel Fuchs; Uncle Tom's Children, Native Son, and Black Boy, by Richard Wright; and Sterile Sun, by Caroline Slade. Here I am talking about backgrounds and themes and not trying to make a complete literary analysis, which would take into account those qualities in writing which I would critically defend. Among those perhaps more pleasing to others than to me, which can also be cited, are The Daring Young Man on the Flying Trapeze, by William Saroyan; the books of Albert Halper and Thomas Bell; Tortilla Flat, by John Steinbeck; Little Caesar, by W. R. Burnett; and The Land of Plenty, by Robert Cantwell. For some further views of mine on this subject, see my essay "The Short Story" in The League of Frightened Philistines and Other Papers (New York: Vanguard Press, 1945).

tion. Just as life here is less secure, it often happens that the personality, also, is less secure. This lack of security commonly exacerbates tempers. The struggle for place, money, and social position on the upper rungs is often transformed into the naked struggle of individual vanities on the lower plane. This is all revealed in the violence described in some of the realistic writings of American plebeian writers. A clear example can be found in the short stories of Richard Wright, in *Uncle Tom's Children*, where we can see lynch violence breaking out or threatening to break out over seeming coincidences or accidents. Thus, a white woman sees a colored boy naked after he has been swimming. Coincidences such as these, in a society of acute class and racial tensions, flare into the social tragedy of violence.

Two of the dominant notes in the best of this literature are tension and violence—inner tension, expressed in frustration, frequently that of children, and violence on the physical plane. The class, group, and racial tensions in American society produce frustration and violence when there is a world or society of isolated and more-or-less estranged individuals who express their natures in a savage personal struggle of vanities. When you do not express your vanity through money and social position, you do it by your fists, by your sexual conquests, and by your language of insult and aggression. Even the dialogue of this literature is frequently sharp and violent.

This bottom-dog literature, a literature that is sharply realistic and that depicts conditions of dirt, physical misery, and inner frustration, is also a literature that introduces the plebeian classes on a more human level than was the case (with perhaps a few exceptions) in American writings before the late 1920's and early 1930's. It implicitly asserts the humanity of its characters; this constitutes its most positive value. It boldly introduces men and women and boys and girls of the lowest social stratum as human beings whose problems and whose feelings demand the urgent attention of the serious reading public of America. The boy on the street, the uneducated Negro, the

sharecropper, the worker, and many others are here introduced, irrevocably, into the consciousness of America.

And with *Black Boy*, by Richard Wright, the problem of
awareness, of development, is shown to be as important among
the lower strata of American society as in the world of Henry
James. This bottom-dog literature has now begun to combine
a treatment of awareness with an account of conditions of life
in America.

In this new literature, characterizations are developed without acceptance of prevailing stereotypes. Just as earlier realistic
writing turned upside down the attitudes and editorial affirma-
tions of the American dream, so this literature has done away
with the stereotypes of the stage Irishman, the stage Negro, the
stage Jew of earlier popular writing. One of the social implica-
tions or meanings of this work is that it breaks—in fact, it tears
to ribbons—the earlier stereotypes associated with the American
melting pot. By and large, this literature is one of realistic statement. It states social problems, not in terms of generalizations
but rather in terms of direct characterization, of the immediacy of life described on the printed page. If we define social
causation as the more deeply influential economic and social
forces in a society, which affect all the members in that society,
we can then say that, in this literature, social causation is translated into individual motivation and into immediacy of action,
thought, dream, and word. This literature deals concretely and
directly with the major phases of American life which now
seriously interest scores of sociologists, social workers, psychia-
trists, criminologists, jurists, and others. It seeks to present in
the more humanizing terms of literature much of what the newspapers sensationalize and view with alarm. Often it tells us what
the quality of life is really like among "one-third of the nation."

It is easy to confuse such writings with neo-populist works on
"the common man" that sentimentalize poverty and point up
an editorialized national unity and a verbally formalized affir-
mation of democracy that exudes snobbery when evidence daily
substantiates the conclusion that American class society is torn

apart and exacerbated by class, group, and racial tensions. If one sees the pertinence in the obvious point that, in order to make men better, you must first tell them what they are like, it is easier to make distinctions between these two types of writing. There is always a gap between conventional images of life and life as it is lived. Realistic writing has constantly sought to narrow that gap. Earlier in the present century, American realistic writing had the effect of tearing away conventional images of the American dream, of sex, and of the social snobbery of the upper classes; in the last decade and a half, a major impact of American realistic writing has been the tearing apart of conventional images of life among the lower strata. Thus the realistic writers of America have contributed to social thinking by setting down in fictional form material that can help to create wider consciousness of what life is like in America.

If this literature is appreciated as a fictional account of the quality of many American lives, it may then be a little easier to tear aside conventional false images; it will be possible to make people try to see more directly, more clearly. Literature is not, in itself, a means of solving problems: these can be solved only by action, by social and political action. But realistic literature can and should serve as a means of helping people discover more about themselves and about the conditions of life around them. And the best of American realistic literature can be shown to have contributed toward this effort. This analysis (necessarily sketchy because of the limitation of space) is an attempt to show in what way we should approach the problem of evaluating American literature by seeing it as a body of works that reveal how American realists have struggled to pin down important aspects of the realities of living in America, here and now.

Biographical Notes

HENRY ADAMS (1838–1918). Born at Quincy, Massachusetts, into a family distinguished in American history, Adams was educated at Harvard, served as secretary to his father who was ambassador to England during the Civil War, wrote penetrating studies of contemporary political and economic conditions, inaugurated the study and teaching of medieval history at Harvard, edited the *North American Review,* produced major volumes in American history, and wrote two novels about contemporary American life. After leaving his professorship at Harvard in 1877, he settled in Washington as observer and writer, and remained there until his death. His achievements in fiction, scholarship, journalism, and history were of a high order, but his importance in American intellectual history stems from his early diagnosis of the forces actuating late nineteenth- and early twentieth-century culture. These were summed up in his *Education,* which he subtitled *A Study in Twentieth Century Multiplicity.* For Adams, the modern western world was one in which the disruptive and self-multiplying tensions first released by the Renaissance had reached an apogee, one which denied modern man any unifying scheme of existence whether by religious, intellectual, moral, political, or scientific means. The high degree of Adams's intellectual sophistication, in sharp contrast to the variously panic-stricken or optimistic responses which most of his contemporaries brought to an understanding of their times, gave him a high standing with many twentieth-century writers whose experience confirmed his conclusions and whose intellectual tastes approved his methods. Adams's chief works were *Democracy; An American Novel* (1879); *Esther, A Novel* (1884); *History of the United States of America During the Administration of Thomas Jefferson* (1884–1885); . . . *During the Administration of James Madison* (1888–1889); *Mont St. Michel and Chartres* (1904); *The Education of Henry Adams* (1907); and *The Degradation of the Democratic Dogma* (1919). A useful brief study will be found in Robert Spiller, *et al., Literary History of the United States,* vol. ii. Volume iii of the same work contains a list of references.

SHERWOOD ANDERSON (1876–1941). Born in Camden, Ohio, Anderson grew up largely in the near-by town of Clyde where his father had established himself as a house painter and odd-job man. After service in the Spanish-American War, Anderson finished his schooling at Wittenberg Academy and began his adult work in Chicago as an advertising writer. From 1900 until 1912 Anderson worked as copywriter and merchandiser in Chicago, Cleveland, Elyria, Ohio. In this last place he made a temporarily successful effort to operate a paint merchandising business of his own. In Elyria, also, he began his first serious writing, which dealt, as did almost all his work, with the difficulties put in the way of a sensitive spirit by American middle-class culture. Late in 1912 Anderson acted upon the question he had posed in his writing by deserting his business career and returning to Chicago just in time for the beginnings of the literary awakening in that city. Through his brother Karl, who also set him to reading Gertrude Stein, he was introduced to Floyd Dell, and through Dell to the Chicago literary and bohemian world. He remained a resident of Chicago for some eight years. Thereafter he lived in Fairhope, Alabama, New Orleans, and Marion, Virginia, with periods of residence in Europe and New York. Anderson's writing remained that of the home-grown, Midwestern romantic asserting simultaneously the importance of self-fulfillment and the unlikelihood of achieving it. His characteristic literary attitude was one of high pathos, and his chief complaint against the frustrating plight of modern man. An excellent collection of his shorter work is in Paul Rosenfeld (ed.), *A Sherwood Anderson Reader*. His chief longer works are *Winesburg, Ohio* (1919); *Poor White* (1920); *A Story Teller's Story* (1924); *Dark Laughter* (1925); and *Sherwood Anderson's Memoirs* (1942). Important studies are Irving Howe, *Sherwood Anderson*, and James Scheville, *Sherwood Anderson: The Man and His Work*.

IRVING BABBITT (1865–1933). Born in the Midwest at Dayton, Ohio, Babbitt made his career at Harvard as a professor of romance languages, after preparation at that university and the Sorbonne. His French background was directly reflected in his criticism through its concentration upon French literature and particularly the (to Babbitt) obnoxious writings of Jean Jacques Rousseau. Much of Babbitt's contribution to the New Humanism may be measured as an almost obsessive distaste for Rousseauism in literature or life—for any expression of the free and individualized spirit. The chief tenet of his critical writing was that of the primary necessity for self-discipline and self-control. Babbitt, however, unlike his colleague in the New Humanism, Paul Elmer More, could never accept the necessity for exterior and supernatural discipline through ecclesiastical means which seemed to lie at the end of his chain of logic. His admirations lay in a secularized classical spirit, which Rousseau among others had upset, accepting mannered behavior, aesthetic formality, and social tradition as dikes necessary to channel the flood waters of personality. During the twenties, he and his disciple, Stuart Sherman, were the constant and vociferous opponents of Mencken and the literary radicals, of twentieth-century "romanticism," and of any other manifestations of the ineffable Rousseau in twentieth-century life or thought. His chief works are *Literature and the American College* (1908); *The New Laokoon* (1910); *Rousseau and Romanticism* (1919); and *On Being Creative* (1932). A reference bibliography is in Robert Spiller, *et al.*, *Literary History of the United States,* vol. iii.

VAN WYCK BROOKS (1886–). Born in Plainfield, New Jersey, Brooks took his degree at Harvard in 1907 and thereafter spent some years abroad, where he wrote his *Wine of the Puritans,* the first of a long series of books in which he was concerned with the stultifying influence of American middle-class culture upon the American writer and thinker. Such a thesis informed his earlier critical work and served to link him with the literary radicals whose interests he served. Brooks argued that in its moral narrowness, intellectual shallowness, and imaginative poverty American life has either forced its writers out of everyday reality for their subjects and methods (for example, Henry James) or, in binding them to its standards, has inhibited their possibilities (for example, Mark Twain). Brooks has made a partial recantation of this argument in his later work, trying, apparently, to discover connections between American life and thought which his earlier arguments had missed. A selection of his most interesting work would include *America's Coming of Age* (1915); *The Ordeal of Mark Twain* (1920); *The Pilgrimage of Henry James* (1925); *The Flowering of New England, 1815–1865* (1936); *New England Indian Summer, 1865–1915* (1940); and *Opinions of Oliver Allston* (1941). A list of references will be found in Robert Spiller, *et al.*, *Literary History of the United States,* vol. iii.

HART CRANE (1899–1932). Born in Garretsville, Ohio, Crane went
to school in Warren and Cleveland. Thereafter his literary interests
drew him to New York. There for nine years he held miscellaneous
jobs while engaged in his real career, first, of acquiring poetic knowledge through a wide reading in works approved for the modern
canon—Eliot, Rimbaud, Dostoyevsky, Marlowe, Whitman, Anderson;
and, second, of beginning his own writing. By the middle twenties
his verse was appearing regularly in the literary magazines. In 1925
he gave up jobs for poetry and philanthropic handouts. In 1930 he
published his master-work, *The Bridge*. After this time, however, his
writing grew less sure, and, in profound depression, Crane took his
own life by jumping over the rail of a steamer homeward bound from
Mexico. His work possesses vitality and breadth of experience, but it
suffers from a failure to objectify or realize its subjects. It shows a
strong element of romantic vision-making coupled with a broad acceptance of postsymbolist methods, but the result is that each compromises the other. One misses equally the uninhibited vistas of a
Whitman and the symbolic precision of an Eliot when the two are
confounded in one poem. *The Collected Poems of Hart Crane* appeared in 1933. Philip Horton's *Hart Crane: The Life of an American
Poet* is a good critical biography. Of interest is the chapter on Crane
in the revised edition of Malcolm Cowley's *Exile's Return* (1951).

E. E. CUMMINGS (1894–). Born and raised in a comfortable
academic-clerical family in Cambridge, Massachusetts, Cummings
graduated in 1915 from Harvard, where he had been a member of a
poetical group which included John Dos Passos and Robert Hillyer.
He took a year of graduate work and then entered the Norton-Harjes
volunteer ambulance corps for an eventful wartime service. After the
peace he lived in Paris for a time and then returned to Greenwich
Village and Provincetown, where he has largely continued to the
present. His poetry is one of romantic disillusionment, alternately
mocking and tender, confining itself entirely to minor forms but
within them sounding an authentic note. His typographic innovations
are striking and contribute to the effect of his verse, but there remains a large element of a basic conventionality of attitude. To this,
Cummings has added a strong salt of the modern temper and there
his achievement largely lies. His *Collected Poems* was published in
1938. Since then he has produced *50 Poems* (1940); *1 x 1* (1944);

Santa Claus (1946); and Χαιρε (1950). He is also the author of *The Enormous Room*, a semifictional treatment of his unjust imprisonment during his army years. A list of references will be found in Robert Spiller, *et al., Literary History of the United States,* vol. iii.

JOHN DOS PASSOS (1896–). Dos Passos spent his childhood variously in Chicago, Washington, D. C., and Virginia. He graduated *cum laude* from Harvard in 1916. There he was one of the "Harvard aesthetes," a group which included E. E. Cummings and Robert Hillyer, among others. Starting for Spain to study architecture after his graduation, Dos Passos instead enlisted in the Norton-Harjes Volunteer Ambulance Service, that "finishing school of the lost generation," where his wartime experiences, as described in his first novel, *One Man's Initiation* (1917), turned his attention from the personal world of the aesthete to the sterner experience of a common reality. His literary development from then until the present may be described as that of an aesthetic sensibility which has bound itself by ties of reason and will to the objective features of common existence. Although Dos Passos was an early practitioner of the novel of social consciousness and was for some time an active Marxist, his novels have never been directed overtly to propagandist purposes. Instead he has been the doggedly sensitive recorder of the texture of modern urban and industrial living. Even in his latest, nonfictional work, he has shown much more the talent of awareness than that of the shaping and interpreting imagination. His most important writing is in *Manhattan Transfer* (1925); and the trilogy *U.S.A.,* published *seriatim* in 1930, 1932, and 1936. The best references are the relevant sections in Alfred Kazin, *On Native Grounds,* and Maxwell Geismer, *Writers in Crisis.* A reference bibliography will be found in Robert Spiller, *et al., Literary History of the United States,* vol. iii.

THEODORE DREISER (1871–1945). Born in Terre Haute, Indiana, Dreiser grew up in a poverty-stricken, German, Roman Catholic family which lived in various small towns in Indiana and in Chicago. His adult work began with humble chores on a Chicago newspaper in 1892, and from that time until 1910 he worked as reporter, feature writer, and editor on various newspapers and magazines from Chicago to New York, where he gradually achieved considerable success. As a writer and thinker he was self-taught. The journalistic discipline, a scattered reading in late nineteenth-century fiction and philosophy, both French and English, and a persistent though often inept interest in metaphysics, ethics, and politics were his chief intellectual influences. In 1910 he resigned as editor of the *Delineator* magazine to devote himself to writing. Although Frank Doubleday had published Dreiser's first novel, *Sister Carrie*, in 1900, suppressing it immediately because of its supposed coarseness and brutality, Dreiser's literary career may be said to date from the republication of that novel in 1907. His work has been classified as naturalistic, which in part it is. Dreiser's restless mind, however, led him into the consideration of many and contradictory attitudes, ranging from an unqualified materialism to a serious effort at mysticism. His work, almost without exception, was that of a searching, slow, and dissatisfied intellect trying out in straightforward though often clumsy imaginative ways the ideas and experiences of the life through which he moved. His most significant work lies in his fiction, particularly *Sister Carrie* (1900); *Jennie Gerhardt* (1911); a massive trilogy composed of *The Financier* (1912); *The Titan* (1914), and *The Stoic* (1947); *The "Genius"* (1915); *An American Tragedy* (1925); and *The Bulwark* (1946). Chief studies are Robert Elias, *Theodore Dreiser, Apostle of Nature,* and F. O. Matthiesen, *Theodore Dreiser*.

THOMAS STEARNS ELIOT (1888–). Born of a New England family located in St. Louis, Eliot graduated from Harvard in 1909 and went into graduate work in philosophy at that university. In 1914, however, he moved to England where he was to make his home and where he was to seek the continuing streams of the western religious, political, and literary traditions. Out of this quest, however anachronistically, Eliot emerged as the most radically influential poet and critic of our times. His verse inaugurated a technical revolution by adapting to English use the suprarationalistic devices of the French symbolist and postsymbolist poets. From his highly conservative vantage he described the modern world as a wasteland where persons, values, and reality itself had disappeared behind a dreary illusion nurtured by scientism, industrialism, a commodity culture, and religious vacuity. This view was heartily accepted by all manner of intellectuals who rejected his premises entirely. As critic, he has succeeded in creating a new standard of taste in English poetry, often over strong opposition, one which exalts imaginative immediacy and wholeness at the expense, if necessary, of the accepted canon. As poet he has become the undoubted master of the modern idiom, and perhaps it is the magic of this last achievement which has made all the others possible. For Eliot himself, it cannot be doubted, the key to his position, and the unifying force in it, is his deep acceptance of catholic Christianity as a working, present, and revolutionary world-view. His major poetry is contained in *Collected Poems* (1936) and *Four Quartets* (1943). His chief prose is in *Selected Essays* (1932); *After Strange Gods* (1934); *The Idea of a Christian Society* (1939); and *Notes Toward a Definition of Culture* (1947). Useful references are F. O. Matthiesen, *The Achievement of T. S. Eliot,* Elizabeth Drew, *T. S. Eliot: The Design of His Poetry* and Leonard Unger, *T. S. Eliot: A Selected Critique.*

JAMES T. FARRELL (1904–). Farrell was born and grew up in a lower middle-class Irish neighborhood on Chicago's south side which also provided a milieu for much of his fiction. As he is a naturalist in outlook and method, so in subject he has returned repeatedly to the ground with which he is most familiar, treating it comprehensively and with a systematic detachment. After his early education in Roman Catholic schools, he broke away from the course of his early upbringing and, at the University of Chicago, inaugurated his realistic method and his interest in Marxian sociology—the two staples of his literary and intellectual career. He is a great admirer of Dreiser and represents, perhaps, the highest degree of Dreiserian influence in American fiction. This is shown particularly in his two trilogies. The first, centering around that victim of modern urban rot, Studs Lonigan, consists of *Young Lonigan* (1932), *The Young Manhood of Studs Lonigan* (1934), and *Judgment Day* (1935). The second takes its hero Danny O'Neill, whose adventures, in many respects parallel Farrell's own, through *A World I Never Made* (1936), *No Star Is Lost* (1938), and *Father and Son* (1940). A third trilogy centered around the newspaperman, Bernard Clare, is currently in the making with *Bernard Clare* (1946), and *The Road Between* (1949). In addition, Farrell has produced a number of volumes of short stories and two other novels. His aim in the mass of his writings is "to recreate a sense of American life as I have seen it, as I have imagined it, and as I have reflected upon and evaluated it." The bulk of his criticism, which very directly and fully presents his point of view, is collected in *The League of Frightened Philistines* (1945) and *Literature and Morality* (1947). A reference bibliography will be found in Robert Spiller, *et al., Literary History of the United States,* vol. iii.

WILLIAM FAULKNER (1897–). Early in his childhood, Faulkner was taken to live in Oxford, Mississippi, a town which has been his chief residence since that date and a center of interest for his writing. With family roots penetrating deep into Southern life, Faulkner's great and natural preoccupation has been with his native culture. The bulk of his writing has been given over to exploring the existence of Yoknapatawpha County, a prototype of his home region, as it has developed through various stages from the early nineteenth century to the present. But Faulkner is not primarily a chronicler. He has seen in his native parts a microcosm of human existence and has wrung from them interpretations of life genuinely mythical in their nature—stories, that is, which seem to sum up in themselves critical and representative moments in individual lives as well as those of group, nation, or race. His work, though slow to achieve popularity, has long been held in high critical esteem and was honored by a Nobel Prize in 1951. His principal books are *The Sound and the Fury* (1929); *Sartoris* (1929); *As I Lay Dying* (1930); *Sanctuary* (1931); *Light in August* (1932); *Absalom, Absalom!* (1936); *The Unvanquished* (1938); *The Wild Palms* (1939); *The Hamlet* (1940); *Intruder in the Dust* (1950); and *Knight's Gambit* (1951). His short stories are collected in *Collected Stories of William Faulkner* (1951). A useful group of studies will be found in Frederick J. Hoffman and Olga Vickery (eds.) *William Faulkner: Two Decades of Criticism.*

F. SCOTT FITZGERALD (1896–1941). Scott Fitzgerald grew up in St. Paul, Minnesota. His interest in literature and in writing wakened early and by the time he came to Princeton in 1913 he was prepared to make writing one of the chief means of finding a place in college life. His taste for literature was developed by his undergraduate friendships with Edmund Wilson and John Peale Bishop and by his fascination with the decadent attitudes of the English author Compton Mackenzie and a clerical acquaintance Monsignor Cyril Fay. He left Princeton with a bad academic standing to enter the army in 1917 and there wrote the first version of his first novel. After the armistice, spurred on by a desire to win fame and fortune for himself and his fiancee, Zelda Sayre, he returned to St. Paul, revised his novel, and had it published in 1920. *This Side of Paradise* was an instant success and launched Fitzgerald into a furiously busy and furiously dissipated decade, a considerable part of which he spent in Europe. By 1930 he had returned to America, but his popularity was waning, his health broken, and his wife revealing signs of the incurable insanity that was to keep her hospitalized almost constantly until her death in 1945. Although a large part of Fitzgerald's writing was given over to hack work for magazines and the movies, he achieved in a substantial group of short stories, in two novels, and in the unfinished manuscript of a third high literary distinction marked by a deft and penetrating style and an awareness of heroic tragedy in uncanny contrast to the seeming waste of his life. His best work is found in *The Great Gatsby* (1925); *Tender is the Night* (1934); *The Last Tycoon* (1941); and *The Short Stories of F. Scott Fitzgerald* (1951). The best references are Arthur Mizener, *The Far Side of Paradise*, and Alfred Kazin, *F. Scott Fitzgerald*.

ROBERT FROST (1875–). Though Robert Frost was born in San Francisco, he was brought to New England by his mother at the age of ten and has remained associated with that region ever since. He graduated from high school in Lawrence, Massachusetts, in 1892, and, after a few years of odd jobs, attended Harvard for two years. Between 1900 and 1912 he tried his hand at miscellaneous farming and teaching, but in 1912 went to England for a two-year period. Here, with the friendship and encouragement of a number of the Georgian poets, Edward Thomas especially, he turned seriously to poetry and had his first two volumes, *A Boy's Will* and *North of Boston*, published abroad. Since 1912 he has lived in New Hampshire, Vermont, and Massachusetts, and has been variously engaged in farming, teaching, and lecturing. His poetry has changed very little over the years, being given to a highly personalized exploitation of his particular region, experiences, emotions, and wit. With very little fanfare, Frost has produced some of the best written poetry of our time, although he has restricted himself almost entirely to minor forms. His skill is very considerable, but his poetry is also a magnificent tribute to the personality which has continued over four decades to supply him with the staple of his art. His work is most easily available in *The*

Collected Poems of Robert Frost, 1951. The best study of Frost is Lawrance Thompson, *Fire and Ice: The Art and Thought of Robert Frost.* A reference bibliography will be found in Robert Spiller, *et al., Literary History of the United States,* vol. iii.

ERNEST HEMINGWAY (1898–). Born and brought up in Oak Park, Illinois, Hemingway completed high school there and almost immediately launched himself upon a variegated series of jobs chief among which were a number of newspaper connections. After personally shattering war experiences, he proceeded to Paris in 1921 bearing a letter of introduction from Sherwood Anderson to Gertrude Stein and through her good offices made his debut in exile literary circles. Through the friendship of Scott Fitzgerald, Hemingway's work was introduced to Maxwell Perkins, the great editor of Charles Scribner's Sons, and his career was fully launched. His writing has been among the most influential of our century, largely creating the "hard-boiled" school in American fiction which includes all manner of tales from the high literary to the outright pornographic and sadistic. Hemingway's own work, however, is more than just hard-boiled. His attitude is that of a romantic naturalist, who finds a tight-lipped, melancholy glory in accepting the brute ultimates of human existence while ceaselessly and futilely projecting his will against them. His chief titles are *The Sun Also Rises* (1926); *A Farewell to Arms* (1927); *Death in the Afternoon* (1932); *To Have and Have Not* (1937); *The Fifth Column and the First Forty-Nine Stories* (1938); *For Whom the Bell Tolls* (1940); and *Across the River and into the Trees* (1951). The best references are the relevant sections in Alfred Kazin, *On Native Grounds* and Maxwell Geismar, *Writers in Crisis.* A reference bibliography is contained in Robert Spiller, *et al., Literary History of the United States,* vol. iii.

ROBINSON JEFFERS (1887–). The son of a theologian, Robinson Jeffers attended various schools and colleges, both in this country and abroad, and graduated from Occidental College at eighteen years of age. His interests led him to advanced study in forestry and medicine and to the Universities of Zurich, Washington, and California. By 1912 a legacy had made him financially independent, and from this date his chief concern was poetry. Jeffers's refusal to follow a pattern in education or career-making was evidenced also in his verse which, from the start, spoke his own mind and feelings, in his own idiom, to the exclusion of all else. His constant theme has been that of the alienation of man in the natural world. Where beasts, plants, fishes, oceans, and mountains follow a cosmic economy in which they are, however brutishly, at home, man stands apart from nature, denies it, and disfigures it. Pathetic in his own eyes perhaps, he is only parasitic and perverse to the rest of creation. Jeffers, like a supernaturalist, sees mankind as set apart from nature, but the apartness he evaluates by a naturalist's scale. Following the publication of *The Roan Stallion, Tamar,* and other poems in 1925, a series of volumes followed, columinating in *The Selected Poetry of Robinson Jeffers* issued in 1938. Since that time he has published *Be Angry at the Sun* (1940) and a major verse translation of the *Medea* (1946). The best study of Jeffers is Lawrence C. Powell, *Robinson Jeffers: The Man and His Work* (1940). A list of references is to be found in Robert Spiller, *et al., Literary History of the United States,* vol. iii.

H. L. MENCKEN (1880–). Born in Baltimore, Maryland, Mencken has been associated with that city all his life. He began his newspaper career, which has been his chief occupation, on the *Baltimore Morning Herald,* then moved shortly to the *Sun* where until recently he was an editor and editorial writer. A second interest was in magazine editing and writing. From 1908 to 1923 he served as reviewer and then editor for *The Smart Set,* and from 1923 to 1933 he edited *The American Mercury.* Through these editorial connections, Mencken found opportunity to write the criticism of things in general which has given him his chief fame. His attitude has been that of the total skeptic, almost, indeed, the nihilist. He has been a violent critic of politicians, clergymen, literary critics, editors, writers, reformers, thinkers—everyone in short who could not subscribe to the Menckenian standard of the absolute Menckenian ego. The writers he has supported, like Dreiser and Anderson, have been those who also argued the injustice of any kind of tyranny over the individual self, but when they deviated from Mencken's concept of self or of tyranny, he turned violently against them. His publications have included the *Prejudices;* collections of essays on all manner of subject, published *seriatim* in 1919, 1920, 1922, 1924, 1926, and 1927; and his linguistic work, *The American Language* (4th ed., 1936), and

Supplement One (1945). For a reference bibliography see Robert Spiller, *et al., Literary History of the United States,* vol. iii.

EZRA POUND (1885–). One of the most controversial exponents and practitioners of modern poetry, Pound began his career as a graduate student in romance languages at the University of Pennsylvania. Proceeding to Europe, however, for research materials on Lope de Vega, he soon found a more congenial metier, that of poet and impresario of poets, which he followed in Venice, London, Paris, and Rappallo from 1907 until his tragic return to the United States after the Second World War. His achievements are unquestionably of the first importance. He served as catalyst to such dominant modern figures as T. S. Eliot and William Butler Yeats. He inaugurated the imagist movement and made it a seminal force in modern poetry. His essays were among the first and best definitions of the twentieth-century trends in poetry. His association with such little magazines as *Poetry* and *The Little Review* spread, almost single-handed, poetic modernism to the United States. His own verse, written with immense vitality and skill, must be placed among the best work of our time. His masterpiece, *The Cantos,* is just now beginning to receive the intelligent critical care which it deserves. Over Pound's whole career, however, lies the blight of his activities as a fascist collaborator during the Second World War and the inhumane and antidemocratic doctrines which mar his poetry as well as his life. The matter remains unresolved with Pound hospitalized, as mentally unsound, in governmental custody. His poetry is well represented in *Selected Poems* and *The Cantos* published by New Directions in 1948 and 1949, respectively. His best prose, that of the early period, is unfortunately out of print. *The Letters of Ezra Pound* (1951) serves as a valuable commentary, as does Alice S. Amdur, *The Poetry of Ezra Pound.* A reference bibliography is contained in Robert Spiller, *et al., Literary History of the United States,* vol. iii.

EDWIN ARLINGTON ROBINSON (1869–1935). Reared in Gardiner, Maine, Robinson showed a precocious interest in and devotion to poetry which led to the private publication of his first volume, *The Torrent and the Night Before,* in 1896. Supporting himself at miscellaneous jobs, he continued to write and publish until, in 1905, his work attracted the favorable attention of Theodore Roosevelt, then President of the United States. From this time until his death Robinson's career waxed, albeit quietly, in honor and distinction. His poetic note is characteristically that of the romantic temperament baffled and frustrated by a naturalistic and materialized world. He spoke of a coming light, but without vehemence or clear definition and often, it seemed, without real hope. Despite his achievement, Robinson has had little direct influence upon twentieth-century poets. His work stands at the gateway garbed in properly somber colors, but its obdurate romanticism, plus its trimmed but conservative technique, marks it as transitional. A complete edition, *Collected Poems of Edwin Arlington Robinson,* was published in 1937. The best biographical reference is Hermann Hagedorn, *Edwin Arlington Robinson.* A useful bibliography will be found in Robert Spiller, *et al., Literary History of the United States,* vol. iii.

CARL SANDBURG (1878–). Sandburg grew up in a Midwestern immigrant family, served in the Spanish-American war, and, as the result of a series of accidental events, entered Lombard College in his home town of Galesburg, Illinois. Here he had his first literary encouragement from a Professor Philip Green Wright who organized a student writers' club and helped Sandburg publish his first book, *In Reckless Ecstasy,* in 1904. Sandburg's postcollege years were filled with a variety of vagabondage and laboring jobs which led him into a professional association with the Socialist Party. By 1910 he had become secretary to the Socialist mayor of Milwaukee. His political and journalistic interests took him to Chicago in 1912 just in time to launch him into the Chicago Renaissance and an association with *Poetry* magazine where his reputation was made. From 1917 until 1933 he held various journalistic posts on the *Chicago News.* Since then he has lived in retirement in Michigan and North Carolina. His poetry, except for a trace of imagism, is non-"literary," populistic, and romantic, finding in the common man, the brute vigor of the modern city, and the enduring strength of the land objects of a basic optimism. His manner is loose-jointed and emotional, in the style of Whitman, and relies heavily upon the impact of subject matter for its effect. His chief volumes have been *Chicago Poems* (1916); *Cornhuskers* (1918); *Smoke and Steel* (1920); *Slabs of the Sunburnt West* (1922); *Good Morning, America* (1928); and *The People, Yes* (1936). He published a novel, *Remembrance Rock,* in 1948, and the definitive biography of Lincoln in six volumes, 1926–1939. The only biography is Karl W. Detzer, *Carl Sandburg: A Study in Personality and Background*. A list of references will be found in Robert Spiller, *et al.*, *Literary History of the United States*, vol. iii.

KARL SHAPIRO (1913–). Shapiro was born and reared in Baltimore and educated at the University of Virginia and Johns Hopkins University. He began writing during his year at Virginia and was given his first book publication in *Five Young American Poets* of 1941. Much of his poetry written during the war was concerned directly with his army experience and was composed in the South Pacific area. His war poetry, however, represents no radical intrusion in Shapiro's writing, since he has, almost from his earliest work, given himself over to what may be called a public poetry, verse phrased primarily in terms of common experience rather than from an inward and more strictly lyrical vocabulary. Like W. H. Auden, whom he resembles in this respect, Shapiro writes of the intellectual, moral, and physical strains of our time. Though the poet's feelings and principles are deeply involved, they are given a hard mass of public and contemporary choices with which to deal. The result may be described as a significant new emphasis in twentieth-century verse. His chief volumes are *Person, Place and Thing* (1942); *V-Letter and Other Poems* (1944); *An Essay on Rime* (1945); and *Trial of a Poet* (1947). The best biographical reference is the article in *Current Biography*.

JOHN STEINBECK (1902–). Steinbeck was born and brought up in Salinas, California, where he attended the public schools. He studied at Stanford as a special student from 1919 to 1925, but in the latter year left, without taking a degree, for New York and what he hoped would be a literary career. Instead, there followed several years of miscellaneous jobs and as much writing as he could sandwich in among them. It was not until the publication of *Tortilla Flat* in 1935 that he achieved wide recognition. Steinbeck's work has consistently displayed two characteristic interests. One is in primitivistic character, which he usually draws as lovable or heroic; the other is in the victimized working class. His most impressive novel, *The Grapes of Wrath*, combines these two in a powerful piece of socially conscious and romantic writing. His lesser productions, however, tend in their primitivism toward sentimentality, and in their proletarianism toward undiluted doctrine. Among his more solidly achieved work one would place *Of Mice and Men* (1937); *The Grapes of Wrath* (1939); and most of the stories in *The Red Pony* (1937) and *The Long Valley* (1938). For a list of references see Robert Spiller, *et al.*, *Literary History of the United States*, vol. iii.

WALLACE STEVENS (1879–). Among poets Stevens' career has been as unusual as it has been fruitful. In one aspect, he has achieved a conventional success marked by Harvard graduation and a long and flourishing association with the Hartford Accident and Indemnity Co. In another he is to be measured by a stylized and highly personalized poetry which has increasingly shown a taste for the esoteric and highly aestheticized. Dealing characteristically with minor subjects, Stevens' verse, by the intensity and finish of its methods, has lifted itself into the realm of major work. And this not by Stevens' decorative skill, but by the genuine imaginative power which his talent has discovered in pure poetry. His later work has centered itself around the theme of imagination—that peculiarly human talent for creating order and interest in a world inherently disordered and dull. His volumes are *Harmonium* (1923), reissued in 1931 with extra poems; *Ideas of Order* (1935); *Owl's Clover* (1936); *The Man with the Blue Guitar and Other Poems* (1937); *Parts of a World* (1942); *Notes toward a Supreme Fiction* (1942); *Esthétique du Mal* (1945); *Transport to Summer* (1947). A list of references will be found in Robert Spiller, *et al.*, *Literary History of the United States*, vol. iii.

EDMUND WILSON (1895–). After graduation from Princeton and service in the First World War, Wilson started upon a career which was to combine editorial, creative, and critical interests. He was an editor of *Vanity Fair* from 1919 until 1926 and of *The New Republic* from then until 1931. His criticism, much of it written since 1931, has been distinguished by its original combination of Marxian and Freudian insights. His chief failure has been his inability to concentrate upon writing itself, the literary act as such, in an age which has come to put a major value upon this interest. Nevertheless, a critic of Wilson's genetic or historical bias can often reveal best, in short compass, the continuity and direction of contemporary trends. His chief critical works are *Axel's Castle* (1931) and *The Triple*

Thinkers (1938). The best reference bibliography, although it is now some ten years out of date, will be found in Fred B. Millett, *Contemporary American Authors.*

THOMAS WOLFE (1900–1938). Born into a middle-class in Asheville, North Carolina, Wolfe grew up through a tempestuous childhood to graduate from the University of North Carolina in 1920 and to take a master's degree at Harvard in writing. Although his earliest writing was dramatic, he had begun, after his college years, and while he was an instructor in English at New York University, the long continuous narrative which was to be his lifework. This fabulous creation grew in manuscript far beyond all bounds, and it was only with the faithful editorial supervision of Maxwell Perkins, whose task was largely that of cutting whole chunks from the original manuscript and then restraining Wolfe's too eager hand in writing the necessary links, that Scribners was able to publish Wolfe's work. The result was a series of large volumes in which a spiritual and physical autobiography of Thomas Wolfe unrolls for the reader from the spool of total recall while a spotlight of high romantic passion beats down. His work is unique, the most unabashedly lyrical work in modern American fiction, and one unmatched for intensity and detail. Wolfe's premature death, it would almost seem, was the only force capable of bringing it to an end. The separate novels which contain Wolfe's story (it exists in two narrative frameworks) are *Look Homeward Angel* (1929); *Of Time and the River* (1935); *The Web and the Rock* (1939); *You Can't Go Home Again* (1940); and *The Hills Beyond* (1941). Useful criticism will be found in the relevant sections of Alfred Kazin, *On Native Grounds,* and Maxwell Geismar, *Writers in Crisis.* A list of references is in Robert Spiller, *et al., Literary History of the United States,* vol. iii.

Rinehart Editions